Jonathan,

TITANS
OF THE
TEARDROP
ISLE

Best wishes,

TITANS
OF THE
TEARDROP
ISLE

A SEASON AS A
PRO FOOTBALLER
IN SRI LANKA

SETH BURKETT

Published by Floodlit Dreams Ltd, 2021.

A CIP catalogue record for this book is available from the British Library.

ISBN: 9781838030018

Floodlit Dreams Ltd
5-6 George St
St Albans
Herts
United Kingdom
AL3 4ER

www.floodlitdreams.com

Cover design by Steve Leard

Printed through SS Media Ltd, Rickmansworth,
Hertfordshire, WD3 1RE

Designed and set by seagulls.net

To all of my nanbans

LONDON

'This isn't the Premier League, mate. We're just a small, developing nation.'

I understand what the coach, an enthusiastic young Sri Lankan called Thaabit, is saying. The emphasis, I note, is on 'developing'. However, with me originally scheduled to start playing for his team as a professional footballer in five days' time, I thought they might have sorted a contract by now. Or a visa. Or booked my flight. I'm still sceptical this is about to happen, so I haven't even got my jabs yet.

Sri Lanka isn't renowned for football. It's a cricket country of 21.6 million people. Football isn't even a close second. In the popularity stakes, it comes even lower than rugby. The national football team attracted minor fame in the 2018 World Cup qualifying campaign by losing the first game of qualification against the team ranked the worst (202nd) in the world: Bhutan.

All but one of the national team play their football in Sri Lanka. But my offer isn't to play in the top league. Or the second league. Instead, it's to play in the North Eastern Premier League, which isn't even a league. At least, not in the conventional sense. It's a tournament – five weeks long and played between twelve teams, split into two groups of six, in the predominantly Tamil area of north-east Sri Lanka. The teams are all located in the areas of the country that were most affected during the brutal twenty-six-year civil war, the areas that were bombed and blasted and devastated and that changed hands between the Sri Lankan government and the Liberation Tigers of Tamil Eelam.

From 1983 to 2009, battle raged. The Tamil Tigers, having formed in Jaffna and slowly expanded their territory, fought for an independent state of Tamil Eelam. Snaking down the north-east of Sri Lanka from Jaffna to Amparai, this area was to be their homeland, a place they believed was rightfully theirs, where they would no longer be treated as lesser. Yet over the years tens, maybe even hundreds, of thousands of civilians were murdered. Men, women and children were forced into battle. The mayor of Jaffna, Alfred Duraiappah, former Indian Prime Minister Rajiv Gandhi and Sri Lankan president Ranasinghe Premadasa were just three of the many assassinated. Countless lives were ruined.

After a decade of relative peace, efforts are now being made to regenerate the area and unify its people. One of those efforts is through sport, and in particular the North Eastern Premier League: an outlet for young Sri Lankans to interconnect regardless of race and religion. Players compete for cash prizes. Business owners and celebrities and wealthy Tamils from all over the world bankroll teams. The best players in the region are put on a pedestal, allowing them to progress to bigger and better things. And since its inception in 2018, teams have each been allowed to recruit four foreign professionals to help raise the standard.

That's where I come in.

Like all good stories, this one starts with a tweet. In April 2019 a BBC journalist friend, Owen Amos, sent a request from his personal profile.

> *A friend of mine is looking for foreign players to play in a new competition in July and August in SRI LANKA. Expenses paid for right player. Would suit someone playing university first team / good non-league. RT please*

A second one followed.

> *@sethburkett know anyone who might fancy this? Or even do it yourself…?*

As it happened, I did quite fancy it. I'd just taken voluntary redundancy from my full-time job as a social media manager. The plan was to write, and I could write anywhere. There was nothing holding me back. I let Owen know my interest and then forgot all about it.

Later that month, suicide bombers attacked Colombo, killing 350 people. It was horrible news, a truly devastating display of hatred and intolerance. Revenge attacks took place. The whole country was put under curfew as intercommunal tensions simmered.

In mid-May, with the possibility of going to Sri Lanka to play football out of my mind, an email from an unknown sender arrived in my inbox.

> *Dear Seth,*
>
> *Greetings from Sri Lanka. I write to you upon the recommendation from Owen Amos.*

My name is Thaabit and I'm a football coach by profession. I've recently taken over the management of a football club (Trinco Titans) for the upcoming North Eastern Premier League in Sri Lanka.

The Club's new owners are very supportive of my plans and will back my ideas, which include bringing in foreign players for the tournament. After discussing with Owen, he suggested your name straight away. Someone with your experience would suit our requirements perfectly. I've read your website and it seems like you are keen to travel.

I wanted to write to you about two weeks ago, but Sri Lanka recently went through a sad episode with some terror attacks. I waited for things to settle down before I wrote to you. This seems to be a one-off attack, which has been claimed by a foreign group. We have been assured by the government and ministry of defence that things will go back to normal.

It is with such confidence, I'd like to open this conversation with you and invite you to be a part of my team for the upcoming season. It's a short commitment from 10 June to 10 August (eight weeks). Our team will be based partly in Colombo and Trincomalee.

I feel this will be a great opportunity for you to explore this part of the world through football and you will contribute to this team not just as a squad player but also as a defensive leader on the pitch.

Also included in this email is Andrew Mollitt, a British national who spent four years playing in the Premier League in Sri Lanka whilst working as a maths teacher in an international school here in Colombo. Andrew and

I have known each other since 2006 and he knows how passionate I am about my profession.

Owen has also toured Sri Lanka with his beloved Richmond Mavericks and has fond memories from his time in Sri Lanka. Both Andrew and Owen can be used as referrals if you want to know more about the football culture and life here in Sri Lanka. So feel free to speak to them.

I hope to hear from you soon so we can take this conversation further if there's any interest from you.

Warm wishes,

Thaabit

Well, that was unexpected. It's rare that tweets have consequences. And here was a great big consequence. Sri Lanka: it was exotic, it was exciting and it was different. But it was so, so soon, and I had a great summer of plans ahead of me: my best mate's wedding, holidays, weekends with friends and family. If I accepted this offer, that would all disappear. Still, I replied and said that I was interested, figuring it was neither a firm commitment nor a 'no'.

Five minutes later Thaabit was on the phone.

His passion shone through straight away. They'd love to have me in Sri Lanka. Return flights, food, accommodation and even a salary were all on offer. The more Thaabit talked, the more I listened. Then came the clincher that he must have been holding back as a final means of persuasion.

'Seth, you know, this team is going to be owned by Mahela Jayawardene and Kumar Sangakkara.'

Jayawardene and Sangakkara – Sri Lankan international cricketers who I used to pretend to be when I was in the nets at my local cricket club. They were legends in England, let alone in Sri Lanka. OK, this did sound pretty amazing.

Thaabit went on to offer me a player-coach role, as well as a position as a producer in a documentary he was making about the team with a videographer called Ihshan. The opportunity was looking better and better.

Just so long as they let me fly back halfway through my contract for my best mate's wedding. Just so long as all the details could be sorted. Which, as the weeks went by, looked like less and less of a possibility.

This is why I'm still sceptical. This is why I haven't yet got my injections. And this is why I haven't yet cancelled any of my summer plans.

* * *

Disclaimer: I've been in this situation before. Aged eighteen, I travelled out to Brazil to take on my first-ever contract as a professional footballer. Essentially, I got lucky. A tour with my local youth team, Stamford AFC, led to an offer from Sorriso Esporte Clube to play in their under-18 side for the upcoming Copa Sao Paulo – the Brazilian equivalent of the FA Youth Cup.

Brazilian football is beautiful on the pitch. Off the pitch, it is not efficient. There was no contract before I left the UK. There was no visa. I even had to book my own flights. All I had was people's words. *Yes, of course we'll look after you.* The contract? *Hey, no worries, we'll sort that when you arrive.* What can I say? I was eighteen and desperate to become a professional.

The first problem arrived when I touched down in Brazil. A club official had been sent to the airport but to pick up a Portu-guese goalkeeper. *Seth, an English left-back? Never heard of him.* Reluctantly he bundled me into the back of his car along with the Portuguese goalkeeper and drove us eight hours north to my new home in Sorriso.

Built in cleared rainforest, Sorriso is Brazil's rural outpost. North is nothing but rainforest. South, west and east are nothing but soya bean fields. By Brazilian standards it's a rich place. A high percentage of the population is made up of European immigrants who moved to make the most of the fertile land on offer. Yet there are still high levels of the inequality that plagues the whole of Brazil.

The football club was based in the suburbs, but the club's accommodation was next to the favelas. It wasn't a house, it was actually a garage that the club had converted on the cheap. There were three bedrooms between twenty-eight players, each of them with barred windows and space at a premium. The shower was a concrete block. The toilets had no doors. For some reason, the one toilet brush in the house took up permanent residence on the dining room table. But tough circumstances bring teams together. Over the weeks, I learned to embrace my surroundings. Music was played constantly, my teammates sambaed down the corridors and everyone seemed to be smiling at all times. I loved it.

A contract was shoved in my face. It was all in Portuguese so I couldn't understand it, but I was assured that I was signing a two-year contract that guaranteed me food, accommodation and R$300 per month.

The Brazilian media loved the story. An Englishman in their country, playing in their leagues, for a team of farmers? The coverage hit a crescendo in the week of the Copa Sao Paulo. I was on national TV almost daily. Reporters came to interview me in the hotel. Cameramen filmed me sleeping. Then they realised I wasn't actually very good at football. I didn't play in our first game. Or our second. Or even make the bench for the third.

The media coverage cooled off but, because of the attention I'd given the team, the club chairman offered me a professional contract with the seniors. I was one of the worst players in the under-18 team. I was absolutely the worst player in the senior team. Suddenly I was playing alongside Uefa Super Cup winners and former Brazilian youth internationals. The first-choice left-back had played for Sao Paulo with Kaka. The second-choice left-back had recently been playing in Germany for Hamburg. I was fifth-choice left-back in a squad of thirty-three that had no reserve team.

Minutes were inevitably hard to come by. I managed ten of them in a pre-season friendly. In those minutes I couldn't have turned in a better performance. I created chances and was solid defensively, but it counted for nothing. With such a choice of players, I barely even managed to get minutes in training games. Nor did any of the youth-team graduates. Then came the hammer blow: my visa hadn't been sorted. All this time I'd been on a tourist visa. The contract I'd signed wasn't worth the paper it had been written on. I was officially an illegal immigrant.

The club's advice was to fly to Paraguay and then fly back to Brazil to get a new tourist visa. I decided not to. If the club couldn't even sort my visa when the police station was a hundred metres away, why would they sort it when I returned? Especially now I was neither playing nor getting them media attention. There were only a couple of weeks left of the season and so I decided to go home. At the airport it was recognised that my passport wasn't eligible and that I was an illegal immigrant. Two police officers took me underground and sat me down at a table. Two further police officers stood behind them, machine guns strapped to their uniform. I was absolutely terrified. I told them the story, pleading with them, asking them to believe me. Thankfully it worked and they just issued me with a fine then allowed me to fly home. Until I've paid that fine, though, I'm not allowed back in the country.

If Brazil taught me anything it's that everything always happens for the best. A few months after I left Brazil, one of the directors of the club was murdered, stabbed fifteen times by his boyfriend. That's the official line anyway; the strong rumour was that the rival political party to the director – who was a local councillor – had ordered the hit, concerned he was gaining too much political power. And then a few months after that horrible incident, Sorriso Esporte Clube ceased to exist. Suspicious activity alerted the authorities to money-laundering, and as a result the club was shut down.

And so, although football had been my dream, university became my reality.

* * *

They say it isn't *what* you know but *who* you know in football. If my Sri Lanka trip ever happens, I feel I'll be pushing that saying to the extreme. I'm friends with Owen Amos, who tweeted about the football opportunity in Sri Lanka. Owen is mates with Andrew Mollitt. Andrew is an Englishman who taught in a Sri Lankan international school for eight years. Thaabit was one of his best pupils.

A phone call to Andrew helped ease my misgivings about Sri Lanka. He told me a bit about the country and the people, let me know what a great student Thaabit was and advised me not to worry about security. The Foreign Office was advising against all but essential travel when he first arrived too. He asked if I had any questions. I had plenty, but there was one in particular that I was desperate to ask: just how good is Sri Lankan football?

Nobody wants to be an imposter. When I returned from Brazil, I still dreamed of a life as a professional footballer. Even while at university, plenty of offers came in from Brazil. Usually I said yes, but always insisted on a work permit and contract being sorted prior to my arrival. That never happened, and so instead I played football at university and returned to playing for Stamford in the Evo-Stik Northern league. I started playing futsal, too, and was progressing well. In my first season I was called up to the England development squad. To wear the kit and train at St George's Park was an incredible experience.

Then, just as it looked like I might get a chance with the senior England squad, disaster struck. An ill-timed Cruyff turn led to a spiral fracture and ruptured ligaments. The recovery was lengthy, my leg reinforced with plates and screws and all sorts. When I eventually did return to the pitch, nothing was the same.

It took months to get back to the level I'd been at before. On the futsal court, I had to totally change my game, eschewing my one-on-one style in favour of a pass-and-move philosophy that left me less likely to be lumped by an opponent. I returned to playing football for the university but struggled with the frequency of training and matches for both disciplines. Every time I put strain on my right leg, the ankle would swell up, and the stress was affecting other parts of my body.

When university football finished I decided to return to non-league with Mickleover Sports. Three games in, I dislocated my elbow, leaving me out for the rest of the season and missing vital futsal games. It was a sign. I was cheating my body, putting it under too much strain. I had to make a choice: I could carry on picking up pocket money by playing football or have a real go at playing futsal for my country. I chose futsal. And I don't regret that. I've never been capped at senior level, but the experiences I've had surpass anything I could have done in football. And I still manage to play the odd game of eleven-a-side.

I shared my fears with Andrew and he immediately put me at ease. He was an amateur player in England but managed to play for one of the best teams in the Sri Lankan Premier League. The standard wasn't great, he told me, and the standard of the North Eastern Premier League would be even lower. Only north-eastern Sri Lankans are allowed to play in it. Those from Colombo would also count as foreign players. I'd have nothing to worry about.

Nothing except the visa, contracts, salary, food, accommodation, flights and training, that is.

* * *

Today is the day that I'm supposed to fly out to Sri Lanka. Instead, I'm sitting at home in my shorts. Nothing is sorted. I suppose there's been progress of sorts. Thaabit asked me for a copy of my passport today, although I don't know if it's to book the flights or to sort my visa or whatever.

I have a new date of departure: two weeks from now, with the tournament starting in three weeks. At least, that's what's supposed to be happening. News has come out that the Macau national team has refused to travel to Sri Lanka to play the second leg of their World Cup qualifying match. Their officials can't guarantee the players' safety. It hardly fills me with confidence. Following the recent Colombo bombings, security has been a big concern. The Foreign Office still advises against all but essential travel. People I've spoken to in Sri Lanka are adamant the country is safe, but it's hard to fully believe them. If it isn't safe for Macau, is it safe for me? My mates tell me I'm going to be kidnapped. My family fear for my safety. But none of them can deny it's a great opportunity.

It's a classic risk-versus-reward scenario. The risk is my safety, as well as the comforting security of a life in England. The reward is an incredible experience, the opportunity to have been paid to play football on a third different continent, the chance to meet new people, learn new stories and grow as a person. And I'm pretty excited to meet Mahela Jayawardene and Kumar Sangakkara.

If I don't find out this week, it's not happening. OK, I've thought that for the last three weeks, but this time I mean it. Apparently the delay has been due to the player auction getting moved back by a week, which has put the Trinco Titans' training camp back by a week. For some reason, that's put the foreign players' arrival back by two weeks. There are two of us: me and an Irish midfielder called Dean. All I know about him is that he's six foot two. Thaabit seems very happy about this. He likes tall players, it seems. If I was an inch smaller I'm not sure I'd have been offered anything in Sri Lanka.

Maybe it'd be easier if it didn't happen. The best-case scenario is that it gets pushed back by a year. That way I'd get to keep all of my summer plans and have enough time to prepare for a proper adventure. I'd be able to get the injections with plenty of time, give notice to my part-time roles, work around the dates.

If only life was so simple.

I bite the bullet and get my injections. If none of this happens then I'll just have to go on holiday in South East Asia to make them worthwhile. There isn't enough time to get them on the NHS. The next appointment is almost a month away, and then it takes up to six weeks for all the injections to be done. I have to go private, which means I have to open my wallet. In reality, there isn't enough time to get them privately either. The pharmacist informs me that after the injections my body will need at least four weeks to build up enough antibodies. I tell him I don't have four weeks, that I might only have ten days. He umms and ahhs, then tells me how some of his patients risk it after just a few days.

'Look,' he says, 'give it two weeks and you should be OK.'

The injections don't half hurt. Days later I still feel like someone has punched me very hard in my left shoulder.

Straight after the injections I told Thaabit I needed to wait at least two weeks before arriving in Sri Lanka.

'Ten days will be all right,' he said.

I replied that no, I needed to wait at least two weeks. No reply. Until today.

Visa work is underway… should have by thurs or fri… pack your bags… flights already booked for this Sunday.

I read the message and then read it again. So many questions, so few answers. I start with the most important ones:

Where is the contract?
When does training now start?
What are the fixture dates?
Please move the flights back by a few days.

No reply.

I still don't think this is going to happen, but I'm beginning to get a little less sure.

* * *

Tonight is the first exercise I've done in a week. My recently dislocated elbow is bandaged, my foam roller packed and my hamstrings tight.

My hamstrings in particular are giving me grief. They have been for the last few years on and off. And on my first 'get fit for Sri Lanka' run last week they almost gave up on me. Every time I take a step they twinge. It's not preventative, just annoying.

My body is another source of self-doubt. When I played in Brazil everything was different. I was eighteen, injury-free and driven by the belief that I could have a career in professional football. Ten years later, having broken my leg, dislocated my left elbow numerous times and suffered multiple hamstring niggles, I'm under no illusions. This Sri Lanka experience isn't going to lead to a lengthy professional career. The hope has died, replaced by concern. There are possibilities but, unlike in Brazil, they are outweighed by fears.

There's only so much I can rest. Is it better to be unfit or injury-free? How am I going to survive consecutive days of double sessions? How can I justify my role as one of the two professional players? To be honest, I don't really have an option.

I lace up and pray that my body can survive for just a bit longer.

* * *

A flurry of activity. Thaabit sends me the first proof of paperwork from this whole process.

Mahela Jayawardene, co-founder of Trinco Titans, has requested the Ministry of Telecommunications, Foreign Employment and Sports to recommend the Business visa and Multiple Entry Visa for Mr Dean P. Curran and Mr Seth Lawson Burkett, who have been contracted to Trinco Titans as overseas players for the upcoming North Eastern Premier League Tournament.

It feels grand to have Mahela Jayawardene – *the* Mahela Jayawardene – request my presence, almost as if I'm royalty. And now, as well as knowing that Dean is an Irish midfielder who's tall, I also know his surname. But a Google search leaves me none the wiser; not even 'Dean Curran football Ireland' works.

I catch Thaabit at a good time. I send him another picture of my passport and a few more details are shared. I won't be staying in a hotel but at the house of one of the board members. Yes, I will still be paid a salary and it'll be the same as everyone else gets, though he won't tell me what that figure is. The owners aren't happy that I don't want to fly on Sunday but he'll try and change it to next Tuesday, arriving on Wednesday. I might have to go to the Sri Lankan embassy in London.

This is the first time I've felt that Sri Lanka is actually going to happen. I have seven days until my potential new departure date. So much to sort. Travel insurance, sprays, kit. Do my boots still even fit? I haven't worn my soft-ground studs for several years. There's no going back from here.

Another message from Thaabit follows. He's going to meet the employment lawyer tomorrow. If all goes well, he'll confirm my visa...

* * *

It's happening. It's actually happening. My visa has been approved. The green light has been given. I'm going to Sri Lanka.

Those flights that were booked for Sunday? They were never really booked. Thaabit tells me he'll book my actual flights by tomorrow. I don't call him out and instead ask about my contract.

Thaabit: Hahaha. You won't let go of this, will you?

Well, no, not really. I doubt Paul Pogba arrived at Manchester United and played his first few games without knowing his employment details. A contract gives certainty. If I have to wait until I'm in Sri Lanka to sort a contract then I'll be pretty stuck and not really in a strong negotiating position. Most of all, though, I'm scared they won't let me come back to England for my best mate's wedding. In Brazil I was told that I had signed a two-year contract. Four months later I was being interrogated by police at Brasilia airport. Let's just say I've got history with contract issues.

I ask Thaabit what I need to bring. Will there be training kit provided? He tells me he'll let me know. After a few more questions, he promises he's talking to another lawyer tomorrow about finalising the player contracts.

The list of things that need to be done in Sri Lanka never seems to end. Three days before I leave there are still no flights. Still no contract. But then a response from Thaabit: he's had to cancel the Sri Lankan Airway flights that were booked. He doesn't know why but that's what's happened. He promises I'm still going to be flying on Tuesday. He has to have me on the training pitch by Thursday and refuses to delay any further. The player auction that happened last Saturday is now happening next Saturday. Once that's concluded they'll sort the player contracts. He tells me to trust him, which is becoming harder and harder as the days go by and the information changes.

Any sensible person would have abandoned this weeks ago.

The North Eastern Premier League website has been taken offline. Am I reading too much into this?

My girlfriend has no sympathy with my situation. 'You choose to associate with these people,' she tells me. 'So any frustration you're feeling is your own fault.'

* * *

Midday, the day before I fly. Thaabit finally responds to my message. The flights are booked, he assures me.

'Great, what time am I flying?'

He'll let me know in three hours.

Seven hours later the message comes through. It's good news. I've got flights. I've actually got flights! And there's proof. Not only are there flights, but there's also my official visa and the outline of an official contract. I'm now flying this Thursday. Seventeen days after my original departure date and three days from now. It's an Emirates flight, too, so no budget airline. That feels safe, at least.

My salary is 50,000 Sri Lankan rupees. Nuts! Excitedly, I search Google for the exchange rate. My face falls: 50,000 LKR is £222, or £27.75 per week. That's about the same as I was getting paid to be an unused sub for my local non-league team as a seventeen-year-old. I'll end up losing money by going to Sri Lanka, especially as I have to fund my own return flights for the wedding. But this isn't about money. It's almost a free holiday – and it should be a great experience.

The player contracts will be presented upon arrival. Thaabit summarises it as:

- » one set of return flights and visa entry to Sri Lanka
- » full-board accommodation
- » player allowance of 50,000 LKR plus win bonuses
- » medical insurance
- » training and playing kit

A list of what to pack is included:

- » personal training gear
- » shinpads, football boots, trainers and flip-flops
- » comfortable casual clothing
- » at least one pair of jeans and a formal shirt
- » beachwear
- » sunblock and insect repellent
- » personal toiletries
- » vaccination card and medical history
- » details of allergies
- » medical prescriptions

Minutes after this email lands Thaabit calls. He's excited, and by this stage so am I. He's just led the first day of training with twenty-four triallists. People have travelled eight hours to try out. The standard is good, but the pitch is like a paddy field. He says I won't believe how wet it is.

He might take me and Dean to Jaffna for the player auction this weekend. He wants me to help with the media side of things, but if I'm too tired then I'll stay behind with Dean and train on the beach before starting properly on Monday. Sounds good to me.

Dean messages me later. He needs to book his own flight over from Ireland. Can he stay with me the night before we leave? I say yes.

'Oh great, a strange person you've never met staying in our house. Let's hope he doesn't rob us.'

I think that means my girlfriend is OK with the arrangement.

* * *

Thaabit is right: Dean is tall. He's muscular, too: one flowing expression of strength from head to toe. I catch him roaming the street outside my flat, looking lost with a massive suitcase in tow. I invite him in and am instantly struck by his soft Northern Irish accent. He's from Derry and plays Gaelic football as well as soccer. His mother is Northern Irish and his father is Nigerian. I'm pretty sure we're going to get on. I'm even more sure that he isn't going to rob us.

Dean has never been to London before so I take him on the Tube to meet my dad and sister for dinner in Leicester Square. On the way in, we exchange our disbelief that this is all actually happening. I tell Dean I've only recently got my injections because I didn't think we were ever going to board a plane to Sri Lanka. He looks at me strangely and motions at jabbing his arm.

'What, you mean like, for malaria and stuff?'

'Well, hepatitis A, typhoid and DPT,' I reply. He carries on looking at me. 'You have got them, haven't you?' I ask. He takes a second.

'Nah, I'll be all right.' The accent is so calming that I almost believe him.

He tells me how he had just as much trouble getting detail out of Thaabit. A further complication was his location. On

Monday, the day before we were supposed to take off, he still hadn't heard from Thaabit either. He needed to fly to London from Northern Ireland but couldn't book a flight without confirmation that we were going to Sri Lanka. What was the point? The departure date kept changing. When the flight was eventually booked, it was booked from London. He had no transport to London, however. Thaabit has promised to refund the extra flight, but it still meant Dean had to get a ninety-minute bus to Belfast, a flight to London, a bus from the airport and then find a night's accommodation. Fortunately for him, I have space.

My dad and sister quiz Dean and ask us both lots of questions about Sri Lanka. My sister is particularly concerned about tsunamis. I tell her it's unlikely. If anything bad is going to happen, it's probably going to be typhoid-related and happening to Dean. Fortunately, there's still time to go to the pharmacy before our flight.

The next morning, reasoning that a sleep might have made him see sense, I try again to make Dean get his jabs. No luck. He assures me he had plenty of jabs as a child so he'll be fine. If they are absolutely necessary then he'll just get them done in Sri Lanka. Considering this the closest I'll get to a compromise, I shrug my shoulders and suggest we head to Primrose Hill with a ball.

When Dean pings a ball, everything seems all right. His technique is faultless, one fluid motion from foot to ball that sends it spiralling through the air. I could watch it all day. In those moments, the action makes me forget everything – including the genuine possibility that he might get typhoid. Two hours later and worryingly sunburnt, we head home. Dean accepts half a tortilla wrap for lunch – his first meal of the day. Such an appetite suggests I may be getting plenty of his leftovers in the weeks to come. As far as I'm concerned, that makes for a perfect travel partner. Although I'm still not fully used to his accent, and there are words and phrases that I don't catch. He's fond of 'grand' and 'gent', as well as rapping at random intervals. He's also taken to outbursts of 'Trinco, Trinco Titans', which prove infectious.

On the packed Tube to Heathrow we remain sceptical. I assure him that if the tickets don't exist he can always stay at mine again, then we can just have another kickabout on Primrose Hill and he definitely won't catch typhoid.

We get off to a bad start at the airport. The self check-in doesn't recognise either of our passports, so we head to the desks, where – eventually – we're told that we do actually have flights. Mine have been booked under my middle name rather than my surname but, after much back-and-forth between staff members, they suggest that I'll be OK.

And then we're through. Security done. Wait done. Boarding done. Flight taken off. The adventure begins.

COLOMBO

The first immigration officer isn't having any of it. He doesn't care for our business visa, nor even the name of Jayawardene. He sends us away to fill out a form, then sends away three others while we're going about our business.

We queue again and let another passenger in front of us so we get a different officer. Dean is starting to worry. He hasn't printed out his visa, his phone is dead and he doesn't even have a bank card on him.

But this one is more impressed. We tell him we're going to be playing football for a Sri Lankan team and he asks how much they're paying us. I say not much and instantly curse myself in case I'm being disrespectful. Maybe it's a good salary over here.

'50,000,' Dean adds.

'Pounds or LKR?' the officer asks. 'Lankan rupees,' he explains after seeing our blank looks.

'Rupees.'

The officer laughs at that. 'Why would you come here for that?'

He lets us through, but only after we exchange numbers and agree to come and coach one of his school football teams for a training session. He tells us how he's always loved football, none of this cricket where only two players out of twenty-two get to play at any one time.

The airport is filled with posters warning against drugs. 'Love your island, protect against drugs,' a leaflet advises us. I tell Dean about an article I read on the flight, which warned of a rising problem with narcotic shipments across the Indian Ocean. It claimed that as many as 300,000 Sri Lankans are narcotic users. Considering there are 18 million Sri Lankans, that seems a pretty high proportion.

'What, like weed and that? It doesn't seem too different to the UK,' he replies.

'No, it's more like Class As.'

As soon as I say 'Class As' a keen-eared policeman appears from nowhere. He demands to see our passports. We show them and he wants to know what we're doing in Sri Lanka. We tell him we're here to play football and, convinced we aren't international drug dealers, his demeanour changes instantly.

'We need more British like you,' he says. 'It's great to have you over to our country to play football.'

* * *

Colombo is one mad rush. Traffic converges from everywhere. Scooters weave in and out. Buses barge in wherever they want. Tuk-tuks chug along. Pedestrians saunter along the sides of the road. And our taxi driver has a serious affection for his horn.

The buildings look like they've been put together in a rush. They're stacked in tightly, with shop displays spilling out onto the road and people just hanging about inside. In plenty of ways it's not unlike Brazil, and I wonder how much impact the Portuguese colonial past has had on the country. The British legacy is evident everywhere – from Norfolk Hotel to British Salons and teaching courses proudly claiming to be approved by Birmingham College (UK). They drive on the left-hand side of the road and even have the same road signs as us. The models on all the advertising boards are white, which seems strange because I still haven't seen another white person since leaving the UK.

Every now and then there's a large projector at the roadside showing the Cricket World Cup. Sri Lanka are in a bad way at 160-6 in a game against South Africa that they really need to win to stand a chance of qualifying for the knockout stage of the tournament.

It's so green here. Trees are everywhere. Where there are no buildings there are trees. The vegetation is lush, even in the hustle and bustle of the capital.

Dean is busily spotting all of the sights from the passenger seat next to me: 'Look, KFC… and hey, there's a Burger King.'

I start to look at the prices advertised as we hoot our way through the outskirts. There's a restaurant promoting an all-you-can-eat buffet for 240 LKR, a shop selling 'moovees and DVDs' for 70 LKR and a roadside stall shifting fruits at 3 LKR a piece, which works out at less than a penny. Maybe the salary isn't so bad after all.

When we arrive in Kalutara, a city 60km south of Colombo and the location of our week-long training camp, I immediately see why Thaabit was so keen to recruit tall players. I feel like a giant among men as the coaching staff walk out to greet us. In English football I'm slightly below average height and a little skinny. Here, with the exception of Dean, it seems I'm going to be the tallest player and probably the biggest. It's certainly enough to drop the 'almost' from saying I'm six foot tall.

'I hope you like to head the ball, boys,' Thaabit says. 'You'll be bigger than everyone here. A big advantage on set-pieces.' Maybe I do like heading. Everything is different here. Up is down, left is right, Seth is physically imposing. I never thought I'd see the day.

Thaabit is tall for a Sri Lankan but still a good few inches shorter than me, despite us being the same age. He's relaxed and excited at the same time, perfectly at ease with the situation. His long hair is brushed back, and a sarong covers his lower half. His eyes sparkle with possibility.

The team are buzzing to meet us, he says. There are so many of them, all with names that I'm hearing for the first time. I don't know how I'm going to remember them.

They're all staying in a dormitory by the training pitch for the next week of our camp. But me and Dean, well, we're given special treatment: we get to stay in the coaches' house. I don't want to think about the state of the dormitories because, on first appearance, the coaches' house isn't great. The communal areas are nice and there is a pool but the bedroom is basic: three beds with bedding that seems as if it hasn't been washed for a while, and a waterlogged en suite that becomes more waterlogged as you wee into the toilet. Am I becoming more demanding as I get older? After all, it's better than what I had to deal with in Brazil.

Kapila introduces himself next. He's the assistant coach and older than Thaabit by at least two decades. An air of quiet authority surrounds him. He's efficient with his words, speaking when he needs to. Though he's not a fluent speaker of English, he's got enough of a grasp on the language to make himself understood. I can tell that patience is a virtue of his. I imagine him sitting in front of a dictionary for hours on end, learning at his own pace. His eyes flit between me and Dean, making sure we take in the information he gives us. His voice is soft and gentle. I take an instant liking to him.

The other coach in the house is called Rimzy. He emerges from behind Thaabit and Kapila, smiling shyly as he shakes our hands lightly before casting his eyes to the floor and returning to his place behind the two others. I catch enough of a glimpse of him to note that his face is pockmarked. As with Kapila, there's a gentle nature about him, though he lacks the authority of Kapila and Thaabit. There's no doubt that Thaabit is the leader.

'Rimzy is the only member of the coaching staff from last season that we've kept on for this season,' Thaabit explains. 'He is going to be very valuable for us. Nobody knows Trinco-malee like him and few people are as respected there as he is. You'll see once we get to the north-east. Rimzy will help us to get the local community supporting the Titans and also liaise with the local players, making sure they're getting everything they need.'

'How did youse do last season?' Dean asks to the gap where we can just about see Rimzy.

'Terribly,' Thaabit replies before Rimzy has the chance to answer, which probably suits Rimzy just fine. 'Like, so bad. But they had many things against them. This season will be different.'

'How terribly?' I'm glad Dean asks the question, though I already know the answer. I've already spent hours trawling the league website, trying to pick up as much information as possible.

'Ninth out of twelve. Eleven games played, fourty-four goals conceded. That's why you're here, Seth.' Thaabit winks at me and I try to share in his confidence but I just can't. Not until I've seen the standard.

'Did youse not have foreign pros last year?' Dean continues.

'There were two Nigerians. Highly paid. Not quite the talent to match,' Thaabit replies while the other coaches watch on. 'I wanted to get two players from Europe this season. A solid defender – that's you, Seth – and a goalscoring midfielder.' Thaabit puts his arm around Dean. 'Anyway, enough of that. I've got a proposition for you. Jai!'

We walk into a spacious living room. The walls are plain white and it feels continental in style. The back door is open and I can see the swimming pool glistening in the artificial light. A television blares in the corner with a couple of sofas surrounding it. There's a big table with dining chairs surrounding it and heaps of coaching notes strewn on top. I can instantly tell that the notes are Thaabit's, while the zipped-up pencil case and neat stack of A4 sheets are most likely to belong to Kapila.

'Jai!' Thaabit shouts again and this time a body emerges from one of the bedrooms on the side. It moves slowly, as if just awoken from a nap. I can see a mop of hair, mainly spiking up but pointing in all directions. I can see a muscular figure, wearing a vest as if to emphasise their bulging biceps. He looks young, only just out of school. 'This is Jai,' Thaabit explains.

'All right?' Jai asks and I'm taken aback. His voice has a slight American twang, though he's unmistakably Sri Lankan. I presume he's privately educated. The voice and the confidence are a giveaway. He holds out his fist and me and Dean take turns to bump it.

'Jai is one of my players from the Thaabit Ahmed Football Academy,' Thaabit continues. 'He's been with me since he was a kid. Now he's nineteen and training with the team to try and win a contract. He'll be sharing that room with you while you're here. Anyway, that proposition.'

It took us two and a half hours to get to Kalutara from Colombo airport, so you can imagine how thrilled we are when Thaabit suggests we return to Colombo for the weekend. We have the option of staying in the coaches' house – where we've barely been for fifteen minutes – but, as there is no training scheduled over the weekend, everyone else is going home. Jai is from Colombo and heading back home. Thaabit suggests we go with Jai and stay in his house. He'll show us the sights. What do we want to do? I take one look at the spartan bedroom with its waterlogged en suite and stained bedsheets, consider there may well be no wifi and that neither of us has any Sri Lankan money, and then jump at Jai's offer. What better way to be shown round Colombo than by a local?

Thaabit drives us back in his Toyota Prius. It's a good chance to get to know him. He proves knowledgeable, enthusiastic, respectful and composed while Jai decides to catch up on the sleep that I presume our arrival woke him from. Thaabit doesn't let that put him off his stride. He has big plans for me and Dean and feels that our height and experience will give them a decent advantage. Not even Dean's acknowledgement that he has had no injections done can put him off.

I fear Thaabit may be bigging us up too much and so I ask what Sri Lankan football is like.

'Terrible,' comes the frank response.

* * *

Jai warns us it's impossible to get a Sri Lankan footballer to relax. They're relentless, flurries of limbs whirring and scores of bodies going to ground in last-ditch slide tackles. If they ever stopped to think, he says, they'd realise that just by standing in the right position they wouldn't have to slide tackle. Five players were unable to complete training on Friday due to injury. All five injuries were sustained from bad tackles. Dean and I are unanimous that we won't accept bad tackles in training. I tell Jai I'll walk off the pitch; Dean says he'll lamp the tackler.

This is the first senior team that Jai has played for. He's just completed his first year of university and has ambitions to study in Australia. It's no surprise when he reveals that he went to a fancy international school in Colombo. He certainly has the accent to prove it – and the house. A gate surrounds the house, separating it from the hustle and bustle of the outside world and keeping private the sizeable amount of land the family owns. The house is so big that there's even enough room to house a cleaner and her entire family. Her six-year-old son, Dhawan, is one ball of energy. He's up and down and up and down and round and round the large communal area. He shoots Dean with a toy gun then insists on racing me. After two 20-metre jogs outside in flip-flops, I'm spent. I call for Dean to replace me, then sit inside my air-conditioned room and glug water for five minutes to return to normal. I'm so sweaty I even have to change my shorts.

Fortunately Dean embraces the opportunity, just as he's embraced everything – except the vaccinations – that's come his way so far. His positivity is infectious and his happy-go-lucky nature reassuring in foreign surroundings. He's been up since 6 a.m., using the four hours before I rise to play with Dhawan and entertain Jai's grandmother. She's in her eighties and is the mainstay of Jai's life when he's in Colombo. Much of her family is in Australia, while Jai's mum runs a hotel business just north of Trincomalee, enabling Jai to qualify as a 'local' player for the Titans. Any player without links to the north-east, we are told, counts as a foreign professional and teams are only allowed four foreign professionals in their squad. She tells Dean of how her husband died from a heart attack on the golf course twenty-two years ago. She talks at length about Galle, providing Dean with plenty of travel recommendations. Before I've even had my first yawn of the morning, the two of them have built a strong bond.

When we have lunch, I note that Dean now eats with his fingers rather than with cutlery, just as regular Sri Lankans do. As we're finishing off, Jai makes an appearance. After letting us into the house he went out into Colombo, partying with friends. He didn't get back until the early hours and needed the rest. His hair is just as dishevelled as when we first saw him.

Jai suggests we go in his family's Porsche SUV so he can give us a tour of his city. We move slowly, the traffic always seeming to be building. The air conditioning is a godsend. After crawling our way along the roads we get out at Independence Square. Despite its central location in Colombo's Cinnamon Gardens district, the square is calm and peaceful. At its centre is the Independence Memorial Hall, a beautiful building with an eye-catching pagoda roof. Statues and carvings of lions surround the building, and Dean and I pose in front of them so we can later post our tourist pictures on Instagram. The memorial was built in 1948, the year that Ceylon achieved independence from Britain. (The country's name only changed to Sri Lanka in 1972.) Jai encourages us to look closer and we see further carvings, sculptures and columns that depict the history of Sri Lanka. The architecture, we're told, is Kandyan. The Kingdom of Kandy was the last native kingdom in Sri Lanka and included within its boundaries the majority of the island before being taken over by the British in 1815. We look and nod and take more pictures before walking the surrounding lawns.

As we walk, Jai tells us of the tense political situation between the three main Sri Lankan groups: the Sinhalese (about 75 per cent of the population), the Tamils and the Muslims. Each needs to be represented in government, but the balancing act is tricky. In fact, it's been tricky ever since independence back in 1948. When the British left, the Sinhalese majority set about creating a new country in their own image. The new flag, taken from that of the Kandyan Kingdom, was dominated by the Sinhalese lion. An orange stripe to represent the Tamils and a green one to represent the Muslims were only added to the flag much later.

Sinhalese nationalism picked up pace after independence. Galvanised by S.W.R.D. Bandaranaike, a growing consensus developed that the island was rightly Sinhalese, and therefore rightly Buddhist and Sinhalese-speaking. In 1956, an official Sinhala Only Act was passed, making the official language of the island Sinhala rather than English. All civil duties would now be conducted in Sinhala rather than English, having a great impact on the Tamils in particular, who held as many as two-thirds of civil service jobs despite making up just 15 per cent of the total population. The vast majority of Tamils didn't speak Sinhala. Neither did Muslims. Protests followed. For many, the Sinhala Only Act appeared to be a move by the dominant Sinhalese to assert their dominance further. The Tamils' and Muslims' language, culture and livelihood were under threat.

Riots followed in 1958, with as many as 1,500 killed. A hasty revision was made to the act: 'Sinhala Only, Tamil Also'. Yet still tensions boiled. S.W.R.D. Bandaranaike was assassinated by a Buddhist monk, who then converted to Christianity. Bandaranaike's legacy, though, lived on. Sinhala nationalist frustrations turned towards Tamils' disproportionate place in higher education. In 1969 Tamils made up half of all medical and engineering students in the country. The government reacted by making universities demand higher admission marks from Tamil students.

Discontent was growing in the north of the island, where Tamils outnumbered all other demographics. Murmurs started about creating a separate state in the north-east of the island, Tamil Eelam, where they would no longer have to be second-class citizens. Armed groups popped up: the Tamil Eelam Liberation Organisation, the People's Liberation Organisation of Tamil Eelam, the Eelam People's Revolutionary Liberation Front, the Eelam Revolutionary Organisation, the Eelam National Democratic Liberation Front and, in 1975, the Liberation Tigers of Tamil Eelam. Many believed they could never achieve sovereignty through political pressure alone; violence had to be the answer – even if it was against fellow Tamils. And so it was that the Liberation Tigers of Tamil Eelam waged war against the other armed Tamil groups. Then, when they emerged victorious, they took on the government in a twenty-six-year civil war. Even after winning the brutal civil war, things have rarely been smooth for the Sinhalese government.

'Yeah, but we've got it pretty bad too,' Dean points out in reference to Brexit. 'And so have Americans.'

* * *

We're becoming paranoid about mosquitoes. Dean has already had five big chunks taken out of him and I'm scared of getting Japanese Encephalitis, the one jab I didn't get. It's spread by mosquitoes and causes swelling of the brain, followed by possible death. It's low risk but the risk is still there. There is no cure.

We turn off the light in Jai's spare room and try to sleep, only to hear a low buzz. Straight away the light is back on and we're hunting. Eventually I spot it and Dean slaps it against the whitewashed wall. The buzz is no more and so the light goes off again. Twenty minutes later we're up again. In the middle of the night I'm awoken by a low buzzing in my ear. I fend it away, only for Dean to shout 'I've got one, I've got one.' I presume he's awake rather than talking in his sleep, which he's prone to do, but I'm not sure.

In the morning I have no bites. Dean has three new ones. Compared to Kalutara, we're told, these mosquitoes are nothing.

* * *

We were supposed to meet Thaabit yesterday. Then we were supposed to meet him today. He was also supposed to go to Jaffna for the player auction. But there's been a lot of 'supposed tos' so far, none of which has happened. Thaabit tells Jai he's too busy, so instead we go for plan B and Jai drives us to meet two of his friends that he went to international school with. Their house is the biggest house I've ever seen. Every bedroom has an en suite. There are several living rooms and several storeys to the house. As with every house we've seen so far in Sri Lanka, there's a family of cleaners in residence and, as we've seen so far in Sri Lanka, every single one of these cleaners is darker skinned than the homeowners. They avoid eye contact when they enter the same room and go about their business as if they were a ghost. It's all a little unsettling.

From there we pick up Yani from the hotel his parents own. His mum comes into the reception area to greet us and soon enough she's chatting away as if we're old friends. She can't speak highly enough of Colombo. The family have been here for five years now and she can't see them moving back to Australia. Sure, there are some things they miss but the positives outweigh the negatives by far. 'Isn't that right, Yani?' she asks. Yani nods. Me and Dean are enjoying ourselves, sitting back and talking about our new home. Jai, meanwhile, is constantly checking his phone. It turns out there's an emergency, and soon enough Jai has to excuse himself. He's considered the peacemaker in his friendship group and right now there's peace that needs to be made. He asks his friends to take me and Dean to eat at a pizzeria. He'll follow later on, he promises.

The pizza offers a respite from Sri Lankan food. Everything so far has been nice enough, but even the mildest of meals has had a kick to it. Back home I usually order a korma or tikka masala from the takeaway menu, while Dean got a carbonara the last time he went to an Indian restaurant. That's what our Sri Lankan hosts are working with here.

Yani is the first white person I've met in Sri Lanka. As we walk the short distance to the pizzeria, he tells us he feels safer in Colombo than he did back in Australia. Following the Easter bombings in Colombo and the subsequent retaliatory attacks that have only just fizzled out, it helps to reassure us. Yani is still in school, the same one that Jai went to, and is coached by Thaabit. He speaks highly of Thaabit's coaching, which – unlike much of Sri Lanka – actually involves organisation.

'It is the same for everyone in Sri Lanka,' one of the friends adds. 'None of us is organised. If you agree to meet at a certain time and then get there at that time that is considered rude.'

'My tutor was meant to come to me at 9 a.m. yesterday and turned up at 3 p.m. instead,' says Yani. 'It's just the way it is over here.'

I can deal with a lack of punctuality. What I really want to know about is the football, though. Yani smiles. 'It's aggressive. Like, really aggressive. They kick and fight and punch. They don't play fair. It kind of works, though. They're pretty good.'

He's the first person so far to tell us that Sri Lankans are pretty good at football.

Dean isn't listening any more. His gaze is fixed on two mosquitoes that he's spotted on my shoulder. He urges me to stay very still, before they dart away and he follows them, splatting them against the wall. Satisfied, he then turns to the rest of the party.

'These aren't too bad, right?' he asks, pointing to his numerous bites. The people around him umm and ahh and none of them tries to comfort him.

'They kind of are,' Yani concludes. 'Those are pretty big and they look like the kind I had last year when I got dengue fever. That was real bad. I was in bed for two months. No school, no football, nothing. It saps your energy.'

From my research, I already know that dengue fever doesn't just sap your energy. Spread by mosquitoes, dengue fever is the country's biggest killer. There's no vaccination against it; you just have to get to the hospital as soon as you can. The fever shuts off your immune system and makes you weak. I don't quite panic but Yani's words don't fill me with confidence. I tell Dean we have to sign our contracts as soon as possible so we get medical insurance in case the very worst happens, but he's only mildly worried. All this time he's been happily sipping from the water that the Sri Lankans among us strongly suspect is directly from the tap. They doubt it's been filtered and therefore it runs the risk of carrying typhoid. Dean, of course, hasn't been vaccinated against typhoid. He's backing his chances. Yani won't have the water anywhere near him.

Talk around the table turns to Sri Lanka's political situation. Currently, there's a lot of racial tension. The burka has been banned; women aren't allowed in the country if they're wearing it. Many Muslims feel uneasy, vulnerable.

Once again, we're told how the government is a mess. For the electorate, the choice is between bad and very bad. In Sri Lanka they vote for candidates rather than political parties. It seems that the current president and prime minister are not well received. Even more questions are being asked of them after the Easter bombings, especially given that Indian intelligence had warned of the attacks.

Our new friends paint a dismal picture of their country. It's a picture that isn't at all in keeping with what we've seen so far.

Later that evening I find Dean considering a one-way flight to Australia after the tournament. After all, when else are we going to be this close to the other side of the world? Many Sri Lankans head to Australia for work or university due to its relative closeness. Why shouldn't Dean? His ideal scenario is to be spotted by a top-flight Sri Lankan team and offered a contract. If that doesn't happen he has family in Australia – a country that he's never visited before but has never heard a bad word about.

Before Sri Lanka he'd been in Boston, USA, for nine months to play Gaelic football. His accommodation had been provided by the club and he'd earned good money on the side as a trainee tiler. Then, back in Ireland, he'd earned little more than £50 a day as a trainee tiler and was bored with life. He was prevented from returning to the USA after overstaying his visa, but then he saw a Facebook post: football players needed for Sri Lanka. He messaged the poster and ten minutes later Thaabit was on the phone.

The one thing now holding him back is Meghan, the girl he started dating before he flew to South East Asia. She's still in Ireland, completing her masters degree in accountancy.

I tell him Sri Lanka will give him opportunities that he never could have imagined – both in Ireland and in foreign countries. Whatever he decides, his life certainly won't be dull any more.

KALUTARA

Back at Kalutara there's the bulk of last season's squad that performed so underwhelmingly. There are a few new additions, but mainly everyone is staring at me and Dean. That's because the bulk of this season's squad hasn't shown up to their first official training session. Neither has Thaabit. Instead there are eight of us taking part in a light session with assistant coach Kapila.

In some ways our new surroundings are regal. We're at the Vernon U Fernando stadium, home to Kalutara Blue Star and built thanks to a generous grant from FIFA. That generous grant may well have had something to do with Vernon U Fernando himself, the former Football Federation of Sri Lanka President currently serving a lifelong ban from football for violating FIFA's ethics. Still, he knew how to develop an impressive stadium. Five separate stands take up just over a quarter of the circumference of the grounds, with palm trees poking over the fence that surrounds the other three quarters. The stands are grand and distinctly Asian, capable of hosting a capacity crowd of 2,000. Looking up at them, it feels as if I'm in a temple. Multi-coloured seats curve around the corner, blue and yellow columns dramatically holding up the stadium roof.

In many other ways, however, the surroundings are far from regal. The athletics track that surrounds the pitch is made of baked mud, with wonky lines painted onto the earth to indicate where the lanes should begin and end. Between the track and the pitch, there's a cattle grid. It obviously doesn't work too well, because standing behind me are two cows. They're happily grazing in the eighteen-yard box, though on what I'm not too sure. The grass around the pitch is thick and lush, but step onto the pitch and it becomes distinctly barer. Between the eighteen-yard box and the centre circle there's a large square of sand. Random areas have been filled with sand, while many others are just firm dirt. There's absolutely no chance that it'll 'take a stud'. What grass that is left won't be there for much longer if the cows have their way. I note that the goal behind them has no net. Nor does the other goal.

We start the session with a simple exercise in threes, one player working in the middle and volleying back to each player. It progresses to a thigh control and volley, then a chest and volley, then a header. It's low intensity but I'm fading fast. Dean's over to the left of me with his hands on his knees, breathing deeply. This is only the warm-up.

Kapila – or Kaps, as he prefers to be known – is Sinahelse and from Gampaha near Colombo. He speaks Sinhala and instructs in English. The players are all Trincomalee locals who have spent their entire lives on the other side of the island, in the coastal city of 100,000. They're either Muslim or Tamil and speak Tamil, while some understand parts of English. Hardly any understand Sinhala.

After some 'light' technical work, we're put into a four-a-side game with small goals. I join three Trinco veterans, Kalua, Sakhti and Priyan, a trio who grew up together and played for the Titans the previous season. Kalua and Priyan are equally wary yet intrigued by my presence. Kalua reminds me of a pirate. It must be the facial hair. He's fashionable, having arrived for training with a snapback cap perched on top of his slicked-back hair, and possesses an impressive beard and moustache combination, which he wears with a mouth always poised to smile. Priyan, meanwhile, is ultra-focused on the task at hand. He has not come here to have a laugh. He's come here to train and he wants to train hard. His eyes are already fixed on the ball, even though Kaps hasn't yet blown the whistle to start. Sakhti has no such reservations. 'Your name,' he demands. 'Sala?' he asks when I tell him. 'Seth,' I reply. 'OK, you are Sala,' he announces before suggesting we chest-bump. There's a wild look about him, the kind that suggests he's either the kind of person that would lead me to war or that he's unhinged. Soon enough, I find out it's both.

Dean and Jai, who has elected to play while wearing his glasses, are on the other team with Banda and last season's captain, Chinna. Banda is a skinny striker with a mischievous look and size 4.5 feet. Already I see him laughing and joking with Dean. He's dressed in a blue Chelsea kit with bright-yellow football socks. As soon as the whistle goes, the mischievous look disappears and one of intense concentration replaces it. Like Priyan, Banda has come here to work. So has the devout Christian, Chinna. He has the air of calm authority that you'd expect from a captain. He's wearing a black beaded chain with a crucifix that bounces up and down on his chest, along with a grey and orange kit. Solid SC, the badge says, and I presume it's another of the teams he plays for. The other players have a great deal of respect for him, that much is obvious. Every one of his movements is considered, yet as the game begins I note that he's also prone to short bursts of intense unpredictability. At thirty-two he's the oldest member of the group, and his serious nature is perhaps a result of his age.

Kaps has created a small area on the part of the pitch with the most grass yet the surface is deceptively tricky. It's rock-solid with an unpredictable bounce. I miscontrol the first pass I receive and give the ball away to Dean, who gratefully rolls it through the metre-long goal that Kaps has created from cones. 1-0 to them.

A few touches later, I'm starting to read the pitch. My confidence is high. I'm knackered but I've seen from the warm-up that my technique is better than the Sri Lankans'. Soon enough, my teammates look for me to pass the ball to. I nutmeg Banda and my teammates whoop and holler. I'm making things happen. So is Dean. He smashes Sakthi and tells him it isn't a foul. It isn't, to be fair, but Sakthi doesn't take it well, squaring up to Dean and insisting it's an illegal challenge. Dean doesn't back down. Quickly realising he's picking a fight he'll never win, Sakthi smiles and refocuses his wiry frame back on the game.

Sakthi has without doubt emerged as the biggest character in the team. Not put off by the altercation, he takes to screaming 'yes' every time he touches the ball, mimicking Dean. Occasionally he throws in a 'nice' too. He's small, thin, sinewy and a bag full of energy. 'Sala! Sala!' he calls to me when he wants a pass. Which seems to be all the time. In defence he chases the ball as it moves around the area, showing little regard for holding his position. With the heat, I'm quite happy for Sakhti to do my defending for me.

My team is adept at keeping the ball but struggles to penetrate. At least it means we rarely need to defend. Our opponents perhaps typify Sri Lankan football more. They play off our mistakes and work relentlessly, Chinna dictating his team's movements from the back. It's the technical side of the game that lets them down. They love a back-heel. If in doubt, they back-heel.

We go to only three touches allowed and the frequency of back-heels from both teams increases still further. Then, just as the session is winding down and I think it's about to end, coach Kaps calls two touches only for the final five minutes. Five minutes. The cogs in my head whirr. Five minutes. Three hundred seconds. That's a long time. I need water. I can't last five minutes. Yet I have to.

The relief I feel when I remove my boots and down my water at the end of the session is immense. My new teammates laugh as Dean and I gasp for air. But it doesn't matter – we survived.

We're all smiles as we say our goodbyes so we can head back to the house to shower and rest. Sakhti insists we chest-bump again. I worry that he's so skinny he'll bounce straight back off me but he takes the contact well. Dean shares a final joke with Banda and then we're off. This is my first time walking in Kalutara. Jai's mum dropped us at the stadium and Thaabit has the coaches' car. The house is ten minutes away, just the other side of the main road. As I walk through the town with Kaps, Jai and Dean, it feels like everyone is stopping to stare at me. I'm the only white face. I keep my eyes towards the ground and avoid contact. I know they're all going to be friendly to me. I just don't yet feel confident enough.

We make it to the gate of the house without incident. Kaps already has the key in his hand and reaches over the top of the iron gate to unlock it. He slides the gate across and we walk up the driveway. Maybe it was the travel fatigue when I dismissed this house before. Sure, we've just walked past an open drain giving off a terrible stench at the front gate, but there is a swimming pool out the back. The leak in our en-suite wasn't a leak after all; the floor had actually been washed in preparation for our arrival. The communal area is comfortable and has satellite TV. Football is on 24/7. Unfortunately, there's no subscription for the channel showing the Cricket World Cup. My bed still has stains but they look cleaner. The bedroom is at least functional.

There's also a caretaker, Joseph. You hear him before you see him. If he isn't laughing then he's talking excitedly. Most important, he's been preparing the swimming pool for us. Kaps suggests we dive in the pool to cool off after our first session. I remove my shirt and then a thought crosses my mind: 'Is there chlorine in the pool?' You can never be too safe in a foreign country. The message does the rounds and makes its way to Joseph, who bends down and scoops up a handful of water. He lifts it towards his mouth and takes a gulp.

'See? Safe,' he insists.

In the warm glow of dusk I want to swim in the hopefully chlorinated water for hours, but Kaps reminds us that we must return to the stadium for dinner. All of our meals will be taken in the stadium's canteen. The locals have offered to do the catering for the entire squad at a cut price that Thaabit couldn't refuse. We dry off and put on our casual clothes then retrace our steps back to the stadium. Cars merge across the lanes of the main road and beep their horns, yet the overwhelming busyness of pedestrians from just an hour earlier has calmed. Men still shout into the night, hoping for the last few sales of their fish or fruit or vegetables. The cows have disappeared from the pavement. I even feel confident enough to take my eyes off the ground every now and again.

We're stopped in our tracks outside the stadium entrance by five figures and a smartphone. One races up to bump chests and it immediately becomes obvious the figures are our new teammates. 'Photo, photo,' they insist. Me and Dean, the tallest by far, are instructed to pose for a picture with each one of them in turn, then a group photo with everyone. I guess this means we've been accepted.

Under Kaps's guidance we're early for dinner and it's no surprise when we are told the food is going to be late. That's not a problem for the Sri Lankans, though, as it gives them more time to find out everything about us.

'Are you married?' Sakhti asks. 'No? A girlfriend?'

'How many do you have?' Banda chimes in.

They smile approvingly when Dean jokes he has two. They're impressed when I tell them I've had the same girlfriend for seven years, though also disappointed when I tell them there is no second. 'Well, while you're in Sri Lanka…' they suggest. Sakhti tells us he likes all women but that he likes aunties best of all. Apparently that's the Sri Lankan version of MILFs. Banda shows us photos of various European ex-girlfriends in various states of undress.

It's sobering to discover I'm the second-oldest of the eight, after Chinna. Most are twenty-three. I'm asked to tell them more about England, football, which team I support, about my opinion of Sri Lanka, cricket. By the time the food arrives in blue plastic buckets, we've been quizzed for forty-five minutes and a bond has been built. We share Instagram handles. They promise to tag us in their pictures.

There's no cutlery. For the first time I eat with my hands, just like all of my teammates.

* * *

I thought everyone was joking when they said we would train at 7 a.m., and I still think it's some kind of sick joke when our alarm goes off at 5.30, otherwise known as 1 a.m. in England. I roll over and go back to sleep. Nobody wakes me until it's time to leave. Coach Kaps doesn't look best pleased that I'm not ready. Maybe that's as angry as they get in Sri Lanka. It certainly seems to be the angriest Kaps will ever get. He's a Buddhist, deeply in touch with his inner peace.

We're the first ones out on the pitch. Nobody joins us for at least twenty minutes. Slowly they filter out. All six of them. We're up to nine players now that a new arrival, Mindron, has joined us. He's fresh off a twelve-hour overnight bus journey from Trincomalee and jumps straight into the session as if it's the most normal thing in the world, barely even saying hello to his teammates.

Still no Thaabit.

Considering this is the first official week of training, with the previous week consisting of trials, you'd have thought the whole twenty-man squad would be raring to go. Especially as they still haven't signed a contract.

The nine of us start off with rondos: football's own version of piggy-in-the-middle. There's no better test to see who can play. Are they happy to take the ball under pressure? Do they just ping it to the other side of the circle? Are they happy to play off one touch? The answers are soon revealed as no, yes, no. That makes the task of defending in the middle easy: just stand still and wait for them to mess up. The ball is a hot potato all around me. Players pass it as far as possible as often as possible, which makes it difficult to control on the hard, uneven ground and leads to mistakes. By contrast, when I receive the ball I keep it under the sole of my foot and roll it to the player next to me, drawing in the pressure. Mindron picks it up quickly. Gradually the rest of my new teammates start to copy. By the end we've even made it to ten passes.

The ball goes away. That's it for the morning. I haven't changed out of my running shoes, which is just as well. We have to run two laps of the 400-metre track that circles the pitch, then do twenty push-ups, twenty squat jumps and twenty lunges. Then repeat. Twenty times. That's 16km, 400 push-ups, 400 squat jumps and 400 lunges.

We run just above walking pace. It's slow but deceptively tough. After the first set we switch to running on the outside of the pitch, which proves tougher. The grass is thick and hard to cut through.

So much sweat. My kit is weighing me down. It feels like my shorts are about to fall to the floor, they're that heavy. And it's a mild day; there's no sun, only cloud. I ran out of water a long time ago. I'm left with a tough choice of dehydration or accepting my teammates' tap water. I look over to see Dean glugging and decide to do the same. The odds are stacked more against him.

We watch the cows move across the pitch as we wait for the call to start our final set. Yesterday they were grazing in the eighteen-yard box and today they're wisely heading to the corner of the ground where the grass is much more plentiful. I'm not sure this is what FIFA had in mind ten years ago when they funded the development of the stadium.

The distraction of the cows helps take my mind off the pain. Soon enough Kaps has his whistle in his mouth and it's time to start the final set. Wearily I push my legs forward as I set about my last laps, cursing with every step. I don't collapse, and I make it to the end. My legs are burning. But worst of all, we train twice a day so I have to do it all again in six hours' time.

Breakfast is served afterwards in the stadium kitchen. Chickpeas, boiled eggs and coconut sambal, which is essentially a mix of grated coconut and chilli. There's nowhere to wash my hands and no cutlery so I just dig in with my dusty hands once more.

The plates all come with plastic bags wrapped around them. At the end of the meal you wrap up any leftovers in the plastic bag and throw it in the bin. When I ask Jai why they do it, he tells me it's to keep the plates clean. 'It's not great for the environment,' he laughs. It isn't, but then if they're that desperate to keep the plates clean I fear they never get washed.

Almost the whole squad has appeared from nowhere for breakfast, and they're all eating alongside us. More specifically, they're all scrolling alongside us. Everywhere I look, smartphones are in hands. While the new members of the squad look fresh, I feel like I've just had a two-hour shower of sweat. Big black bags hang under my eyes. I'm still struggling with jet lag. Last night I didn't get to sleep until 2 a.m.

One of the new players has started calling me Thomas Muller. Apparently we look alike. The rest are equally fascinated by me and Dean. Many point their smartphones in our direction, covertly filming us for their Instagram Stories without working up the courage to ask for a photo. I'm too shattered to entertain them much and Dean feels the same. Priyan, sitting on the table with me, Jai and Dean, assures us that the training session is exactly what we need to win the tournament. I hope he's wrong. I'm not sure I can put my body through that again. It's a relief when Kaps tells us it's time to return to the coaches' house for rest before the afternoon session. My bed has rarely felt more appealing.

The streets of Kalutara have come to life by the time we walk back. Stalls, shops, pedestrians and roads merge as one.

Buildings are in various states of disrepair. Adverts shout from all directions. Everywhere you look, people are selling goods. Rambutan, a red hairy ball of a fruit from the lychee family, goes by the cart load. A mountain of fish sits on top of a cardboard box in the raging sunlight. Music plays and people shout, horns sound while tuk-tuk drivers attempt to lure us in. To cross the road is to dance with death: some cars wait, but most don't. Even the buses drop off and pick up passengers while on the move. It's the busiest laid-back country I've been to. It seems Sri Lankans either do frantic or relaxed and nothing in between.

For the next few hours I do relaxed. Even then, the afternoon training session comes around much sooner than I expect. By the time I've laced up my boots – an act I take as long as possible to do in an attempt to save my aching legs – I notice that 'grenades' are raining down on Dean, who's already out on the pitch. The 'grenades' are passes of various speeds coming in at all angles, flying into his shin and striking his knee. The culprit is a young Sri Lankan called Aflal. He's wearing a CR7 kit and has obviously modelled himself on the Portuguese forward. There's no doubt that Aflal is doing it on purpose. Dean's body is moving at all angles as he does his best to bring the grenades under control and pass them back.

'Hey!' calls Dinesh, a big-bellied Trinco native with a cheery expression and a purple Real Madrid kit, blasting his own grenade in my direction as I walk onto the pitch. I bring it under control. Just.

'Are these boys sure?' I ask Dean.

'Madness, isn't it?' he replies. 'They best be good.'

'Grenades' are an often-used tactic in English football too. Established players in a team test new players by giving them bad passes on purpose. If the new players manage to control the ball, they become accepted. If not, it can lead to jokes and often something more malicious.

Today's grenade-givers are among the players who have just arrived. As their welcome, they're gathered together and instructed to do our run from this morning. After receiving those grenades, I have no sympathy for them. While they run, those who took part in the morning session are put into a rondo.

There are nine of us once more so this time we decide to have two defenders in the middle. As a result, those on the outside are allowed to take two touches. The extra touch changes everything. Suddenly passes are being made and defenders are being forced to work. Mindron, already marked out as a quick learner, is very good in the rondo. He happily takes the ball under pressure and draws in defenders. He's almost Brazilian in his technique. The standard is relatively high – better than many rondos I've played in at a semi-professional level in England. While I get four nutmegs in, Dean is on a one-man mission to bust the myth that Sri Lankan footballers are aggressive. When defending in the middle he goes charging about like a Sri Lankan bus trying to overtake a tuk-tuk. His mission is successful. Players – notably including Sakhti – soon jump out of his way rather than risk any contact. They tell him to calm down and he ignores them. He's defending in a style that'd be called 'hard but fair' in England. In Sri Lanka it's probably GBH.

'Bloody softies. I knew it was mash. I knew they was all soft,' Dean concludes when the rondo is stopped so we can play a training game.

Thaabit has arrived, at last, with Ihshan in tow. Ihshan's camera is already rolling when Thaabit greets his players. There's no denying that he has a certain aura. He wears a green Titans t-shirt, sunglasses and a backwards baseball cap.

He smiles and high-fives, laughing with players and making them feel a million dollars. His presence instantly lights up the stadium. Few of these players have ever had a proper coach to learn their craft from.

With Thaabit perched high in the stands to get a tactical view, and the free-roaming cows moved from the pitch, we're split into two teams and placed into a training game. Dean and I are on opposing teams. I'm told to play sweeper with new arrivals Hizam to my left, Balaya in front and Priyan to my right. Hizam and Balaya both play with the supreme confidence you'd expect from players wearing bright-red boots, if not the skills to match, while Priyan huffs and puffs up and down the wing.

Dinesh is anchoring the midfield. He seems thrilled to be there. He runs up to me and thrusts his arm next to mine with a gleeful expression. He can't believe how white I am. Then the call comes for our team to take our tops off so we can 'play skins', and he does a double-take. My belly is whiter than white and my shoulders are already peeling.

Coach Rimzy takes the whistle and is made to suffer the cries of anguish and screams of disbelief that inevitably come from having no linesmen. Shouts of 'Rimzy Nana!' – Tamil for brother – ring through the air, usually a mark of respect yet often said in this instance with an undertone of frustration. 'Sir!' come further cries, the usual reference term for a Sri Lankan referee.

Despite the refereeing decisions, my team is the better of the two and I rarely have to leave my comfort zone. The gap between defence and attack is big, making it hard for midfielders to get on the ball. When they do, the surface inevitably plays its part. Our defence is solid enough. Hazim listens to everything I say, Priyan plays with strength, and Balaya is assured if a little kamikaze. I suggest we play left and right centre-back instead but Balaya dismisses it as too complicated. Instead he marks and I sweep. In theory.

Tactics are few and far between. Players understand the concepts of defence, midfield and attack but don't necessarily practise them. The majority have never received any formal coaching, instead relying on the games they see on TV to teach them. I yell myself hoarse as I take on the role of in-game coach, gesturing in every direction and doing my best to move all my teammates into the correct positions. Yet with some there's little hope.

We're 2-0 up when I roll the ball back to our young goalkeeper, Ranoos, who still has the body of a child and the innocent smile of someone so young. That innocent smile is quickly wiped off his face as he inexplicably panics. This is his first experience of playing adult football and it shows. He's about as comfortable with a ball at his feet as my pale skin is with the hot sun. In his world, goalkeepers use their hands and their hands only. Ranoos takes at least three touches too many, allowing Banda to successfully close him down, steal the ball and tap the ball into the empty net. My team erupts. Balaya, one of the team's main players last season, accuses me of having a slow touch. With a hint of English arrogance, I point out I haven't missed a pass so far.

We go on to win the game. Thaabit comes down for the post-match wrap-up and expresses his delight at our defence, as Ihshan and the camera follow his every move. The players hold deep respect for both. They have done since the first day they met Thaabit and his coaching staff. For them, this is a great opportunity. Even Ihshan is referred to as 'coach' or 'brother'.

There's a real deference to teachers and coaches, which Thaabit later tells me is a common trait in the north-east. As the exhausted players lap up Thaabit's every word, he asks them to congratulate themselves on their effort in the game. It's then asked that we all applaud Dinesh, the heaviest of the Sri Lankans by far, who is aiming to lose 6kg in the pre-season camp and has already lost 3kg. Impressed, we clap. Dinesh smiles.

'Of course,' Thaabit adds, 'Dinesh is aiming to be 65kg. He currently weights 68kg.'

If he weighs 68kg I dread to think what our other team-mates weigh. Dean looks equally perplexed. As we walk back to the changing rooms, I tell Thaabit that Dean and I both weigh 80kg. Thaabit stops and looks at me, my training shirt still off.

'Yes, but Dean is a much more muscular 80kg.'

I can't think of a reply.

* * *

It's amazing what football can do to your mood. A few days ago I enjoyed being in Sri Lanka; now I love it. One decent performance in a training session and I feel on top of the world. I love Sri Lanka, love the people, love the food, love the accommodation, and most of all I love the football.

That evening, Thaabit apologises for all the delays. It's past midnight and we're gathered around the TV in preparation for the England v USA women's World Cup final. We'll be up again in a few hours to watch the Copa America semi-final between Brazil and Argentina. There's no doubt that Thaabit loves football.

Dean and I sit either side of Thaabit. He's excited to see Alex Morgan in action for the USA. He talks at speed, his words tumbling into one another. Making the most of our time with him, we ask Thaabit about the tournament. He replies that his hands have been tied by administration, particularly from the tournament provider. He sighs and thrusts out his arms. The impatience is obvious. This is Thaabit's first role managing a senior team and he can't wait to get started. Most of the issues have stemmed from the player auction, which has been pushed back once again and will now take place at the coming weekend. Until that has taken place, Thaabit cannot confirm his final squad. Each team in the tournament is only allowed to retain five players from the previous season; all other players are automatically entered into the auction, and the highest bidder gets the player.

Thaabit has tried to work round the problem by building a squad of local players from the Trincomalee region who didn't play in the tournament last season. Still, eight of the players in our training camp are up for auction, including Banda and Sakhti. It's a delicate situation that has left Thaabit wary of secrets being shared. He doesn't want to be outbid for a player from our training camp, then have that same player reveal our tactics to their new team. That's why we're mainly working on fitness and playing training matches. There won't be any tactical work until after the auction.

There's a real danger that Thaabit will be outbid for some of our players. The owners, seeing this as more of a charitable venture to benefit the players of Trincomalee rather than a stab at winning the tournament, have limited him to a maximum bid of 50,000 LKR per player. He has no plans to bid for players not in the camp.

Considering this is the first official week of training, with the previous week consisting of trials, I'm surprised to hear another player has been cut tonight: Mindron. Technically he was one of the best players, though he was quiet in the game. Thaabit goes on to explain that he doesn't like Mindron's attitude. Last season Mindron played for the champions of the North Eastern Premier League. He's apparently been telling his new teammates that they were awful last season, they still aren't great this season, and he's come back to rescue them.

There was already friction between Mindron and his new teammates before he even opened his mouth. They lost respect for him last season when he moved from Trinco to the team that would go on to be champions, despite them being based six hours away in Jaffna. Though good money was on offer, his Trinco teammates felt he should have stayed loyal to Trinco. Local pride and loyalty, it seems, are important beyond all else in the north-east. But now Mindron has no option: he can't stay loyal to Trinco because Trinco hasn't stayed loyal to him. Thaabit suspects Mindron heard about the new owners and the money they were investing and decided to return. It turns out that 50,000 LKR is considered a decent wage in Sri Lanka.

While I'm surprised and a little disappointed, Dean is thrilled by the news. Mindron is the only player he's taken a dislike to so far. And now he's gone.

* * *

What started as a swim and stretch has become a selfie session. Every single player has to have a picture wearing Hizam's designer sunglasses. Every single player needs a picture in the pool with the two foreign players. Dean clocks it early and escapes back to bed. I'm too slow and end up having to smile and smile and smile again. Arms grab me from nowhere and point to the camera. Hizam, taking charge of the photographs, is in his element. Appearance means everything to him. Even the elder statesman of the team, Chinna, wants a photograph that he can share on his social media pages. It feels like an age before I finally escape and head back to bed. Having watched the England v USA game until 2 a.m., and then lain awake staring at the dark ceiling and cursing jet lag, I only managed a couple of hours' sleep before my 6.55 a.m. wake-up call. The whole team was supposed to arrive at 6 a.m. to watch the Brazil game on our communal TV and then have a team-bonding session in the pool, but fortunately they were almost an hour late. Right now I'm at the stage where every second of sleep counts. I drop off as soon as my head hits the pillow.

I awake re-energised and get up to check the time on my phone, which I had left charging in the corner. Dean is still out like a light and I can't help but feel jealous. The phone flashes and the energy drains from me when I see the screen. 10:45 a.m. Not even an hour's sleep. Nowhere near enough. I want to creep back to bed, but Thaabit spots me.

'Seth, I'm going to check out a futsal court. I want you to come. Can you be ready in two minutes?'

I tell him yes.

We battle the manic traffic as we head south down the coast towards Beruwala. Thaabit makes gentle conversation as I stare out of the window at the Laccadive Sea, which stretches across to the Maldives, and then all the way to Somalia.

When we arrive I find that the court is narrow but has its charm. Tropical plants and trees flank the far end, giving a beautiful view. A lone basketball hoop stands isolated in front. It is all still a couple of weeks from being ready. The flooring is yet to be laid, the goals yet to be bought, the changing rooms yet to be built, the car park yet to be landscaped. I feel this could be another example of Sri Lankan punctuality. Many men are standing around, many men are talking, but few men are working. I count twenty-six in total.

The futsal court is the first for Beruwala, a historic town famed for gem trading. Arabian settlers first came more than a thousand years ago. To this day it's a predominantly Muslim area. The majority of its population work in the world-renowned international gem market, with cutting and trading the main forms of business. Over time Beruwala has established itself as the Sri Lankan version of Hatton Gardens.

After admiring the futsal court we head into the town where a friend of Thaabit's works. It's modern, clean and very white. Everyone seems to be wearing white. A steady procession of prospective sellers comes and goes through the doors of the trading offices. Removing their shoes at the entrance, they shove small white packets containing rare stones towards the owners. I see one set of traders demand 1,300,000 LKR. They barely look old enough to be out of school. The dealer entertains them. He removes his Ray-Bans, gets his torch out and spends some time inspecting the fine details. All eyes are on him. He shakes his head and hands the stones back to the boys. The next trader is taken more seriously. The dealer disappears out the back so he can inspect the stone in natural light. It's the best way to assess quality, although stones that look beautiful in bright places such as Sri Lanka look less so in Europe – especially in the winter months.

Hundreds and hundreds of people line the street. Traffic is reduced to a few frantic traders attempting to weave through on mopeds. People ignore them. It's quicker to walk. Nearly everyone is wearing a white sarong. It's traditional, but it's also pure and gem traders want to be associated with the purity of white. Torches constantly flash on and off. Stones are held to the sky. Sri Lankan streets are synonymous with hustle and bustle, none more so than this. Sellers rush from one trader to the next, hoping to get the sale they so desperately need. In one corner a trader has dropped a stone and several people are on their hands and knees in search. A Chinese lady draws attention. The guess is that she's looking for something unique and has money to burn.

Among the excitement nobody notices me. They're too busy looking at their gems. Just as no one pays much attention to the loose cow grazing on the pedestrian crossing of Kalutara's main road – nobody knows who it belongs to and nobody is trying to move it, as cars, tuk-tuks, mopeds and even buses manoeuvre their way around it – people no longer seem to stare at me either. Sometimes people come up to me, tap me on the shoulder and say 'hello'. When it first happened I thought they wanted to sell me something. Now I know they just genuinely want to say hello and smile at me. This is the kind of place Sri Lanka is.

* * *

I've always thought of myself as a cultured player fond of a short pass. Now I find myself on a one-man mission to teach every Sri Lankan 'the diag'. Often hit from one's own half, the diag is a long and searching ball aimed between the opponents' full-back and centre-half. At worst you give away a throw-in in a dangerous area for your opponent and 'box them in'. Better still, you win a throw-in in an attacking position. And best of all, your winger breaks free of the defence and runs on to the pass to score. When your full-backs mark the winger incorrectly, the latter often happens. When your full-backs mark touch-tight – and not even goal side – it's a recipe for disaster. Sri Lankan full-backs tick all the boxes. Their positioning is basic, to say the least. On opposing teams once more, Dean and I take it in turns to hit diags over each other's defence. They always come off.

Today's session is a training match. I'm first pick, which at least means I'm not considered an imposter by my new teammates, but things soon go downhill from there. I'm playing in the centre of a three-man defence with Hizam and Balaya either side of me. I tell them not to get touch-tight to their winger when the ball is on the other side of the pitch, urging them to take their position off me so they're around halfway between me and the winger. Hizam listens, Balaya doesn't. Hizam starts to block diags and so Dean starts to drive forward with the ball from midfield. He's met with little resistance. Since yesterday's rondo, his opponents would rather jump out of his way than tackle him. When I try the same thing from centre-back I'm also met with similar resistance. Until I run into Dean, that is, which brings about a fifty–fifty of such intensity that few Sri Lankans will ever have seen. Dean is playing in skins today and I slide straight off, failing to hold on to the shirt that he isn't wearing.

Dean is dominating. He's on the better team today and he's their best player. I spend most of my time mopping up mistakes from players being out of position. My frustration grows as my teammates refuse to pass forwards. They're happy to go sideways and back but that is all. They don't dribble much either. When my team has a six-on-two counter-attack they opt to pass backwards. My frustration grows further still.

I play a diag and we're through on goal. Priyan holds on to the ball. He passes to Naleem – a part-time rugby player alongside his teaching with the physique to match – who holds on to it. We've gone from being two-on-one to four-on-four.

'Master, master,' my teammates shout in honour of Naleem's profession. Naleem obliges and passes the ball sideways, only to receive it again with the next pass. The ball is being passed sideways and sideways again ten yards from the goal. It's as if they're too scared to shoot. I charge forward from centre-back, demand the ball and instantly shoot. It gets blocked and we would get counter-attacked if our opponents possessed any urgency. Instead, the ball ends up being dished around midfield. We have a lot of work to do if we're going to get anywhere in this tournament.

The lethargy is worrying, though it is at least explaina-ble. It's been there since the start of the session, when we were greeted by the sight of an angry Thaabit driving away from the stadium with Ihshan. He'd stumbled across Mindron, who he had ordered to leave the night before. Instead, the Trinco players had agreed to hide him in the stadium. They didn't do a good job. Thaabit, unsurprisingly, lost it at the sight of Mindron. He needs the players on his side, not Mindron's. He needs his players to take this whole tournament seriously. The only way to control his emotions before doing something he regretted was to drive away from the situation, leaving Coach Kaps to take the session instead.

Thaabit isn't at the house when we return from training. He isn't even in Kalutara. Apparently he was so angry that he drove back to his house in Colombo. It can't just have been Mindron's presence that angered him. Something else must have happened.

We wait up all evening, each of us offering our theories as to what really happened. Eventually Thaabit walks through the front door just as we're about to retire to our room for the night. He says hello and tells us we were late to training in a voice that is far from his usual excitable tone. There isn't much conversation from him. He dismisses the afternoon's issue as team politics. We want to hear more but he doesn't give us an option. He heads straight to bed. The tension remains high.

The next day Thaabit takes the lead in the early-morning session and the team is full of spirit. It's as if yesterday has been forgotten by everyone. Dinesh greets me as 'Peter Parker' and the nickname sticks, which I'm pretty sure is just because I'm also white. Chinna is missing and Jai is sick. Other than that, everyone takes part in five sets of 400-metre runs followed by the usual twenty push-ups, squats and lunges. It takes thirty minutes and while we wait for breakfast to be delivered to the ground Thaabit calls us into a circle.

He says a few words in Tamil and then tells me and Dean what he said. It's all motivational, praising the togetherness of the team and expressing his desire to keep everyone together after the auction. This appears to be where Thaabit is at his happiest. He invites Kaps to say something, then Dinesh, then Priyan. Dinesh and Priyan speak in Tamil, Kaps in Sinhala that's translated by Thaabit. Next up is Dean, who unsurprisingly opts to speak in English. He thanks his teammates for the welcome and says he's ready to go to war with them. Once it's been translated by Thaabit there are roars of encouragement. Then Sakhti speaks, then Balaya, and finally Thaabit asks me to speak. I knew this was coming. I compose myself, look around the circle, and then open my mouth.

'This is going to be a long tournament of many games. It's a marathon and not a sprint. We have to believe in ourselves and believe that we can win it. If we trust the process that the coaches have put in place then we will succeed. We will make the final.' I stop speaking to find silence. There is no immediate reaction and I wonder if I've misspoken. A few more seconds pass and there's polite applause. Then Thaabit translates what I've said into Tamil and the polite applause become more emphatic. I breathe a sigh of relief. Another test passed. We finish by joining hands and expressing our gratitude. Mindron is nowhere to be seen.

On the way back to the coaches' house after the session, Dean and I are stopped by a police officer. Dinesh bumps into us as the officer breaks off from writing a traffic ticket to start angrily gesticulating towards Dean and me. We're mesmerised as he embarks on a back-and-forth with Dinesh. It turns out he's ordering Dean to put his top back on. We're told it's disrespectful to be topless on the street. Dean appears to think it's more disrespectful that he's been stopped. Fortunately Dinesh manages to calm all parties and we are free to go.

We have a few hours of free time before the day's second session, and I need to do some washing back at the house. When I asked Thaabit if I'd be able to wash my clothes regularly when I got to Sri Lanka he told me yes, of course I would, and that Sri Lanka may be a developing nation but they do at least have some basic hygiene standards. What he actually meant, though, was that I'd have to stand in the hot garden – roasting at 84 per cent humidity – with my sweaty clothes bundled together under the garden tap. A bar of detergent soap is in my hands. An army of red ants is crawling over my feet. I soak each garment then rub it with the soap, rinse it out, squeeze, then lay it on the floor to dry. The cycle repeats. It takes me ages. It'll be revolutionary once washing machines come to Sri Lanka en masse. But until then I'll be washing my clothes with soap. It's not exactly the life you imagine for a professional footballer.

As I wait for my clothes to dry I join Dean and Thaabit by the pool. Thaabit is all hands and smiles. He's in a great mood – the disappointment of yesterday has been forgotten after this morning's session. Again he dismisses it as team politics, but we probe deeper and as we do so he opens up. He tells us it wasn't just the fact that Mindron had stayed, but that he'd been hidden. Despite his obvious talent, Mindron hadn't made the cut for this week's squad and had already been asked to leave. He was allowed to return to the dormitory to pick up his bags. Thaabit was furious when he saw that Mindron was still training, but Kaps assured him that Mindron just wanted a runabout. Not wanting to risk his chances of being seen again, Mindron instead stayed in the dormitory the next day. He wouldn't have been found had Thaabit not come to his room to ask the masseuse to stay for longer. Thaabit wasn't just angry because Mindron was still there. Mindron is friends with Chinna, who he has pinned the blame on. Their friendship outweighed Chinna's loyalty to the coach, so Chinna agreed to hide Mindron's presence. As a result, Chinna has also been asked to leave by Thaabit, which has caused waves around the squad. Last season's captain – gone! With that move, Thaabit has shown that he means business. Unlike Mindron, Chinna wasn't up for hanging around. The pair are already back in Trincomalee. Thaabit still plans to speak to Chinna. It isn't over for him. Thaabit will still ask him to be part of the squad, but he also has plenty of options to cover his position.

Chinna struck me as a proper captain. Hard-working, respectful and always leading by example, he's the kind of person you want on your team. He's loyal. But it seems he's more loyal to his friends than his football. Who can blame him? With the respect Chinna commands in the changing room, Thaabit is aware the Mindron situation could lead Chinna to turn a number of players against his leadership. It's a delicate situation that requires delicate handling. I don't envy Thaabit one bit.

* * *

My body is sore but not injured. My mind is drained but still working. My lip, however, is bleeding heavily. I've just received my first bad challenge in Sri Lanka and it hasn't come from a Sri Lankan.

Excited by the prospect of a goal, Dean swung his arm out to hold me off at centre-back. As he did so, his elbow caught my lip. It worked. I went down and Dean rolled me. There's no apology and there's no need for one. We both understand it was just one of those things that happens when you play football. However, the Sri Lankans treat it as GBH and my teammates insist the game be stopped. Sakhti sprints to get me some water. The incident motivates them further.

The standard is much higher today. Yesterday I could run with the ball at will. Now I'm being hounded by Priyan, Banda and Dean. I barely get a second to think. Our team is also playing with intensity. Everyone desperately wants to prove themselves.

Thaabit has been clever here. He's kept the players on their toes. Now he's clearly split the teams to play his first-choice defence against his first-choice attack. It makes for an even game. We're up against it as wave after wave comes at us, but whenever we do get to make a forward pass it slices through our opponents' defence at will.

With the score at 2-2, Thaabit orders us to play the game on the full pitch. We've been trying different formations through-out and now he wants my team to play 3-4-3. He tells me to set up my team as the captain. I hold total responsibility for what happens. Thaabit wants me to take all the free-kicks, tell the players where to stand and even take the goal-kicks. I'm not used to this. It's like I'm the manager's son in a Sunday-league side.

We concede within ten seconds. From the kick-off the ball is played to Sakhti at right-back. He makes a hash of passing forward, then gives a hospital pass to our Cristiano Ronaldo idoliser Aflal in central midfield. With Dean snarling down his neck, Aflal shouts 'Seth' and aims a pass in my direction. He aims but he doesn't execute. The loose ball falls to Banda, who gleefully strikes it home. Twenty seconds later it's 1-1 as the same thing happens at the other end. This is my first experience of Sri Lankan football on a full-sized pitch.

The mistakes settle down. The team that makes the fewest will win. Dean and Banda are pulling me all over the place but aren't being played the right balls. We're on the front foot. Our long balls are coming off. The only player on the other team who heads the ball is Dean, and he's usually up next to me. We score from a long ball, then score again. It ends up being a comfortable if not deserved victory. Dean is left to rue the state of his team's defence.

Several players head home after the session. Balaya – Chinna's brother and my defensive partner – says his goodbye. When I say I'll see him in Trincomalee he looks evasive. A post-training discussion is being held on the pitch by the senior players who are most friendly with Chinna. They're there for half an hour. This doesn't seem right.

* * *

We've discovered the supermarket. There are shelves and shelves of beautiful, glorious refined sugar. Dean goes crazy. He gets two ice creams, a bottle of Sprite, two tubes of Pringles and a packet of Maltesers. I get a Fanta, a bottle of water and a Mars Bar. Our bodies are being pushed to the limits. They deserve a treat.

Hizam and Aflal bump into us in the aisle. Hizam stares at our sugary snacks.

'Coach say no fizzy drinks,' he tells us. We reply that it's OK. He smiles and disappears. The next minute he's standing behind us in the queue with a bottle of Coke and a tube of Pringles.

I curse myself. I've proved myself on the training pitch yet I still feel like an imposter. The reality is that our teammates look up to me and Dean. Hizam does everything I tell him to on the pitch and is always grateful for any direction. Our teammates are impressionable and see us as role models, which feels crazy. I'm not used to this. I feel so guilty that I put my Mars Bar back on the shelf and get a banana instead. I keep the Fanta, though.

That afternoon we arrive five minutes early at the stadium. There are hundreds of people out there exercising, doing drills, balancing in headstands, running round the athletics track and playing football. But none of them belongs to the Titans. Something isn't right.

Dinesh walks past in flip-flops and shorts as if he doesn't have a care in the world. Kaps follows him up to the dorms and lets loose. Stern words are said. Slowly the players filter out for training. Ten minutes after the scheduled start time, six of us are warming up. The number eventually rises to sixteen.

We're split into two teams for what is set to be our last training session in Kalutara. The two goalkeepers are captains and are tasked with picking. I'm among the last few to be selected. Something isn't right. I've been the first pick for the last two days and I know that me and Dean, who isn't fit to train, are two of the Titans' best players. There are four players here now that I've never seen before, and they're the first four picks. The game starts and I see that three of them are very decent. One is a composed centre-back who demands the ball, another bosses the game and gets on the ball at every opportunity, combining well with the third, who has a comfort in possession rarely seen in Sri Lankans. One of the four, Iham, is the best player I've seen so far.

From the sidelines Dean is coaching Banda, who's giving me a tough time. In much the same way that Hizam's development has become my personal project, Banda has become Dean's. Banda is a little 49kg ball of energy. There's not a gram of fat on his body. He chases everything and doesn't give me any time on the ball. Dean is teaching him to come short to go long and how to run the channels.

My body is worn out. I haven't been sleeping at night. I spend my whole time drinking water but am constantly dehydrated. I lack energy. And now I have to try and catch up with Banda. I take a couple of bad touches, but Banda doesn't punish them. He breaks clear and I block his goalbound shot. It's a good contest, which is more than can be said for the rest of the game. Iham dominates.

*   *   *

Traders shove flowers in my face from all angles. Thaabit laps them up and buys twenty-five bunches, all of them either pink or white varieties of lotus flower. There's a reason for the assertive traders: we're next to the main Buddhist temple in Kalutara. Thaabit has ordered us here to give an offering ahead of the tournament, which – from a team of Tamils and Muslims – is a powerful symbol of unity. It's the last thing we're due to do in Kalutara before making the journey to our new home in the north-east, Trincomalee. With flowers in hand, we take to the street in pairs. I'm with Kalua, who I'm growing to like more by the day. Sure, he's crazy, but he's always laughing and tries to include me and Dean in what's going on.

Everyone is security-checked before entering the temple's grounds. It's a new measure introduced since the Easter bombings. Buddhism in Sri Lanka, we're told, is always wary of being under attack. After the first four boys get caught with their phone in their pocket, Thaabit instructs everyone else to hold their phone when they get checked. Safely through, we remove our flip-flops at the entrance. We walk up whitewashed steps and then take turns throwing water over our flowers. There's a Buddha statue behind us that is illuminated by a halo of multi-coloured electric lights. Back in our pairs, we queue up for the Buddha statue then, two by two, we remove the petals from our flowers and leave them as an offering before saying a quick prayer.

Other than Kaps, there are no Buddhists in the team. Buddhism is the Sinhalese religion, the religion of the state. Our players, however, are all Tamil (so either Hindu or Christian) and Muslim. Still, a few of the team pray in front of a line of candles while the rest of us wait.

The temple grounds are large. We walk up and down stairs, observing the quiet peace all around us. Ihshan captures every moment, trying his hardest not to laugh as the players fail to carry out the simple directions he gives. We must be some of the toughest actors he's worked with. Up-and-coming in the film industry, Ihshan is an assistant director fresh from working on ITV's *Good Karma Hospital*. Everything about him screams 'creative'. Every time I see him he looks like he's leapt out of bed and dressed in a rush. He's constantly restless, prone to laughter and usually has a can of Coke in his hand. You can almost hear his mind whirring. Most importantly, he's great company: sociable, open and funny. There's not a bad bone in his body.

Our offerings given, we leave the temple. As far as some of the boys are concerned, whatever happens in the tournament is now out of our hands.

I walk back with Iham. There's a composed aura about him. He's one of the taller members of the team, with a thick head of soft, dark hair and the kind of figure that comes from a comfortable upbringing. He wears a pleased expression, as if life is going exactly the way he planned. The other new boys – friends of his, I presume – join us and suddenly there's a group of seven using Iham to ask me questions in English. Iham learned his English in university, where lectures were conducted in a mix of Sinhalese and English. He has no shame in jumping straight in with the questioning. After asking where I'm from, he asks how much I'm being paid to play for Trinco. I tell him that I'm getting paid the same as everyone else. Iham tells me that some players are getting more. He uses Priyan as an example. I reply that Thaabit told me all players would earn the same, which is again dismissed.

I change approach, telling the surrounding group that my flights were paid for. That seems to satisfy them. I add that this is basically just a free holiday for me. They ask if I'm a professional footballer in England and I tell them about Brazil, then I tell them that I'm now a writer. Immediately Iham asks how much I earn. I try and avoid telling them. I say it's hard to know because the pay isn't regular. But he won't let up and the surrounding group is relentless. I say I earn around the average salary in the UK. Still, the pressure comes. Yet how can I talk money when the average salary of the two countries just doesn't compare? How can I talk money when I'm in a team of fishermen, painters and kitchen assistants scraping by on a tourist industry that has deserted them since the bombings? In the end I significantly lower the amount of the average salary in the UK, yet still their shock is evident.

Back at the stadium Dean heads inside to change from his long trousers worn for the temple into his shorts. As he opens his bag, all packed up for the evening's bus journey, five of the boys who had been in the group quizzing me gather round and stare. They can't believe how big his bag is. We're not rich by UK standards but we certainly are by Sri Lankan standards. Dean doesn't mince his words when he tells them where to go.

A special dinner is planned for our last meal at the stadium. Dean and I line up as usual with our plates covered in plastic bags, but when we get to the front of the line we're not given the Sri Lankan food. No, this is a special dinner. Instead we're handed two loaves of bread and a thick wad of butter each. When we try and get meat we're told the bread is our dinner. This is what Sri Lankans think English people eat. After a bit of back-and-forth, we're served string hoppers straight out of a cardboard box and allowed some meat. Our teammates are ecstatic that we leave the bread. They lap it up and – when they think Thaabit isn't watching – they pour sugar on top, making themselves a sweet sandwich. Some even stuff sweet sandwiches in their pockets. They'll need them for the long journey.

As we thank our chefs and hosts, a sense of excitement fills the air. The training camp is over. We're done in Kalutara. From here on in, we're going to be based in the north-east. A bus is already waiting for us outside. A sign at the front reads 'Special' and that sounds about right. The bus is like no other I've seen in my life. It's painted about a hundred different shades of sky blue. The lights are multi-coloured. There's stuff everywhere. Golden decorations adorn the front window, so much so that I wonder how the driver will possibly be able to see the road ahead.

Twenty-two players walk onto the bus. The time is 9 p.m. and yet we aren't expected to arrive until 4 a.m. It's not a long way, just 291km by road, but it's going to feel like it on this bus. Inside we find there's no air conditioning. There's no leg room. Anyone wanting to sleep has to contend with a toxic mixture of Pitbull and traditional Tamil music being pumped at full volume over the speakers. There's even a disco light. It seems that expense has been spared. Dean and I sit together at the front. His limbs are contorted into ridiculous angles as he attempts to fit into his window seat, and because he's bigger than me he inevitably manouevres himself to take up part of my seat too. This is going to be even worse for my legs than one of coach Kaps's sessions.

I dare not let go of my bag. Not for fear of it being stolen, but for fear of it falling out of the open door. We have two drivers, and the co-driver prefers to stand at the door so that he can smoke, as well as hop in and out of the bus every now and again to wee or buy food and drink. I'm very aware that one hard turn and my bag will go flying.

And the uncertainty isn't just regarding my belongings. At the end of the journey, we're pretty much being dumped in Trinco. None of the others who will be staying with us are on this bus. The coaches are all in Thaabit's car heading to Colombo. Jai is with them. Initially we were told we'd be staying at the owner's house in Trincomalee. Now we're being told we are to stay at a hotel. Before we boarded, Dean and I were looking at each other frantically. What are we supposed to do when we get there? Where are we going? Where are we being left? Banda has now been tasked with taking us to our accommodation. The coaches will follow in a few days.

With at least four hours of the journey still to go, my hamstrings won't stop cramping up. When you factor in the time lost to a punctured tyre, filling up with diesel, toilet breaks and pineapple stops, it could be a lot more. I'm sweating so much.

The bus also keeps moving while passengers get on and off. The co-driver attempts to disembark once more, only to miss his landing, falling and rolling to the floor. We laugh, then check he's OK, but he just shakes it off like it isn't the first time this has happened and jumps back up to his position next to the open door.

I close my eyes and pray that the monotonous beats of Pitbull will send me to sleep. They don't. In his sleep, Dean takes up more of the little room that I have. I attempt to push back but even in his sleep he's too strong for me. I check my phone constantly to track our location, following our blue location dot as we move diagonally across the island that's shaped just like a teardrop. Right at its northern tip lies Jaffna, a former kingdom within the island and the home to many teams within the North Eastern Premier League. Less than 80km to the east is India. At its closest point, India is within 30km of Sri Lanka. Not that many tourists get close enough to find out. The south and west of the island make up the majority of the country's tourism industry. Tourists head to Galle and Kandy and Colombo and Ella and Mirissa. They may venture north and east enough to visit the wondrous rock fortress of Sigiriya but they rarely come further. The beaches of the northeast are just as beautiful but they're less accessible. The only international airport is in Negombo, just north of Colombo, and journeys to the north-east, as I'm finding out, are long and slow. And, of course, there's the legacy of the war.

We continue along the A6, past Dambulla and Sigiriya. As we get closer to our final destination we wind east through the towns and villages of Trincomalee district, dropping off players at places with names like Kantale and Mutur and Kinniya. I expect to see extreme poverty in these rural areas, but I don't. There are no decrepit shacks in the style of Brazilian favelas, only buildings of cement – admittedly small – that provide comfortable homes. Some towns we pass are traditionally Muslim. Many have illuminated Buddha statues at their centre, despite few people being Buddhist in this area. There's visible excitement when we cross what Banda loudly proclaims to be Sri Lanka's longest bridge, Kinniya Bridge, built in 2009 with assistance from the Saudi Arabian government and standing at almost 400 metres in length. Soon enough we're driving past China Bay, a name indicative of the direction that the Trincomalee region is heading. Chinese investment has ramped up in recent years and shows few signs of slowing down. Several people have already joked that Sri Lanka is owned by China. Now Sakhti makes that very joke, although there's a hint of anger in his voice. His eyes remain peeled to the window, watching out in the dark for the familiar sights of his hometown. It's 4:30 a.m. but nobody is sleeping. Not even Dean.

TRINCOMALEE

'Before the bombs, this road was full of white people,' says Priyan, gesturing up the track at the stalls and the gifts and the juice bars that lead to the Koneswaram Temple. 'Now, just you,' he laments.

We remove our helmets and park the moped. Monkeys jump up and down on a parked tuk-tuk and scour the bins for food. We get close but not too close, as Priyan warns me they're dangerous. Some of the stall owners attempt to lure me in, but most are resigned to defeat. Business has fallen drastically. The whole area is struggling.

Before entering the temple we remove our flip-flops out of respect. This is a Hindu temple located in the naval base of Fort Frederick. It's beautiful, its colourful depictions of the religion guarded by a 10-metre statue of Shiva. A stone indicates that the temple has stood on this very spot since 1580 BC. Few historical artefacts remain, however.

It was the Portuguese who destroyed Koneswaram. They came in the seventeenth century with their desire to form trade routes and spread Catholicism through the country. As they raged war on the king of Jaffna, Koneswaram was just one of a vast number of temples and shrines destroyed on the island.

The vast majority of Koneswaram's thousand columns and three stone temples disappeared into the sea as the Portuguese used the land to build Fort Frederick.

It wasn't until the 1950s that the temple was rebuilt. After the Portuguese, the Kandyans came, then the Dutch, the French, the Dutch again, the French again, and then the British, who described Trincomalee as having 'the finest natural harbour in the world'. They had a point. Trincomalee's accessibility by water and ability to hold as many as twenty large battleships in its natural harbour gives it a great deal of strategic importance. Yet such a blessing is also a curse: for much of the past two millenia, Sri Lanka has been occupied, invaded or at war. Due to its strategic importance, Trincomalee has often taken the brunt of any fighting.

If things had worked out differently, Trincomalee could have been the British version of Pearl Harbour. But for a tip-off from intelligence, the 129 Japanese planes that attacked Trincomalee in 1942 would have caused chaos to the British fleet of naval ships. The attack was successfully repelled, but many more attacks would come during the civil war, with Fort Frederick occupied by the Sri Lankan navy, the Sri Lankan army holding their own base, and China Bay (just south of the town) occupied by the Sri Lankan airforce.

Despite such attempted destruction, the land that Koneswaram sits on has remained spiritual throughout time. Pilgrimages take place regularly, although not since the bombs. As we walk around the temple's interior we're joined by a small group who are each carrying candles in broken coconut shells. Priyan tells me they're doing so to ward off evil. At the back of the temple, where all the coconut shells are discarded, a tree is covered with cradles. They've been hung by couples hopeful that Lord Shiva will grant them a baby. Back around the front we linger at Lover's Leap, where legend has it that Francina van Reed, the daughter of a Dutch civil servant, threw herself into the sea after seeing her Dutch lover sail back to Europe, breaking their engagement in the process.

From up here, there's a panoramic view of the city and its surroundings. It's a lot calmer than in Kalutara and Colombo. It's much more beautiful too. The natural harbour covers the town on three sides. White sandy beaches stretch for miles, with clear sea water and plentiful coral making it a perfect place for snorkelling and scuba diving. There's no hustle and bustle. Nobody shouts. Stall owners sit and watch rather than stand and gesticulate. Cricket matches take place throughout the city. The houses are pink and blue and green. Dense green jungle land lingers on the periphery. Further afield, crocodiles patrol the marshes and elephants rampage through the wilderness. This is the closest I've been to paradise.

Priyan hands me my flip-flops and a helmet that's at least two sizes too big. It's time to move on. We walk back to the bottom of the track, where the moped is parked, to find Dean and Banda. Dean is wide-eyed and Banda is laughing.

'This place is mad, you know, lad,' Dean announces as he jumps off Banda's scooter. 'You'll never guess what happened.'

'Dean go crazy,' Banda adds.

'Shut up!' Dean, with a smile on his face, goes to slap Banda and Banda cowers in mock fear. 'This policeman just pulled us over, right. That's because mash-for-brains over here,' he gestures at Banda, 'overtook a tuk-tuk on a pedestrian crossing, while a load of people were crossing.'

'I have much room,' Banda points out. They're already becoming quite the double act.

'You would have had lots of room. If there weren't people crossing. And the tuk-tuk. And if there wasn't a police officer on the other side of the crossing. And get this: the police officer was already writing out a ticket. For Mindron!'

'Mindron very bad man,' says Banda.

'Mindron was with your boy Sakhti and the two of them had been riding on the same scooter. But their scooter didn't have a licence plate. Mindron had just stuck a piece of paper over where the licence plate should have been. The police officer flagged us down and gave Mindron the ticket. But fortunately mash-for-brains knew him – just like he seems to know every-one in this place! We spend so much time talking to other people driving scooters or tuk-tuks or just walking.'

'I famous.'

'So Banda's high-fiving the policeman and giving it the big 'un, but the policeman is still telling him off and warning him that he'd get in trouble with a different policeman. At the same time Mindron is complaining to the policeman that there is nothing wrong with his paper licence plate, and Sakhti is trying to talk him around. In the middle of all that madness, Coach Rimzy drives through. He hops off, has a word with the policeman and everything is good. Crazy!'

Trincomalee, we're finding out, isn't a big place. It's the kind of city where everybody knows everybody and they all look out for each other. The sense of community is strong. Word gets around quickly. Mindron ended up being let off his offence and making a powerful new connection. We leave Banda to show Dean around Koneswaram and agree to meet on the town beach once they're done.

I tentatively put my leg over the back of Priyan's moped and perch myself on the seat. I've never been on a moped before today and I feel far from safe. I grip on tightly to Priyan as he pulls the throttle and catapults us back down the hill. As the wind beats against my bare arms and legs, I stare at Priyan's back rather than the road ahead or the views to the side. It feels safer this way. Rather than remain alert to any oncoming traffic, Priyan prefers to scroll his Facebook feed, talk into his phone or point out various sites, all while turning blindly into corners and beeping his horn.

'Seth, are you OK?' he asks as we drive into the town.

No, I want to say, but I tell him yes.

'You are holding very tight,' he smiles. 'Very strong.'

We arrive without major incident. Banda and Dean soon join us on the beach, both calmed since our earlier meeting. Priyan buys us all ice creams and jackfruit nuts from a local seller, which we eat while sitting on the soft sand. More sites are pointed out to us, then we're told more about Trincomalee's past. Priyan and Banda were just children during the civil war. Priyan lost both of his parents when he was just a child. His aunt brought him up. I don't ask how they died.

Trinco witnessed its fair share of violence during the civil war. The town sits almost perfectly between the northern and eastern provinces that make up the intended Tamil Eelam. 'Trincomalee is crucial to us. It is the capital of our Eelam,' the leader of the Tamil Tigers, Velupillai Prabhakaran said in the early stages of the war. The government reacted accordingly, taking charge of the town and then heavily reinforcing, using the natural harbour to successfully repel the Tigers. At their height, the Tigers controlled all the land around Trincomalee. But, try as they might, they couldn't take their proposed capital.

It wasn't for want of effort. A series of massacres in the town and surrounding district caused havoc in 1985, just two years into the war. Yet it was reported that the massacres weren't the work of the Tamil Tigers (depending which side you were on); instead, hundreds of Tamil civilians were allegedly murdered by the Sinhalese home guard while as many as 1,500 Tamil properties were looted and burned. With 86,342 Sinhalas and 86,743 Tamils living locally, the army believed control of Trincomalee was imperative in preventing the spread of Tamil nationalism. That way they could stop the Tamils from linking up the eastern and northern Tamil-speaking provinces and creating their new capital – especially as the Tamil Tigers already held Nilaveli just to the north and Muttur just to the south.

The government managed to hold Trinco. Regular outbreaks of violence continued – some of it directed at Tamils, some retaliatory attacks on Sinhalese, much of it the sound of shells and rockets being fired from the harbour. In time, the violence became normalised. But still, lone incidents could shock.

In 2004 came the tsunami, sweeping aside thousands of homes and killing hundreds of people. The following year, while the civil war was still officially at a ceasefire, the erection of a Buddha statue in the town market started a domino effect where sixteen Sinhalese locals were killed in an explosion, which led to hundreds of Tamil properties being burned to the ground and tens of murders. It was an incident at the very end of that year, though, that most scarred Trincomalee. Even now, Priyan and Banda struggle to articulate just why it happened. Five students were the victims. Every night they would sit in the exact spot we are sitting in now on the town beach and talk. One December day it is alleged that the army drove past on the way to the naval base and stopped when they saw the students. They got out of the car, walked up to them and shot them. There had been no provocation. The government claimed the students were Tamil Tigers and were about to launch a grenade. Two witnesses came forward to suggest otherwise. One, a photographer, 'disappeared', while the other has received multiple death threats. Thirteen years later the inquiry is still ongoing.

The end of the civil war didn't bring with it an end to the violence. Revenge attacks, murders and abductions were regularly carried out in the city for several years after the last gun was fired. The 2005 split in the eastern and northern ranks of the Tamil Tigers (LTTE), occurring after perceived lack of resources allocated to the east, accelerated the withdrawal of the LTTE from Trincomalee as early as 2007 after the Karuna group (named after the senior LTTE commander who caused the split) went on to attack the LTTE. So did the government forces. Tamils were detained and taken to Plantain Point on Orr's Hill – just a few hundred metres away from us – to be 'questioned': the official line for what was rumoured to be rape, torture and disappearances. Eventually, though, life was allowed to return to some form of normality. Under heavy police and army presence – there are now as many as one police or army officer for every eleven people in the north-east – Priyan and Banda were allowed to leave their house without fearing for their life. A new chapter could begin.

Now the town's violent past is drifting away in place of a brighter future on the horizon. Tourism is on the up. Development projects have been invested in. The local economy is becoming healthier. There's still a long way to go. The biggest development project – a complex of sport stadiums that sits at the town's centre, one of which was intended to be capable of hosting international football matches – sits unfinished and unused. Ethnic tensions haven't truly gone away. Unemployment is still high. Wages remain low, a 2012 census revealing a median monthly salary of 5,500 LKR (about £25). But at least people are now talking about Trincomalee – and not just for its strategic importance. Instead they speak of the white beaches, the character, the potential. It isn't crazy to imagine a future where the town serves as a tourist hotspot, revitalising the economy and bringing plenty of employment opportunities. With such beautiful surroundings it's maybe even inevitable.

* * *

Mothers are the same all over the world. I find myself sitting in Kalua's house with Priyan, Kalua's sister and his mother. As soon as she hears Kalua's old schoolmate Priyan is in her home with some English boy, she rushes in. Immediately the tea comes out. It's Ceylon Tea, of course. She's laughing and joking with her boys, finding out the latest gossip and asking all about my life back in England. Kalua's life, she laments, is football, football, football and no work. He attended St Joseph's College, the largest secondary school in Trincomalee and one renowned for its footballing prowess. Unlike the rest of the country, football is the biggest sport in Trincomalee. All youngsters grow up playing it, and the St Joseph's College team have been national champions on several occasions, including during Kalua and Priyan's time. School was where they developed their love of football, where they began to play the game that would shape their lives. It had to be at school. In Sri Lanka, all youth football is school football. There are no youth clubs or academies. Games are irregular and training is rarely structured or organised. Few receive proper coaching.

Several times, Kalua's mum strongly hints that he needs a job that isn't football. Kalua is so close to securing a contract for the tournament, but it seems his mum doesn't count that as work. Her words are never malicious, though. Mums never are.

A two-minute walk downhill from Kalua's house brings us to the most beautiful beach I've ever visited, flanked by tropical paradise on all sides. Fishermen are coming in from a day at sea and unloading their catch. One has found a 3kg lobster that should fetch 10,000 LKR. The business drives the local community.

Located far from the tourist hotspot, this isn't a rich neighbourhood but nor is it gripped by extreme poverty. The buildings lining the beach have steel roofs and appear to be one single room. Closer inspection shows them to be fitted with relatively modern appliances and would suggest they're comfortable homes, though still a million miles from my sheltered life in England. Not for the first time, I'm reminded of my privilege.

We head straight for the beach volleyball court. Dean and Banda are waiting there for us. They arrived just before us after spending the afternoon with Banda's friends. As well as Dean and I get on, it's good for us to be separated every now and again. That way we really get to immerse ourselves in this new culture.

Dean and I are the tallest there so we're placed on opposite teams and instructed to play at the net. It has the feel of a village kickabout. The ages of those playing range from eleven to sixty. The community stops to watch. Old men perch on top of boats. Fishermen lie out on the sand. The play is fierce. At the end of each game we're brought fizzy drinks and a new person joins in.

We play until it's too dark to see the ball and then head for the water. I leave my bag with my phone and my money in it by the court. I'm assured there's no need to worry and so I don't worry. This is a country and a community that looks out for its own; everybody clubs in together.

The sun is down and the moon is out yet the sea remains so clear I can see everything. The Sri Lankans are catching fish in the water with their bare hands. I give it a go but am hopeless. Instead I turn onto my back and allow myself to drift. I could stay here all night. I could stay here for ever.

That evening we go to an Italian restaurant with our tour guides Banda, Kalua and Priyan because Dean has been craving spaghetti carbonara. We eat on the beach and laugh and joke. At the end of the meal we pay for everyone's food to show our gratitude. Later we find out that the cost of spaghetti carbonara is the equivalent of two days' wages for Banda. Though Sri Lanka has very low levels of extreme poverty – especially compared to their neighbouring countries – as recently as 2013 up to 45 per cent of the country was surviving on less than $5 per day. Yet all day Banda didn't say anything and didn't complain. He was happy to come and eat with us despite the cost. The level our new friends go to to make sure we're happy is incredible.

* * *

The squad has assembled in the reception of the hotel we're staying in with the coaches until a suitable house is found. Everyone is beaming. They've made the final twenty-five and their contract is all but confirmed. At first I'm slightly nervous to see who will walk through the door, but in the end I can't think of anyone who is missing.

There's one new player I haven't seen before. He's got a tattoo of a star on his neck and also a sleeve tattoo on his arm as well as the classic footballer's fade haircut. His name is

Anushaht, and he's quit his job to be part of the Trinco Titans. Most of the players have an agreement with their employers to take extended leave, but when Anushaht requested leave he was refused. The only option, he decided, was to risk his livelihood as a kitchen assistant and give everything to make it as a Titan. This decision was made just for the trials. There was no certainty that he was going to get selected, but he assured Thaabit that even if he didn't make the final squad the risk would have been worth it. Thankfully the risk paid off and, though he was injured at the end of the trial week, he proved to Thaabit that he has enough ability to be a Titan.

Thaabit retained all the players he wanted to at the auction and refused to spend any extra to entice players away from rival clubs, despite all players from the north-east being available for purchase. The owners have made it clear they want the Titans to be a team made up of local Trincomalee players, complemented by me and Dean. The owners have also made it clear that, despite their impressive backgrounds in sport and business, they won't be stumping up the money to spend on expensive new imports. If we are to succeed, we will have to do so through coaching, spirit, and pride. Out of our local players, Banda and Dinesh were the most expensive at 31,000 LKR, with Banda the subject of a three-club bidding war. The others were sold between 21,000 and 30,000 LKR. The most expensive player was sold to Northern Elite for 330,000 LKR. To put that into perspective, our entire squad cost half that amount.

With Trinco finishing third from bottom last season, their players weren't taken seriously by the other clubs. A few bids were made, but nothing to worry the Trinco purse strings. Three former Trinco players were bought by other teams, but as I hadn't heard of them I presume Thaabit wasn't too bothered.

After being told about the auction and then listening to a speech from Thaabit, we're presented with our official green Titans training shirts. The mood is raucous. Someone has brought an air horn, and when Dean and I are invited up first to collect our shirts we're met with whoops and hollers. Cheers meet the names of our teammates as they walk up for their moment and shake the hands of the coaches. Smartphones are held out by the dozen.

Once all the shirts have been given out, Thaabit pulls everyone together for a special announcement. Chinna, who isn't here, has been retained and will once again be squad captain. It seems the emphasis, however, is on 'squad'. There will be three vice captains: one each from the forwards, the midfield and defence. Priyan is the first, then Dinesh, and finally my name is called. I'm to be a vice captain and am taken aback by the reaction. It's truly humbling. Imposter syndrome has long been forgotten.

That evening the celebrations continue. It's Priyan's birthday and all day there have been whispers about drinking a beer. Having had Priyan down as a super-focused athlete willing to do whatever it takes, I'm surprised that he is game. Some of the other players, though, are less keen, with Banda particularly vociferous. They want to be as disciplined as possible.

Priyan, Kalua and Banda hang around in the hotel reception while Dean and I shower. By the time we're done, Kalua's cousins have arrived in the street on their mopeds. They're loud and excitable. The coaches have clocked that something is going on. Dean and I bypass it all by walking the short distance to the restaurant that serves spaghetti, as Kaps watches on from the balcony. Banda and Priyan join us shortly. They're arguing, getting more and more animated all the time. Priyan wants to have a single beer but Banda still isn't keen. One suggestion is to go to a beach far away but they fear the coaches will see them all getting on their bikes. Banda refuses to drink, whatever happens. They're speaking in Tamil so we're only getting a flavour of what's going on. Banda disappears then reappears five minutes later. Priyan orders a milkshake and helps himself to a piece of naan bread.

When we're done we walk a short way down the beach. All Priyan's friends are waiting there with a cake. It's the first cake he has been asked to cut since he was a child, when his parents were still alive. He poses for a photo with each of us. Tradition states that he has to feed us a mouthful in each photo. Things soon escalate when the cream is rubbed all over his face.

With the cake finished, the beers come out to a mixture of elation and silence. Kalua's cousins have brought bags full. Priyan and Dean both accept a single beer, but Kalua and Banda refuse. After all, the opening match of the tournament is supposedly only six days away.

We call it a night at 11 p.m. but still have to scale our hotel wall to get into our room. Thaabit watches on from the hotel balcony but doesn't tell us off as me and Dean head to our room. After all, why would he?

* * *

Still no contract. Still no fixtures. And still no long-term accommodation. Everything should be happening. Nothing is. The six of us living in the hotel – me, Thaabit, Ihshan, Kaps, Dean and Jai, all of whom had stayed in the coaches' house in Kalutara – can no longer stay at the owner's house in Trincomalee, as had apparently been the plan. Thaabit's days are spent driving around Trinco with Banda, Priyan and Kalua, attempting to find a house big enough to rent for all of us. They're haemorrhaging money on the hotel we're staying in and paying for us to eat at restaurants every meal of the day until a solution is found. I love the hotel but appreciate there's a budget to work to. The place we're currently in is on the beach, right next to the stadium and within a few metres of a top-quality restaurant that serves something other than rice. Most importantly, its satellite TV shows the Cricket World Cup.

At lunch Thaabit tells us more about the auction. Each club was allowed to spend no more than a million rupees on players. Northern Elite FC, who finished in last place the previous tournament, spent 995,000 LKR on eleven players. Tamil United spent 994,000 on twelve. Four other teams spent well over half a million LKR on players. The remaining six spent no more than 206,000. There's a clear split in terms of budget: one club, Maathodaam, didn't spend a single rupee.

With the amount of money floating about, the power is seemingly with the clubs. They've spent big and therefore want to be able to call the shots. An actual fight broke out at the auction when the bidding was closed on one player after a team had actually increased their bid but hadn't been seen by the auctioneer. In that instance there was a re-auction, but that episode is the least of the league's worries. One team is threatening to pull out altogether because their foreign players haven't shown up. I'm not sure what the league committee can do about that, but it seems they're giving in. If they continue to give in then who knows how long it'll be before the tournament starts. Or ends. It could be a week. It could be a month. These are amateur footballers whose lives are being played with. They'd all told their employers they'd be back to work on 11 August. Now the delays put that in jeopardy.

Thaabit changes the conversation and reminds us of the huge influence we have over our teammates. He says we have no clue how much power we have and he's probably right. What we do while we're in Trinco, he says, may affect our teammates – especially the young ones – for the rest of their lives. He asks us to stress the levels of practice we've done to get to our position, to say how often we go to the gym, to do everything right. Sure, we can do stuff that isn't right – we just need to make sure that it's done out of sight. If we stay behind after training, he assures us, our teammates will too. Help them get better by being better ourselves. I wonder how much of this speech is a result of us coming back late last night.

That afternoon proves just how right Thaabit is. We assemble on the beach with the locally based players. Priyan, Kalua and Banda take a break from looking for houses to attend. We sweep the beach for as much of the shards of glass and dangerous debris we can find, then play a game of 'two touch', keeping the ball up in one big Titans circle. To finish, we split into teams to play football tennis on the white sand.

The session ends and we jump into the sea. I lie on my back and take in my tropical surroundings. I could have been in an office right now. I could be working at the same desk, then making the same Tube journey home to make the same dinner and return to the same routine the next day. Instead I'm here. Paradise.

Banda stays behind after we dry off. At first we play keepy-uppies, but soon he's asking me to teach him skills. We work on how to roll a defender, footwork drills and one-on-ones. He's eager to learn and hangs off my every word. It makes you wonder just how much better Sri Lanka could be if a nationwide infrastructure of coaches were to be put in place.

We stay until it's too dark to see.

* * *

Our first official training session in Trincomalee begins. The tournament is supposed to start tomorrow but there's still been no contract to sign and no fixture schedule put in place. All we can do is work hard. We just can't work hard tactically, because we're still not out of the public eye.

We're training at the communal stadium in Trincomalee, Ehamparam, also our home venue for the tournament. The pitch has no grass. It's a mixture of sand, soil and rock. Guessing how the ball is going to roll is like picking between red and black. Closer inspection finds actual bricks laid into the ground. Stones poke out all over the place. A makeshift cricket wicket of coarse carpet is hammered into the earth. It's amazing that this is considered fit for a professional tournament. To slide tackle is to risk your lower limbs.

Around thirty people have gathered in the sole concrete stand. There's a pick-up game going on in one corner, a handful of teenagers playing basketball on the far side, and about ten cricketers practising in the nets in another corner. Three cows remain by the wall where they're shaded. There's no grass for them to graze on anyway. According to Thaabit, those in the stands are a mixture of opposition players and jealous Trinco natives who didn't pass the trial for the team. They spend the entire session laughing at us and booing, which is far from the heroic homecoming I'd expected. Unsurprisingly, it gets to some of the players.

We start off with speed and agility work, then ballwork in pairs. It's sweaty stuff but nowhere near as bad as the climate in Kalutara. It's hotter here but the humidity levels are much lower. While the west of the island is going through its wet season, Trinco enjoys its dry season. Hence no grass.

As always, we finish with a match. As always, Coach Rimzy takes the whistle and has a tough task on his hands. Even though attendance is compulsory, only sixteen have showed up and so we play eight-a-side. Dean and I are on opposite teams again. Within five minutes he's given someone a firm shoulder barge in a fifty–fifty. The recipient, Aflal, goes down screaming and stays down in a style that makes me wonder if he's re-enacting something he's seen on TV. Dean towers over him.

'Next time it'll be harder, lad,' he warns.

My teammates are in uproar, yelling 'Rimzy Nana, it's a foul, a foul.' Even those on Dean's side are convinced. Yet Rimzy waves play on. At half-time I tell them it was a perfectly fair challenge that wouldn't have been a foul in England. Dean tells Thaabit his players are all as soft as mash.

The second half restarts and the ball breaks free between Dean and Anushaht. To his credit, Anushaht goes for it. But Dean goes for it harder. There was only ever going to be one winner. Anushaht's lean figure is left in a heap and is carried off the pitch by a remorseless Dean and Priyan. The myth that Sri Lankan players are aggressive is well and truly broken.

At the end of the session we return to our hotel. We were supposed to move into our new accommodation yesterday, then this morning, now tomorrow morning. I wouldn't be surprised if we're still here next week. The house we're supposedly renting is only going to be available once we've paid up front.

Coach Rimzy, whose house is just around the corner from Ehamparam, hosts us for dinner. He's got a humble house but makes an extravagant meal. I'd expect nothing less from him; he's a true gentleman with a kind heart – especially when he refuses to whistle for fouls that I make. There's also the added bonus that eating at Rimzy's is much cheaper than eating at a restaurant. While waiting for the food, Dean and I play basket-ball with Rimzy's boisterous eight-year-old son, Razan, though play is regularly halted for ball cleaning every time it lands in the open drain. When we're called into the dining room we find a generous spread of freshly caught fish, rice, chicken, string hoppers, coconut sambal, aubergine, various curries and bread. The flavours are exceptional, and as there's no cutlery they remain on my fingers for a long time. We talk for a long time and are full of compliments for Rimzy and the cooks. Rimzy's wife and mother prepared the food, but they only show themselves at the very end to say goodbye. They're warm and welcoming and it's a shame they didn't join us. Here in the north-east, women are often almost as invisible as domestic cleaners. I make sure to give them eye contact and smile but still feel uneasy about their place in such a culture.

And that's not all I feel uneasy about. The uncertainty around everything makes it hard to relax. The accommodation, the fixtures, the tournament delay. Football is about controlling the controllables but, as the days go by, more things are being taken out of our control. Last season's North Eastern Premier League started on 30 May and finished on 26 August. Are they really going to condense that into one month this year? My flight home is in five weeks' time and we still don't have any fixtures scheduled.

Dean is similarly uncomfortable, though his discomfort is more to do with the food. The meal at Rimzy's was too spicy for him and so we make the short walk back out to his favourite restaurant for his favourite spaghetti carbonara.

* * *

I wondered why Dean got up so early and left our hotel room. Now I know: I arrive at our new accommodation to find that he's already nabbed the best room.

Our hosts have done a good job in finding this place. Our new accommodation is big and spacious yet spartan. A short walk up a small dirt track from the main road, it's just minutes from the beach yet far enough from the main town for us to have some privacy. A large iron gate separates us from the outside world. Immediately outside, a sign reads 'tsunami evacuation area', which doesn't fill me with confidence. Our neighbours' houses are large and appear to have a never-ending supply of loudly barking guard dogs, while on the other side of the dirt track is a field of coconut trees that sway back and forth in the wind. Men are climbing up the trees with just their feet and hands. Their bare feet are tied with cloth, which they use to push themselves up while reaching higher. It takes them a matter of seconds to reach the top, where they reach for coconuts and throw them to the ground for collection. The area is littered with discarded coconut shells and foil and plastic and paper. As with much of Sri Lanka, people choose to throw their rubbish to the side of the road, from where it's occasionally gathered and burned. There are few bins and even fewer bin collections. Down the track it looks like the used contents of a corner shop. There are Coke bottles, chocolate wrappers, crisp packets, fruit skins, newspapers.

Inside, my room contains a double bed and that's it. No wardrobe, no cupboards, no curtains, not even any decoration. There's a fan but no air conditioning. There's also a power cut. I'm sweating so much.

Dean's room is the same as mine but is better lit and has a king-size bed. The power sockets in both rooms are on the part of the wall that meets the ceiling. If I get on Dean's shoulders I might just be able to plug my phone in, though the cable is nowhere near long enough to reach the floor or even the bed.

In the communal area there's one long table, four chairs and a dusty floor. We have no washing machine or television. This comes across as a place to sleep and to sleep only. Grand plans are laid to buy new appliances and make the house a home. I'll believe it when I see it.

Kaps and Ihshan are also on our floor. Ihshan's room is the nicest: it features an en-suite and air conditioning. Thaabit is on the ground floor, while Banda has talked himself into the room upstairs, traditionally the servants' quarters but providing spacious enough accommodation. The house is advertised as having 'sea views', which is pushing it. From the balcony on Banda's floor you can just about see a slither of sea. Obscured by palm trees and coconut trees is the beach, a long expanse of white sand that joins the city centre with the out-of-city tourist hotbed a few kilometres north. Our particular slice of beach, neither in the city nor the tourist area, combines sand with scattered shards of glass and fishermen's leftovers. Not that Banda is too bothered by the lack of view.

Up until now, Banda has told Dean that he's a chef, a tour guide, a diver, a fisherman and a barber. Banda has also told Dean that he doesn't know how to cook rice. You have to admire the guy's hustle. Now, thanks to that hustle, he is our official team chef. He managed to talk himself into living with us so he can cook all our meals. Thaabit has placed him on a two-day trial that, if successful, will see a significant boost to his wages. He might even learn to cook rice.

Sitting on my new bed, I draft an email to Nomi, a club director and head of logistics. I'm yet to meet him but I've said hello on the phone. All I know is that he lives in Jaffna. In the email I stress the importance of knowing the tournament dates and ask whether he can start applying pressure to the league through our connections with Jayawardene and Sangakkara.

Dean sticks his head around the door and asks what I'm doing. As soon as I tell him, he urges me not to send it. Nomi's daughter was born last night. She died this morning. I don't know what to say. All I know is that our situation matters not one bit compared to what Nomi must be going through. I delete the draft.

Later that morning, Priyan arrives to pick me up on his moped as usual. Banda follows him on his own moped with a spare helmet for Dean. The two of them head off in one direction, while me and Priyan head back into the city. He wants to introduce me to his family.

The journey doesn't take longer than five minutes and when we arrive we are warmly greeted and ushered into the front room of Priyan's family home. It reminds me of Rimzy's front room: a small television, plastic chairs for guests, and family pictures hung high up the wall, just below a roof made of corrugated iron. There we find his aunt and six cousins, five of them girls. The girls initiate handshakes and we're all offered a mug of warm malted milk. Priyan's five-year-old cousin is relishing the opportunity to practise his English with me. Literacy rates in Sri Lanka are impressive and it's obvious their schooling system is good. We talk for a while before he returns to watch the post-match analysis of India's nineteen-run defeat to New Zealand in the Cricket World Cup. 'Virat!' he screams every now and again. I ask the girls about cricket and they respond positively. They played at school and occasionally play club matches. They love the sport.

Speaking to Priyan's cousins – all of them laughing, smiling and initiating conversation – I realise it isn't Sri Lankan culture that hides women. It's just the different religions. Priyan's family are Hindu, while Rimzy's are Muslim. Both are exceptional families, warm, welcoming and full of good humour. It brings home to me the importance of adapting. I can't judge what I see against western values. I have to embrace what's in front of me.

* * *

That afternoon we have our training session on the beach instead of whatever you'd call the surface at the stadium. Thaabit is concerned about hostility from the stands. I understand the move but also believe that you can't keep protecting players. Professional footballers have to be able to perform against a backdrop of hostility. Even if it is on a dangerous blend of bricks, stones and cow poo.

We're assured that the hunt is on for alternative training venues. Talks are advanced with the naval base, but we can't train there at the moment because the Sri Lankan president is visiting for the next few days. Still, I can't really complain about a session on the sand.

We start off with a speed and agility session. The focus soon changes, however, when Thaabit spots the local fishermen. They're hauling in their catch for the day, just as they do every day at this time. Two sets of ten men stand around a hundred metres apart, each pulling a length of rope connected to a fishing boat out at sea. A light switches on in Thaabit's head: strength workout.

The squad splits in half and helps pull each rope. Sensing a photo opportunity, Ihshan follows with his camera. It's back-breaking stuff – until I'm shown the proper technique. Gradually I learn to step back and inside in time with the man in front, rhythmically pulling the rope along with me, which then closes the gap between us and the other set of fishermen. The catch is getting closer. I can see fish jumping from the net and swimming to freedom. Jai, standing behind me, estimates these men catch a million rupees' worth of fish a day. They should be rich men but they're not. It's just the way the world economy works.

After training, the coaches leave for Jaffna to pay their respects to Nomi's family. The death has put everything into perspective for me. I no longer feel frustrated. I understand that I have to accept whatever happens and do my best to enjoy it. After all, life's too short not to.

We wander a kilometre up the road to the main tourist area and the Coconut Beach Club, where Banda was last employed. There are white people everywhere. It's like a different world. This is the same beach, the same city, but nothing else is the same. They sprawl around the tables set out for them on the beach, laughing into their cocktails and long dinners before heading back to their artificial chalets in the coconut trees. We pull up chairs on a table alongside them. Banda and Priyan are the only two Sri Lankans who are not serving or cooking. Banda orders, then invites the chef who will cook our meal out to the table for a quick introduction. We soon learn that Banda wasn't a chef but was instead a kitchen assistant. Banda points out that he may have been slightly exaggerating before, but he now really is a chef because he's officially the chef for the Trinco Titans. I can already feel my insides going.

* * *

'It's all politics,' Priyan says across the breakfast table. 'No Tamil, no Muslim. Only Buddhist and some Christian.'

We're discussing the state of Sri Lankan sport. The cricket team, he claims, is plagued by it. So is football. And so is society as a whole. This is a country that many still believe to be a nation of Sinhala Buddhists – even more so after the conclusion of the civil war. The ethos of the Sri Lanka Freedom Party that inspired the Sinhala Only Act continues to inspire many: according to this ethos, the entire island of Sri Lanka is Sinhala Theravada Buddhist and anyone who isn't is therefore an invader. Christians? Invaders. Hindus? Invaders. Muslims? Invaders. Tamils? Ha.

Sinhalese Buddhists, Priyan says, now make up much of the country's public sector. Long gone are the days when Tamils enjoyed a disproportionate share of civil service jobs – a legacy of British colonial divide and rule that favoured minorities. Instead the Sinhalese choose the cricket team, the football team, make the rules, run the country.

Not that it stops Priyan from dreaming. After all, the North Eastern Premier League is a chance for him to stand out. Sri Lankan national team players will be taking part. If he can get the better of them, sparkle with his talent, then perhaps politics can be overlooked.

'And what about Trinco,' I ask, 'is there politics here?' Though the players are different religions, none are Sinhalese.

'Hmm,' Priyan replies in the distinctly Tamil manner. It's a sound that expresses both disapproval and concern. 'Last season we have many problems. The coach was no strong and Chinna runs the team. Chinna refuse to play if certain players play. Coach gives in and only picks Chinna and his friends.' Priyan made just two appearances. Now he's one of the vice captains.

The ethnic tensions aren't just between Sinhalese and the country's minorities. They're even between Tamils – Sri

Lankan Tamils believing themselves superior to the Indian Tamils shipped over by the British in the nineteenth century to work on the tea plantations in the hills – as well as between Tamils and Muslims. Many Tamils are Hindu. Many are Catholic, while most of the country's Muslims speak Tamil. Though they share a language, these Tamil-speaking Muslims are not seen as ethnic Tamils by Sri Lankan Tamils, however, and are often subordinated within Tamil culture. Nor do these same Muslims see themselves as ethnic Tamils. Instead, many believe themselves to be the descendents of Arab traders.

Tensions between Tamils and Muslims truly exploded during the civil war. Throughout the early stages of conflict, the Tamil Tigers tried to recruit the Muslims of the north and east to fight for their cause. The Sinhalese, they suggested, were a common enemy, and they attempted to rally Muslims through their shared language of Tamil. It largely failed. Many Muslims remained bystanders in the war, committing to neither side. And so in 1990, desperate measures were taken.

It started in Jaffna. All Muslims – as many as 46,000 of them – were given two hours to leave the peninsula. They were officially being expelled from Tamil Eelam lands due to fears that they were being used by the government as informers. All property and businesses were left behind, and the majority were relieved of their possessions as they left. Those who didn't leave immediately suffered worse fates. Thirty-five wealthy business-men were kidnapped in Jaffna. In total, the Muslims of Jaffna peninsula lost an estimated $110 million due to their expulsion.

As the years went by, Muslims slowly trickled back to the areas they were expelled from. Gradually, they were accepted. Yet still they are the subject of attacks. After the Colombo bombings, the retaliatory attacks largely focused on the 10 per cent of the population that is Muslim. Mosques and Muslim businesses were targeted for looting and burning as mobs rampaged through towns.

As I learn more about these tensions, my head starts to hurt. What seems to be a peaceful, welcoming country is actually a complex spider's web of discrimination, religious animosity and persecution. In truth I'm a little scared. I wish I had known about all this before I flew to the country, but I barely knew the difference between a Tamil and a Sinhalese until arriving in Colombo. And now here I am, trying to make sense of everything while keeping a low profile and staying out of trouble, which by all accounts seems easy to find.

We run back home along the almost empty beach. It stretches for miles and distracts me from what I've just heard. Coconut trees line the sky. A couple of puffer fish from the previous night's catch are lying motionless on the sand, their last breath long gone. The day is just beginning but the sun is already hot – just like it always is in Trinco.

* * *

Our first dinner at the house is a takeaway. Dean has spent the whole day telling Thaabit that Banda isn't a chef and is actually a kitchen assistant. It seems he's got through. Banda is still going to live with us, but from tomorrow we'll be eating lunch and dinner at Rimzy's house. Banda tells us that means he's still the breakfast chef, which is fine with me because Thaabit tells us that breakfast will now be cereal and toast.

Later I see Banda washing up. He rinses our sauce-filled plates, rubs them a couple of times with the hand he's just licked, then stacks the plates on top of each other. Kaps has to show him how to use washing-up liquid and a scourer. I ask him how long he's been a kitchen assistant. Five years, he tells us.

The takeaway is well received by the Sri Lankans but Dean and I are still starving. We essentially had a couple of bits of bread – one with egg in the middle – and a relatively spicy gravy. I send him a WhatsApp message.

Seth: Could be the smallest dinner I've ever had – you fancy shop?

Dean: It made me angry so I had to go up to the room hahaha. Sounds good.

Seth: 5 mins?

Dean: Sweet aye lad.

We open the gate and Thaabit pops his head out of the door. I wave to acknowledge him, not sure whether we're breaking his rules by heading outside at 9 p.m.

It's not a long walk to the shop. We're little more than twenty metres from the main road. From there, we turn left and head past the Hindu temple that enjoys playing loud music through its speakers at what always seem to be the most inappropriate times. Worshippers wander the grounds, some sweeping the floor, others with offerings. They ignore us, all too focused on the task at hand. Across the way, the roadside stalls have long since been abandoned. Rogue rambutans, a spiky red ball of a fruit, are left behind along with a mass of sliding cardboard boxes. The traders will be back when the sun rises, armed with fresh batches of coconuts and mangoes and dragon fruit and rambutans.

Dean gets a Sprite at the shop while I go for a bag of cashew nuts and a coconut water. Truth be told, I don't want to upset Thaabit by getting a fizzy drink – not until I've returned from the wedding at least. We carry on walking and discussing everything that is happening. Dean is worried about the food. The food at Rimzy's is excellent but it's very Sri Lankan and quite spicy. Dean can't go to his usual restaurant for a spaghetti carbonara after every single meal. Our salary will nowhere near cover it, and nor will he be able to get there without relying on someone with a moped. He fears he'll have to stock up on fruit.

Frustration is kicking in. Living with the coaches, being told what to do, when to do it, at all times, is proving tough. Worst of all though – we both agree – is all the changing facts, the moving dates. Dean's girlfriend has booked a flight to land in Sri Lanka the day I am supposed to be flying home. Dean has decided to stay out on holiday for a couple of weeks. Now she's going to be twiddling her thumbs while Dean trains and plays in the tournament – if the tournament ever starts. We wonder how much the coaches actually know about what's going on. There have still been no fixtures despite us being promised them three times already this week. Dean is bored of asking for them. So am I.

Previously Priyan told us the tournament would 'definitely be over by September'. He said there was no chance it'd be delayed by only a week. If he's right, we'll be here an extra three weeks. We've both made commitments back home. As every day passes with no news, it's looking more and more likely that we'll have to cancel those commitments.

* * *

Matchday. We're playing our first official friendly, away at Al Jaya SC in Kantale. It's a 40km journey and we're given a choice of going by bus or by moped. We go everywhere by bike. It's always the same: me and Priyan on one, Dean and Banda on the other. Travelling by bike is thrilling in Sri Lanka. You're out in the open, swallowing in your surroundings as you cruise along at 40km/h in a haze of diesel, navigating wandering cows and meandering tuk-tuks. It's also terrifying. Driving a moped seems to have a very specific set of road instructions:

» never check your mirrors
» never look before turning onto new roads
» use up as much of the road as possible
» always announce your presence by beeping your horn.

Still, it seems preferable to travelling by bus.

On the outskirts of the city we pull up to park at a restaurant. This is a restaurant in the loosest sense of the world. It's dirty by Sri Lankan standards, let alone British standards. The paint job looks like it was done in colonial times. Mess is splattered up the walls and dust gathers in the corner. Meals are displayed in the shop window, intending to entice and doing anything but.

The manager shoves us towards a table that's covered with the previous diner's remains. He unceremoniously sweeps those remains onto the floor and declares our table now clean. Dean has already started to curse Banda.

'Where have you taken us, ya mash?' he asks over and over.

Banda orders three chicken fried rices – Priyan has wisely already eaten – and moments later three big plates of rice are dumped in front of us. Unlike most food in Sri Lanka, chicken fried rice is eaten with cutlery. Banda points out to the manager that I have no spoon. The manager grunts, picks up a dirty spoon from the sink, rubs it up and down a couple of times with his thumb and then gives it a quick rinse under the tap. I shudder when he passes it to me.

I pour ketchup on my plate and then do my best to shovel the food into my mouth without touching the spoon. The blackened meat is, I presume, chicken. What it mainly consists of, however, is bones, followed by salt. Dean eats a quarter of his plate and gives Banda evils throughout every mouthful.

The bill comes to 470 LKR for three dishes and a two-litre bottle of water. It's the equivalent of around £2. You don't pay for the hygiene.

Kantale is a rural area of small houses and large farmlands. Its football pitch isn't a football pitch at all. Rugby posts are wedged into the ground. The football goals are left on the floor at the side of the pitch. Together we lift them up and move them into their rightful position. Neither set of goal posts is complete. They're both missing parts from their frame, though they do at least both have posts and a crossbar. We drape a net over each goal and stand them up. Neither looks stable. I don't envy the goalkeepers tasked with standing under them for the ninety minutes.

The pitch is similarly hazardous. There is grass but mainly it's rock-solid, comprised of earth that's been baked by sun. There are circular holes all over it. Where they've been made, rubble covers the ground. I ask my teammates what they are and Dinesh winks when he says 'snake holes'. I don't take him seriously because I've told everyone that I don't like the thought of playing on the same pitch as snakes. But Jai confirms what I've been told and I trust him. They must be snake holes, which is at least one way to ensure that I never stand still.

In the moments before kick-off we huddle together as a team. Final instructions are given by Thaabit before Priyan, captaining the side, says the last words. 'For the people of Trincomalee, the Titans are their pride. We have to respect that. We have to fight for that. In Trincomalee we have a saying: all or nothing for Trinco,' he announces. 'All or nothing for Trinco!' we respond as one.

The game kicks off and it's immediately obvious that we're the far superior team. We line up in a 1-3-1-2-1-2 formation that relies heavily on its centre.

Fasith (GK)

Seth

Sakhti   Balaya   Inshaht

Dinesh

Kalua   Priyan

Dean

Aflal   Banda

We have almost all the possession. Dean is dominating the play and I'm comfortable as a sweeper. The only trouble is getting the ball in the goal.

From nowhere Dean is fouled. His opponent seems to try and kick his head despite the ball being on the floor. We were warned prior to the game that these opponents were dangerous but we dismissed it as more talk of supposed Sri Lankan aggression. Al Jaya, though, are living up to the stereotype. They're late with their tackles, lead with their elbows in headers and aren't afraid to push and shove.

Fortunately I don't get near enough to the action to be affected. I touch the ball a few times but nothing more. Eventually our goal comes and it's through Aflal, who twists and turns and fires home. Seconds later we're in again. I play a one-two with Dean and then launch a long ball down the line for Banda to chase. He finds Aflal, who once again beats two defenders before Priyan steals it off his toes to strike past the keeper. The linesman's flag is up. Priyan was offside.

At half-time we're told that Al Jaya have drafted in five players from Trincomalee for the game. All five are the most aggressive, and one of the defenders was unsuccessful in the trials to be part of the Titans. He really is out for revenge.

Our opponents are devastated that Dean is removed at half-time. We have a surplus of midfielders that Thaabit needs to assess, but Balaya and I retain our positions.

'Bring me the white boy,' Al Jaya's central midfielder requests as we walk back onto the pitch, 'I want another go at him.' He's talking about Dean. It wouldn't be a contest but the words still irritate Dean.

'I'm not bloody white,' he retaliates. It isn't the first time he's been called white.

The referee continues to let the leading elbows go, but then punishes the smallest of touches in a tackle. With the ball bouncing towards me, the last thing I see is a five-foot-five forward jumping upwards with his elbow aimed at my face. Fortunately he misses. Everything I try is coming off. Even when I aimlessly boot it – often a necessity on this surface – the ball seems to find a teammate. When I make my one mistake of the game, misjudging the amount of space needed to cover and missing a flick-on that sends an opponent free, the substitute Hizam is blamed for not being in line with me from left-back. The attacker, who was almost certainly offside but wasn't flagged, misses anyway.

We could have scored five or six, but the game ends 1-0. Inshaht is deservingly declared Man of the Match. Despite his eye-catching beard and rugged features, I'd barely noticed him before today. Yet now he seems to have played his way into Thaabit's plans. People from all over the pitch and the stands hug me and Dean.

Banda believes our opponents were a very good team, which gives me and Dean – neither of whom had to get out of breath – high hopes for the tournament. Yet Thaabit is much more frank in his assessment. He says they were terrible.

'I don't believe anything that comes out of Banda's mouth,' Dean smiles. 'Next he'll be telling me the sky is green.' Still, you can only beat what's in front of you.

Inshaht provides twenty green coconuts for our cooldown, chopping them with a huge knife before inviting us to drink straight from the hole. The mood is good. Everyone is laughing. The coconut tastes sweeter than any victory possibly could.

* * *

'Seth, buddy, I hope I'm not interrupting.'

I'm lying on my bed in my pants, aimlessly scrolling my phone. I tell Thaabit I couldn't be less busy. He steps into the room with Ihshan and says he has news regarding the tournament. It isn't good.

Rimzy has got through to a different member of the league committee, who has warned that there could be a big delay to the tournament. The Sri Lankan FA Cup is still going on and they don't want to start the North Eastern Premier League until that's finished. Thaabit asks if that will be a problem. Naturally, I ask how long the delay will be. Probably a month, I am told. The opening game will take place in a few weeks.

So many commitments, gone just like that. I can't give up on Sri Lanka. I have to give up on my plans at home. I tell Thaabit it will be fine so long as I can stay in England for a few extra days after the wedding. He gives me his blessing.

Dean is in a good mood at dinner and I know he hasn't been told yet. There's no chance he'll take this well. I wait until we take our usual walk to the shop to share the news.

'Has Thaabit spoken to you, by the way?' I start.

'Nah, why's that?'

'There's a big delay to the tournament. Maybe a month. Seems we aren't going home for a while.'

Dean stops in his tracks, his mouth open. His hands rise to his head.

'I can't... I don't even want to be here any more,' he whispers. Then he's silent. Totally silent. I go into the shop and his hands are still on his head when I emerge with a chocolate bar. 'I'm going to need a Sprite,' he says and so I go back in to pick him up a bottle. When I return, his head is still in his hands.

How can he keep doing this? What about Meghan? She's not going to want to come to Sri Lanka to watch him train, but he doubts whether she can cancel her flights. I suggest he can ask Thaabit to pay for them to stay in a nearby hotel together, but he replies that Thaabit got us individual rooms in the house so Meghan can stay with us. Poor girl.

Then there's his job. He'll almost certainly lose it. He's already on thin ice by coming to Sri Lanka for all this time. I tell him it's not important and that he'll be able to find a new one, which is probably what he least needs to hear right now. We sit for twenty minutes, discussing everything and deciding nothing.

* * *

The next day we learn there are more reasons for the delays. The Sri Lankan Football Federation has got involved and is demanding sign-off after sign-off before the tournament goes ahead. Really, though, it all comes down to money. Money and pride. The prize fund for the North Eastern Premier League is vast: 5,000,000 LKR to the winners, to be precise. That's almost the amount the Sri Lankan Football Federation gives for their premier tournament.

Then there's the issue of it being a Tamil tournament. The Sri Lankan Football Federation doesn't like the fact it's only open to players from the north-east. What would help them to like it is a backhander, which could be coming in the next few days. The tournament has to be over by the end of August so the Sri Lankan league can start. That means the tournament has to start soon.

Dean calls his mum. She calms him and convinces him to stay, which also calms me. This whole experience would be so much harder without him.

I call my girlfriend to tell her the news. We speak for an hour, and by the time I'm done there's another update: the green light has almost been given. The tournament is looking like it'll start on 25 July: a fifteen-day delay. Everything should be confirmed tomorrow.

I've heard it all before but it doesn't mean I'm any less hopeful.

* * *

I get respect from my teammates because I'm English. I also get respect because I'm one of the better footballers in the team. But mainly I get respect because I'm a 'hard-ball cricketer'.

They've all seen my photos on Facebook. There's one of me in full pads, whites and helmet. No matter how regularly I tell them that I'm no good at cricket, that I bat down the order and play in the ninth division of the Hertfordshire Cricket League Regional Division West, that I bowl plenty of wide long hops, they simply reply 'hard-ball cricketer, wow.'

Now the illusion is being shattered. I'm standing on the beach with a bat in my hands. Priyan is keeping wicket behind me and Thaabit is bowling from a makeshift stump placed fifteen yards away. A full circle of fielders is ready, Dinesh poised in the sea.

I dilscoop my first shot in homage to Sri Lanka's famous batsman Tillakaratne Dilshan and run a single.

'Very good player,' come the cries.

Thaabit smirks. He doesn't like being hit for such an expressive shot.

I don't score another run for the rest of the day. The next ball I run myself out, then I'm caught in my following two innings. Bowling goes just as badly. It takes me a while to adjust my length and bowl full tosses. My first ball is hit for six by Dinesh. The over lasts for ten balls due to no-balls and wides. It isn't until my final spell that I pick up two wickets. It's no surprise that they're both caught.

Up and down the beach, games of cricket are taking place. It's a Saturday and the locals are enjoying themselves, their whoops and hollers loud as balls soar into the air. Tourists stop to watch and take photos before heading back to Coconut Beach Club and the other hotels that cater to their needs. Even some of the fishermen join in before they're needed to haul in the catch.

Dean, Banda and Jai arrive as the sun sets and we jump into the sea, my cricketing respect long since diminished. Dean and Banda haven't been seen since the morning. The last thing we knew they were following us to the football stadium to watch the schools' under-19 championships. They didn't arrive and Banda failed to answer his phone all afternoon. Now we find out they went to Jai's mum's hotel in Nilaveli, where Jai has been staying since arriving. Dean describes it as paradise. I tell him Trincomalee is as close as I've been to paradise and he replies that Nilaveli is even better. It's quiet, just a few people on the beach, and is within a stone's throw of Pigeon Island and its beautiful coral reef.

The cricketers call them traitors. They laugh that Dean, Banda and Jai make up the Nilaveli Titans and not the Trinco Titans. Dean is insistent that playing cricket was the last thing he wanted to do no matter who it was with, so he didn't do it.

Pressure is put on me. Jai has come to collect me so I can stay the night at his mum's hotel in paradise and eat something other than rice. But the cricketers want a barbecue on the beach. I tell Thaabit that I'm going to Jai's but he says he wants me at the barbecue.

'The lads are in a good mood,' he says. 'Let's make the most of it.'

Sadly, I tell Jai that I'll have to come along later. Dean escapes to paradise; I remain with the cricketers.

The barbecue is amazing. My teammates go out of their way to do everything they possibly can. They even turn down

Thaabit's offer to finance it and insist on buying the ingredients themselves, despite many of them barely having two rupees to rub together. Anushaht is put in charge of the chicken and cooks it to perfection. Kalua chops the ingredients then controls the fire. Sakhti fizzes around doing whatever is needed. Priyan and Dinesh lay the table and clean up. When we sit down to eat, all those around the table are soon laughing and joking. Stories are told of Banda and I hear Dean's name regularly.

Attention switches to Anushaht, who shows us the tattoo on his arm. It reads Aushaht. Thaabit promises him that if he scores in the tournament he'll pay to have the 'n' inserted so it's no longer misspelled.

We finish with a toast to the Trinco Titans.

'Not the Nilaveli Titans!' Dinesh roars and the room responds in kind.

As does my stomach.

* * *

Even with the fan on full blast, my room is becoming too hot. I unstick myself from the sheets and head downstairs, where I find Thaabit at the kitchen table with someone I've never seen before. She's an Australian called Lisa and they're chatting away like the best of friends while drinking coffee fresh from Colombo. She's blonde, energetic and friendly, her pale skin faintly burnt. Thaabit introduces us. Lisa, it turns out, is just one result of the post-war efforts to develop Trincomalee. She's working for the Australian government right here in Trinco as a digital marketing expert attempting to improve the locals' knowledge so they can lure tourism to the area. In two months she's made progress but has had to adapt in so many different ways.

I'm impressed when she tells me she has a basic understanding of Tamil. I can just about say 'yes' and sing one line of a Tamil song. The words are just so long and complicated and aren't even written in our alphabet.

A mutual friend introduced Lisa to Thaabit. Since moving to the north-east of Sri Lanka she's struggled to socialise. Unlike the more liberal Colombo, Trincomalee is a conservative area when it comes to gender. Women don't really hang around outside of their homes. It's rare to see them walking the streets, almost unheard of for them to be alone in public. People have stopped Lisa for selfies. They've leered and tried it on, but increasing familiarity has numbed their attention. By the age of twenty-five most of the local women have married within their own community and moved into their husband's family home. Their life's purpose is then to cook for their husband's entire family and look after the home. There's no time for paid work, no time to leave the house, no time to hang out with Australians at the weekend.

Lisa is happy to be with us and she proves a great addition to the group. Together we jump into Thaabit's Prius and head towards the Nilaveli Titans. Along the way, we discuss local gossip and rumours. Rumours abound in Sri Lanka. 'A well-told lie is worth a thousand facts,' Michael Ondaatje wrote of Sri Lanka. He has a point. Our neighbour, we hear, made his riches in London, where he developed a sophisticated ATM-scamming device. Suitably minted, he returned to Sri Lanka to build a sizeable house. On the way to Nilaveli we pass a golden temple. Lisa has heard that it was paid for by a people smuggler. Over the best part of a decade the smuggler made millions by sending Sri Lankans to Australia. Then, one day he had an epiphany: what he was doing was wrong. To rid himself of guilt, he built a vast golden temple. Who knows if any of it is true? But why let truth get in the way of a good story?

Nilaveli is a fifteen-minute drive from our house. We arrive at Jai's mum's hotel, Nagenahira Beach Villas, to find that Dean wasn't lying. This truly is paradise. The set-up is simple: a handful of clean, white chalets leading to an avenue of tropical trees that pave the way to the ocean. Monkeys jump between the trees and run with freedom between the chalets. The young cling on to their mother's bellies as they scamper across the ground. 'Careful,' Jai says, 'they can cause havoc. Don't leave your flip-flops lying out in the open or they'll take them.' We decide not to linger and instead head straight through the trees and onto the beach. Just like the Trinco beaches, this one has white sand and a beautiful blue sea. Yet there are no people, no tourist traps and as a consequence no rubbish at all. The beach goes on for well over a kilometre yet I count just two fellow bathers and three grazing cows. Pigeon Island dots the ocean. Beneath the sea's surface lies a coral reef where sharks, turtles and whales all swim.

The ball comes out immediately. We start a cultured game of 'red arse' with Dean, Jai, Banda and Kaps, punishing the loser of each round by making them bend over and then blasting the ball at their rear. Sensibly, Lisa and Thaabit decide to swim instead.

A call of lunch comes from the distance. We finish our game and then set up in front of the TV for the next eight hours. The Cricket World Cup final is on. New Zealand have won the toss and elected to bat. I announce that every team batting first at Lord's in this World Cup has won. There's instant uproar from all corners. 'What about 1996!' They haven't heard me correctly. I try to explain but everyone is too busy reminiscing about the one and only time Sri Lanka won the World Cup.

The cricket has us on tenterhooks for the rest of the day. It's one of the greatest sporting matches of all time. Lisa is alone in her support of New Zealand. Everyone else is cheering for England. Banda starts to tell Lisa about his previous career as a chef.

The cricket isn't the only thing keeping us on the edge of our seats. We were expecting confirmation of the fixtures this morning, but there's still no news. Thaabit has extra reason for frustration: he's been invited to Sweden by Manchester City to help in the Gothia Cup, one of Europe's biggest youth tournaments. It's a great opportunity for him but one that he can't take until the fixtures have been released. It's not beyond the tournament organisers to arrange the first game for tomorrow.

We wait and wait. Kaps jokes that maybe they meant nine in the evening rather than the morning. We're still waiting long after England have lifted the trophy.

* * *

'Is this professional, like?' Dean asks.

'Well, it's professional in that it's all of the players' full-time jobs for two months,' I reply.

'Yeah, but nothing else about it is professional.'

The fixtures still haven't come through. Training is supposed to start in an hour but we don't know where it's taking place or what kind of session it is. Many of our team live an hour away from Trincomalee. Chaos or relaxation – you only ever get one or the other in this place.

A message comes through on the team's WhatsApp group: *Training at 4.30 p.m. on the beach.* It's just what we don't need. More fitness: the one element of football that our teammates actually have been coached in. You can't work on tactics or set-pieces on the beach. Tactics remain a mystery to many. We were supposed to be training on the army grounds or the navy grounds. The stadium had already been written off as an option for fear of spying eyes.

Dean laughs. Nothing ever stays the same.

And yet when we get to the beach the chaos is forgotten. So is the need for tactics and proper training.

Dinesh waves down a white man running on the beach: 'Woah, woah. Stop! Seth, this your friend?'

Banda spots two women walking past and starts doing press-ups, loudly shouting '113, 114, 115!'

Sakhti is in the water with his shorts off. He waves them over his head, screaming 'Ladies, ladies.'

We have a royal rumble in the water. Everyone picks a partner to put on their shoulders, then the last man standing is the winner. Inevitably it's Dean.

Beach sessions may not improve our tactical understanding but they don't half bring us together even more as a group.

* * *

Sri Lanka never ceases to amaze me. Every time I think I've just played on the worst pitch in my life, a new one comes along.

Our new training pitch is small. There are patches of grass – most of it knee-high – but mainly it's stones varying from the size of a pea to a knuckle. When we arrive there's a goat urinating in the middle of the pitch. A cockerel struts across the penalty area. Plastic bags and degrading coconuts line the perimeter while a stream of watery rubbish babbles down one touchline. Goat droppings and cow pats are everywhere. It looks like Dr Dolittle's back garden.

Even the Sri Lankans tell me it's the worst pitch they've ever played on. Now I see why Thaabit was so keen to stay on the beach. He assesses the ground and concludes that it's dangerous. He'll still run a session but it'll have to be low-intensity ballwork.

We start just as two cows are released onto the pitch by their owners. One immediately makes a beeline for us. As Thaabit is explaining the exercise we're about to do, the cow picks up a cone in its mouth while its friend loudly moos. Alarmed by the sound, three stray dogs soon join us. It's absolute carnage. We're already taking up the smallest area possible – the part deemed the least unsafe – and are made to feel even more hemmed in. Locals gather to watch us. A few play in one of the goals. I don't know how some of them do it in bare feet.

We survive the two hours with no injuries. My plastic studs have been severely worn, but that's all. It's no wonder my team-mates lack basic ball skills when they've grown up playing on surfaces such as this.

Nomi meets us back at the house. It's the first time I've met him and he instantly strikes me as a calming presence. He's bear-like in build and looks in relatively good spirits given what he's been through. He's desperate to make sure Dean and I are happy and asks what I usually eat back in England. Later that evening we're met with a kitchen full of eggs, bread, jam and cereals. It's only a small touch, but it means a lot. Before returning to Jaffna he reimburses us for all the food and drink we've bought so far.

He also leaves us with good news: the tournament's opening ceremony will be on 27 July. Our first game will be against the biggest spenders, Tamil United, in Jaffna on 29 July. Finally, things are starting to move, even if it means the tournament now won't finish until the end of August. And that's if we're lucky.

This also means I'm now going to fly back to England before the first game. It also means I could have just flown out after the wedding and saved myself £800 in plane tickets. Still, I can at last book my flights back to England. You shall go to the wedding, Seth. It'll just cost you four times your Trinco Titans salary and require you to leave in two days' time, straight after the friendly against Muttur. A return taxi will also cost half your entire salary.

But the flight gives me some positivity in a day of pain and torture. My insides are rebelling against me. Delhi belly. While the Nilaveli Titans head to Jai's little slice of paradise, I'm left dashing back and forth to the toilet. With the hygiene levels out here, it was only a matter of time.

Much of the day is spent laid flat out on my bed. When I do finally emerge in the evening, I'm greeted by Thaabit, Kaps and Lisa at the kitchen table. It's good to see Lisa again. To navigate a foreign place is much easier when there's someone from a similar culture to speak to. I usually have Dean, but Lisa has nobody.

Kaps has bought me a loaf of bread and a kilogram of mixed-fruit jam. I force down two slices, the first food I've eaten all day. They are all concerned about my health, though after the first bite they relax.

Lisa starts to complain about how unreserved her colleagues are. A male colleague today told her she was getting fat. He didn't mean it in a bad way, she assures us, but she still snapped at him. Fighting back felt good.

Our talk turns to the Titans. Thaabit emphasises how little the people of Trinco have. The football club, he says, is truly their family. It's stability, something they can be proud of, a home away from a home that has often been affected by war. Many have lost parents.

Inevitably we are soon talking about Banda. So many stories revolve around him. I mention that he has at least three houses that he calls home in Trinco and Thaabit explains why. Banda's mother died when he was just three. His dad was left to raise him, but his job in the Sri Lankan navy meant he was often away. Much of the burden fell on Banda's aunt and uncle. When Banda's father was back from sea, much of his time was spent with a new woman. Soon he would marry her. Banda's relationship with his father disintegrated as a result. The task of raising him now fell solely to his aunt and uncle, yet at the age of fifteen there was a big falling-out over a trivial issue. Banda stormed out of the home and has been sofa-surfing ever since. Eleven years. Eleven years of living out of bags, of having belongings strewn across various houses of friends in Trincomalee. The Trinco Titans house is Banda's first permanent house in eleven years. He's brought all his possessions, which barely fill a sports bag.

Thaabit is thrilled that Dean has taken Banda under his wing. Now he's living the life in Nilaveli and coming away from his struggle. He's finally settled in a family: the Titans.

* * *

The police flag frantically. They want to pull the car over. We've been warned about it but now it's actually happening. There are so many police about and so many checkpoints that it had to happen eventually.

Jai winds the window down and is immediately asked for his insurance papers. He hands them over. Still, the police aren't satisfied. They demand to see the identity cards of everyone in the car. Nobody has their identity card on them. This angers the policeman. Now an army man is sticking his head through the window.

'Where's he from?' he demands, pointing at Dean. The army man smells of alcohol and is slurring slightly.

'Ireland,' Jai replies. This angers the army man.

'Thailand! Thailand! This man is not from Thailand!'

'No, Ireland. Ire-land.'

Jai has to conclude the conversation soon. The car is too full and so Banda was put in the boot. He's lying there right now, trying to make no noise. Jai has no other option. He pulls out his wallet and gives a green 1,000 LKR note to the policeman.

Satisfied, the policeman waves him through. Everyone is happy: Jai has avoided a 25,000 LKR fine for not carrying his identity card, and the policeman has made 1,000 LKR rather than having to write a ticket and give all 25,000 to the government. Everyone except Dean, that is, for in that moment Dean's whole perception of Sri Lanka has changed.

He tells me all this as we walk to the shop to buy an ice cream. It's still fairly early in the evening but Banda and the coaches have long gone to bed. Dean and Banda returned earlier to play in a game of beach cricket and rest ahead of tomorrow's friendly. That friendly match has now been cancelled. Just like so much we've experienced in Sri Lanka: promise, expectation, no delivery. The cycle continues.

Dean doesn't know how he's going to cope by himself while I'm back in England for the wedding. We've had two training sessions on firm ground and one friendly match in two weeks. Everything else has been on the beach. Now that the friendly has been cancelled, another beach session looms followed by three days of rest. The constant changes are getting to Dean. Why is nothing ever as it seems? And when it does fall through, why is it never anybody's fault?

I suggest it could be to do with the war. If Tamils criticised, if they blamed others, if they were realists, how could they ever forgive those who committed such unspeakable atrocities against them? Maybe they always assume a bright future and shrug their shoulders when it never comes.

The police incident is replaying over and over in Dean's head. It's the fourth run-in he's had with the police, whereas I'm white and have yet to be stopped. I've never been more aware of my white privilege than in Sri Lanka, a country where some women whiten their skin in an attempt to appear more 'attractive', a country that seems in part to hark back to its days of colonialism with its idealised posters and liberal use of 'Ceylon'. The bribe has shocked Dean. It's the kind of thing that you only ever expect to see in movies.

'A country of liars and cheats,' he reflects. 'Corrupt. They're all corrupt.' It's harsh but I see where he's coming from. After all, we're in the land where a well-told lie is worth a thousand facts.

We need football to distract us. Two games a week and a few training sessions on a proper pitch. Without that distraction, the mind begins to wander and criticism comes easily. Is Sri Lanka really more corrupt than the countries surrounding it? Is it really more corrupt than England? As long as we're not being lied to and cheated, I'm happy. I'm not sure the same can be said for Dean. After all, four run-ins can hardly be a coincidence.

And we still haven't seen any sign of a contract.

* * *

'That's it. Final. Tonight I will cut players. We can't carry on like this.'

Thaabit is speaking to the squad. More accurately, Thaabit is speaking to the squad who bothered to turn up. The previous session had ten attendees, today's has thirteen. Our squad has twenty-five players – all of them supposedly full-time professionals. Players have begged Thaabit to sort it out. They fear the team is going the same way as the previous season, when players didn't bother to train and just turned up for matches.

We've just finished a 3km run around the naval base and a whole-body workout. 'Liars!' Dean yelled as players cut corners in the run, 'Cheats!' Turning to me, he asked 'Why can't they just take responsibility for their actions?'

Now Balaya is trying to do just that. He's having a passionate one-to-one with Thaabit. He emerges as the new captain, taking the title from his brother, Chinna.

The players who turned up have faith in the management. They have faith in the foreign players. But they don't have faith in their own. Thaabit assures them that he'd rather play with a committed thirteen players than have twenty-five uninterested squad members.

Later that night, a WhatsApp message confirms that three players yet to turn up to training have been released from the squad. The message signs off with the words 'Let this be a warning.'

* * *

The taxi driver arrives on time, so I can breathe. It's suggested I have dinner first. After all, the airport is only five hours away and so there is plenty of time. I suspect this is another case of misplaced optimism but don't want to turn down a free dinner.

Priyan and Kalua join us. They haven't come to eat. Instead they've turned up so they can accompany me to the airport.

It will be a ten-hour round trip for them in the middle of the night. I can barely bring myself to accompany Banda ten minutes down the road to collect dinner from Rimzy's house. It's been a tough week but, as they join me in the car, an overwhelming sense of gratitude arrives. It's truly humbling.

I do my best to keep them occupied and chat. The driver plays a Spice Girls Greatest Hits CD, supposedly for my benefit, and Priyan and Kalua sing along. I smile but, as the road inches by at a painful 40km/h, the tiredness hits. I just can't keep my eyes open...

Until the car slows to a halt and fingers tap against the window. We're almost at Negombo, right on the other side of the island. Kalua winds the window down.

'Are you Tamil?' the army man asks, though he already knows the answer. Kalua nods and the army man shines his light into the car as if he's trying to find something incriminating. 'Where are you going?'

'The airport.'

'ID, please.'

The other three hand over their identity cards. I sit there, thinking my white skin will absolve me from this like it usually does, but even I'm asked to show my passport. After all, I'm travelling with Tamils. The army man asks plenty of questions. Who am I? Where am I going? Why am I in Sri Lanka? He's more hostile than friendly. There's not a single smile.

I answer through Priyan but still he doesn't seem satisfied. He makes us all get out of the car so he can check it more thoroughly. Then he goes through my bag, furiously rummaging. His machine gun is swinging from his chest as he removes my laptop from the bag. I wonder whether he's assessing how rich I am for how much of a bribe we need to give. But he doesn't.

After going through every one of my possessions, he begrudgingly allows me back in the car.

I ask Priyan if I can have a toilet break while we've stopped. He looks at me like I'm taking the piss. No, he wants to get out of here as soon as possible, just as the others do. There's fear in their eyes.

This is the reality of being Tamil in Sri Lanka. No matter how hard the Tamils try to forget what happened in the past, the Sinhalese government won't allow them to. They were victims of a horrific civil war, now they're victims of suspicion and subordination. Suddenly I understand what the North Eastern Premier League is fighting against to even run the tournament. How can one ever feel free as a Tamil in Sri Lanka?

'Stupid policeman,' Kalua concludes as we speed away into the night.

LONDON

Back in England the work continues. I run, I go to the gym and yes, I even make the wedding. It's so good to be home. Absence makes the heart grow fonder. My country seems greener, more beautiful, and the weather is just perfect.

Still, I can't help but wonder what's happening in Sri Lanka. I follow the content that Ihshan posts on the Trinco Titans' social media pages with interest. It feels like I'm missing out.

Priyan messages me every day, Dinesh gets in touch regularly, and I hear from Kalua often. But many of my teammates go quiet. The majority of them asked me to pick stuff up for them from England. Aunties, brothers and friends making up the millions of displaced Tamils around the world have all kinds of gifts that need taking to Sri Lanka. I promise to meet up with them and collect the gifts but, like so much of what has happened to date, it leads to nothing. None of the aunties, brothers or friends calls me.

Thaabit has also given me a task. He asks me to sort a boot deal. Most of our players wear locally produced PAN boots, made of cheap plastic and with studs worn to the sole. Many have holes in. I use contacts at Nike, ask people on Twitter and try to sort something with Concave, who gave my six-a-side team heaps of free product. Nothing. My leads lead nowhere and so Thaabit decides to get the boots in Colombo. Instead he asks me to pick up thirty boot bags.

On my travels to various Sports Directs around central London, I stumble across a Tamil Tigers demonstration taking place just off Westminster. There must be at least fifty people standing holding banners and LTTE flags, a restless tiger leaping out of a red background, its claw bared in readiness.

RAPE IS USED TO DESTROY OUR NATION.

TAMIL EELAM IS OUR HOMELAND.

EELAM TAMILS ARE A NATION.

UN, STOP PROTECTING GENOCIDAL SRI LANKA.

LET TAMILS DECIDE REFERENDUM NOW!

TAMIL EELAM IS THE ONLY SOLUTION.

THIRTY YEARS SINCE BLACK JULY. SUSPEND
SRI LANKA FROM THE COMMONWEALTH
IMMEDIATELY.

ENOUGH TIME FOR SRI LANKA! TRANSITIONAL
ADMINISTRATION IN EELAM NOW! REFER SRI
LANKA TO INTERNATIONAL CRIMINAL COURT.

This is a minority of the diaspora, the people forced to flee by a brutal war. Leading the group, there's a man with a microphone who's speaking in Tamil. His followers nod and shout and stand in their spot, staring out at those passing by. I take a video and send it to Priyan. He replies straight away.

Bro, I don't like this. It's the worst. It's done for in Sri Lanka and that's good.

Defeated, but not destroyed. Tamil Tiger supporters continue to lobby all around the world. In Germany and Canada and the UK, those who fled from gunfire set up home. The diaspora that formed in faraway places remained critical throughout the war. The Tamil Tigers routinely lobbied them for donations. In his book *Elephant Complex*, John Gimlette reported that from England, where more than 100,000 Sri Lankan Tamils now live, these donations came to around £250,000 a year, though in the final stages of the war they were ramped up to as much as £250,000 every month. This minority of the diaspora continue to raise awareness of Tamil Eelam far away from their home nation. Their guns, thankfully, remain unused but the desire for a separate state remains.

While they continue their peaceful protests in London, developments are taking place in Trinco. Numbers are low for training and several more players are released. Mini shockwaves go around the team when Chinna is one of them. Dean tells me it was mutual. A couple of players told Thaabit they didn't think the team was good enough and so they didn't want to be involved. Their loss.

Just twelve players manage to play in the week's friendly. Three triallists bring the squad to fifteen. Jai takes my place and is awarded Man of the Match. Dean scores twice then goes over on his ankle. Banda has a late third chalked off for offside.

Another win. Another clean sheet. It doesn't matter that the squad is much reduced. Better to have twelve who fight for each other than twenty-five who aren't committed.

TRINCOMALEE

Ihshan picks me up at the airport with his ever-present smile and bottle of Coca-Cola in hand. Kalua, Banda, Priyan, Sakhti and Dinesh wanted to do it, and they'd even gone as far as identifying a van they could use to collect me, but they were thwarted by Thaabit. He reminded them that, as they were now professional footballers, they should probably attend training instead of making a ten-hour round trip to pick up a teammate.

Back at the house, it feels like I've never been away. I get a great reception, then it's back to my room with the windows wide open and the fan turned up to a maximum speed that is never quite maximum enough.

I sleep for thirteen hours, then get straight back into training on the beach. Again, there's a great reception. It's an honour to share a pitch with such teammates. There are two new ones: Vithu, a compact, barrel-shaped defender with one full sleeve of tattoos and a prominent wedding ring who played for the Titans last season, and Roshan, a bony midfielder with a large moustache who played for last week's opponents. Roshan had impressed by squaring up to Dean and not backing down when Dean snarled at him. He's already earned everyone's respect.

The mood is good. The boys are ready. Everything is positive.

And in more good news, I discover we have a washing machine! We actually have a washing machine. The fridge has now broken and the TV is still missing a cable, which means it doesn't work, but who cares? We have a washing machine!

Less positive is the news that Dean has lost his room key – somewhere on the beach by Jai's, he thinks. The hopes of finding it are slim to none. With his door now permanently locked, he has to leave his bedroom window open the whole time, scaling the building and creeping around the small balcony before jumping back in through the window. It's been this way for the last week.

The days are so long, he complains. He's been doing nothing all day except train from 4 p.m. to 6 p.m. when the sun is low in the sky. He's even deleted Instagram and Snapchat from his phone because he found himself spending too much time on them.

'What do you do now then?' I ask.

'It's a good question,' he replies.

* * *

We had a thunderstorm last night. Lightning lit up the sky every few seconds. Thunder rumbled and rain poured. It was enough to bless Ehamparam with a few shoots of grass. Not that we're able to play on much of them. The community stadium's pitch is packed. There's a hard-ball cricket game going on in one half of the pitch. The ball is launched onto the other half of the pitch for six runs with regularity. In one corner the cricket nets are being used. Two more cricket games are taking place on the edges. There's a cow walking round. And in among the carnage we have to set up. Thaabit does the best he can in such a situation. Still, it feels good to get back on the balls and return to work.

This is our first time in the stadium for a long time. The need to shelter our players from the jealousy and boos of those watching in the stands is outweighed by the necessity of sorting some actual tactics. Especially now there is a start date to the tournament. Sure enough, a handful of locals sit high in the stands, ready to provide us with entertainment. Chinna is also lurking. He's the closest thing Trinco has to a celebrity. He arrives at the side of the cricket game and instantly the batsman offers him the bat. He lazily takes a few drives and sweeps, then passes the bat on so that he can watch us.

In the break I say hello and give him a hug. It's crazy – he refused to come to most of the sessions, told the coach we are terrible and yet I still respect him. There's a real aura about him.

'Seth,' he says. 'Australia 85-3.'

He's the fourth person who's told me the score in the first day of the Ashes. I thank him, hoping Thaabit hasn't seen our brief exchange. At least it's less inflammatory than Mindron's actions. Mindron has plastered a challenge across his social media pages, betting any willing taker 50,000 LKR that his team, Valvai, will beat us. We play them in our second game. So confident is Mindron that he's promised Banda he'll come to our bench after the game and remove his pants in celebration. He's desperate for revenge. My teammates need to just shrug and ignore it.

I stay behind with Dean for some extra practice. Thaabit encourages it, hoping the rest of the team will imitate us in the days to come. Maybe they'll use Mindron's actions to drive them on. Or maybe they'll shrink. Those watching in the stands have long since disappeared.

In the car afterwards, Thaabit realises he's driving without having his licence on him. If we were to be stopped by police there could be an issue. I tell him about my own run-ins with the police on the way to the airport and their hostility when finding out Kalua was Tamil. Thaabit replies that the police checks in Jaffna ask passengers if they're Muslim. If they say yes then their name is written in a separate book. I ask if it's because the government fear a Muslim attack more than anything, and Thaabit snorts. I tell him I've always believed Buddhists to be calm, tolerant people in search of enlightenment. But in Sri Lanka, it emerges, some monks are far from the peaceful monks we in the UK associate with the religion. In fact, a minority are the most dangerous, the least peaceful, the most radicalised. And sometimes they're even politicians.

The Jathika Hela Urumaya is a right-wing party made up solely of Buddhist monks. Formed in 2004, it put up 200 monks as candidates and won nine seats in its first election. The party then used its platform to lobby for Sinhala nationalism and against peace talks with the LTTE, instead advocating for its total destruction. The political pressure they applied had a major impact on the Sri Lankan government who – buoyed by a post-9/11 world seeking to eliminate terrorists at all costs – eventually caved in. Since then, further political parties made up of Buddhist monks have sprung up. The Bodu Bala Sena, Sinhala Ravaya, Ravana Balaya, and Mahasohon Balakaya parties are all much of a muchness: right-wing parties that aggressively spout Buddhist nationalist politics. Together they have formed a movement that 'protects the motherland', which often translates into violence and radical methods.

My head hurts again. It's no wonder our team politics are so complex.

* * *

The house is on fire. Thaabit spots it first. I'm sitting at the table with him and Ihshan just before midnight. He turns and a leaping flame catches his eye. It's from the coils that we light every night to try and keep mosquitoes away. Tonight was the first time Banda was trusted to light them. Now the coil has all gone up in flames and the cardboard it's sitting on is alight.

Ihshan is first to react. I'm surprised by his speed as he runs to the kitchen and fills a bottle with water before throwing it on the blaze. It works. The fire comes under control.

It's the first and last time Banda is ever trusted with matches.

* * *

The boys are buzzing. There's no other word to describe them. We're all sitting in the conference room at Skandig Beach Hotel. Nomi has made the trip down from Jaffna and has been joined by two representatives from Kimin Holdings, the company of one of the owners that is pretty much running everything from a financial point of view. There's also the Trincomalee District football secretary and football president, who are acting as third parties to events.

Thaabit is at his engaging best as he introduces everyone and then the secretary reads out the contract. He's supposed to read it first in English and then in Tamil. However, his English is muted at best. Dean and I strain to hear it but have no luck. Thaabit assures us we'll be able to read the contract before signing. But when it comes to it, we can't. We're called up one by one and I'm the third. My name gets a loud cheer and several people pat me on the back and fist-bump me as I walk to the front. It wouldn't be right to ask to read the contract now. I didn't hear much but I did hear that the contract only runs until 1 September. I should be fine.

I sign then pose for a photo with Thaabit. He hands me a personalised water bottle with my new squad number: five.

While everyone else signs, I manage to read the contract. It's nine pages long and seems pretty sound. Other than the pay being less than promised. We're now due to be paid 40,000 LKR rather than 50,000. Essentially, we're being forced to work for one month longer than promised and for less money. But you can't have everything, I suppose. I point this out to Dean.

'Never again,' he smiles. 'This is the first and only time I'll do something like this.'

Neither of us can be angry because the mood is so good. When Banda is awarded the number seven it looks as if he may break down and cry. In a country where Cristiano Ronaldo is revered, where hard work and physical attributes are favoured over technical ability, where Messi will always be seen as second-best, the number seven shirt has an incredible aura. Banda is honoured.

By the time everyone has finished signing, cheques are being waved, jokes are being made and hundreds of selfies are being taken and uploaded immediately to Facebook and Instagram. We've just been handed 40 per cent of our salary: 16,000 LKR. Everyone gets paid the same.

Dean and I are invited to reveal the official match shirts. Anticipation is in the air and as we turn the shirts a big cheer erupts. They don't look half bad. Pretty nice, in fact. The home one is a classy blue and white, while the away kit features the same blue at the top but an eye-catching yellow at the bottom, the two colours separated by a chevron pattern. TRINCO TITANS is splashed across the belly of both, while the NEPL logo is printed on the right of the chest. There's no sponsor, which seems strange. All of the other teams have extra money coming in through selling off shirt sponsorship. In our hands, the shirts both seem tiny, sized for Sri Lankans. As good as they look, I fear I really will have to squeeze into it.

But now it's official: we have a team, we have a kit, and my teammates can all say they've achieved one of their dreams – they're all officially professional footballers. And nobody can ever take that away from them.

* * *

There's been an earthquake off the Indonesian island of Java. It hit 7.0 on the Richter scale and has prompted fears of a tsunami. The south and east of Sri Lanka are especially vulnerable. After the 2004 disaster, which killed 35,000 in Sri Lanka and left many more homeless, everyone in the house is understandably shaky. That tsunami was the result of an earthquake measuring 9.3 on the Richter scale.

We're advised to pack our bags while the coaches monitor further warnings. If a tsunami is coming, we should be warned around 5 a.m. tomorrow. In the worst-case scenario, we'll cram into the car and head for the mountains. Well, almost all of us. Banda suggests we should all go surfing. In all the panic, nobody has even noticed that he's once again lit the coils for the night.

We keep one eye open all night, prepared to jump out of bed in an instant. Eventually the morning comes and we're in luck. The tsunami doesn't materialise. Life goes on as normal, or as normal as life can ever be in Sri Lanka. Since arriving back in Trincomalee from London I've vowed to make the most of my location. Mainly, that means using the beach more. That afternoon I swim in the sea, and that evening I head out alone for a walk along the beach under the stars.

Always wary of dead puffer fish and other rejected creatures left lying on the shore by the fishermen, I tentatively move down the beach, towards Coconut Beach Club. It's quiet tonight. Cloud obscures many of the stars and there are only a few fishermen sleeping by their boats. Maybe the rest have stayed home with the tsunami warning in mind. I turn and make it almost all the way back to my starting point when a voice calls out to me.

'Hello.'

I stop and see someone approaching me. There's nowhere to go and so I say hello back. I'm engaged in conversation immediately. The silhouetted stranger asks where I'm from and then tells me he's a footballer. He turns and shows me the name on the back of the Sri Lankan kit he's wearing: Rifas. We move into the artificial light so a photo can follow. He stands closer than I'm comfortable with. His facial features are harsh, cheek bones prominent. 'I'm the captain,' he proudly informs me.

I ask if he lives in Trincomalee and he invites me to sit, as if he has all the time in the world. When I eventually tell him that I play for the Trinco Titans he isn't surprised. It's as if he's followed my every move.

'Today you have contract signing? How much are you getting paid?' I reply with the truth.

'20,000 LKR a month.'

'20,000 a day?'

'No, a month.'

'20,000 dollars a month?'

'No, rupees.'

This conversation is going nowhere. I sum up that the money is no good but it's a free holiday and that seems to satisfy him. But it isn't long before he's shaking his head once more.

'Trinco team very weak. Last season strong. Now only focused on fitness. No footballers. Only fitness.' Considering the team finished so poorly last season, I guess there's a few holes in his argument. 'My friend Iham very good,' he continues. 'My friend Inshaht OK. Very good fitness but no good football.'

I wonder if Iham – who still hasn't been seen since his sole session at Kalutara – has been feeding Rifas information, or whether he's just been watching us all along. Maybe it's a bit of both. Rifas goes on to tell me he plays for the national under-23 team, for Army SC in the Sri Lankan Champions League, and for Kalutara Blue Star – and all while working in the army and living in Trinco, which seems a bit far-fetched to say the least.

But I don't question how one person can do all of that and play for three teams at once. All my thoughts are on what Rifas said about Trinco. Maybe we aren't any good. After all, our team is unique in that our owners aren't doing this for glory. To them, we're a corporate social responsibility project. They're investing money to develop sport in Trinco and to give our players amazing opportunities. Mahela Jayawardene himself has assured Thaabit that 'expectations bring pressure, and there are no expectations.'

Or maybe there's another reason why so many people keep telling us we're no good: jealousy, uncertainty, suspicion, call it what you will but Trincomalee has in some respects been invaded by outsiders. The club was bought by some fancy owners, its local coaches and back-room staff other than Rimzy were let go in favour of some fancy hotshots from Colombo, a place that few in Trinco have visited and even fewer like. Many from Trinco have rarely if ever travelled out of the district. No wonder they'd like to keep their football club for themselves. If that's what this is all about, anyway.

After half an hour I leave Rifas. I'm intrigued and confused. Once again, there are more questions than answers.

* * *

When we get to the beach for our training session the next day, the volleyball net has been taken down. The hotel has noticed we're the only ones using it when we turn up for our beach sessions.

'These people only care about tourists,' Priyan explains. 'Not the locals, the community.'

Thaabit's father, cousin and uncle join us from Colombo as we opt for a beach football tournament instead. Afterwards we return to our house while Thaabit's family head back to their hotel – the same one that has removed our net – where they're staying for a couple of days. Then the trouble starts.

A waiter asks to see proof of Thaabit's family's room number. A few minutes later a second one asks. When the third stops them and asks for proof, before they've even finished their coconut sambal, Thaabit's cousin loses it. It's racism. In Sri Lanka, local tour guides are given separate hotel rooms to guests, often servant quarters on the top floor with small, basic rooms and holes in the floor you have to squat over for toilets. Just because Thaabit's family have dark-coloured skin, it's assumed they should be in the servant quarters. Why would the three of them be in the main dining room with the white guests, especially as they're all dressed in football kit? Sri Lankans really do seem to lack trust in their own people.

Thaabit hears about it and storms to the hotel. He's met with desperate apologies.

'Please,' the general manager begs him, 'please don't put this on TripAdvisor.'

We don't yet have our volleyball net back, but we do now have unrestricted access to the hotel pool for the next month.

Thaabit's family hope to return to see one of our games. But they won't be staying at the same hotel. They cut short their stay and return to the more tolerant capital, their home.

Thaabit, left in Trincomalee, now stands in the kitchen, calmer and watching me type into my laptop.

'Hey buddy, what are you going to call the book you're writing?'

I stop and press save.

'I was going to go with *Football with the Tamil*. What do you think?'

'I don't think that's a good idea, buddy.'

I try to explain that people in England are interested in the Tamils and their struggles, that by having 'football' and 'Tamil' in the title it immediately attracts people. Thaabit just shakes his head.

'Seth, you need to understand that there are three things here: language, religion and culture. Someone can speak Tamil but not be considered a Tamil. Hinduism is the religion of Tamils yet our team is almost half Muslim and half Christian. Muslims may speak Tamil and identify with Tamil culture, but consider themselves to be Muslim over Tamil. Then many Tamils don't really consider Muslims to be Tamil anyway. You know that the Tamil Tigers expelled Muslims from their area, right?' I nod and he continues: 'So if you call it that, you're alienating a lot of the members of the team. I wouldn't go with that.'

'The Tamil Titans: My Season in Sri Lanka?'

'I'm not sure about the association between Tamils and Titans. Especially with the fighting and all. How about freedom?'

'That could work, but maybe just as a subtitle. We have to make clear it's about football, Sri Lanka and the war.'

'Well, we best get thinking.'

This place is so complex.

* * *

I'm shocked to discover that Kaps is fifty. I'm less shocked to discover that Kaps has been registered to play for us in the upcoming tournament.

'You couldn't write it,' Dean smiles, before smiling even wider when he realises that I am in fact writing everything down.

Ultimately, though, Kaps is good enough to be a squad player. He has the ultimate Buddhist mindset – not the ultra-nationalist one that seeks to sow division but the one that promotes clean living, calmness and contentment. He looks at least ten years younger than his age. He eschews social gatherings in favour of early nights and even earlier mornings, spending hours meditating upon waking. He's fit and healthy, not to mention highly intelligent. Whenever he has joined in with training, he fits in seamlessly and I can tell he used to be a very good player.

The facts remain, though. On the outside, people back home see that I'm playing professional football abroad and assume that I must be excelling, that I'm competing in something high level. The reality is that I'm playing alongside a long-retired fifty-year-old on terrible pitches against tactically naive teams. Yet we live in a world of fake realities, the Instagram age. I'm perfectly happy for the perception back home to continue.

* * *

My first mini-confrontation with Thaabit comes two days before our first matchday of the tournament. After a week-end off, we're planning to train on both days. Thaabit tells us he's booked the whole pitch at Ehamparam so we'll have a hard session. Fine. Then he tells us we'll do a beach session the following morning, working on our cardio and clocking around 7km. Dean and I exchange wary glances. That'll be followed by an afternoon session on tactics and set-pieces.

'Two sessions the day before a game?' I ask. 'Cardio the day before a game?'

And it isn't just the day before a game. It's the day before ten group-stage games in twenty-seven days, possibly followed by quarter-finals, semi-finals and a final. It's crazy, ludicrous, another big ask on what is already ten big tests on our bodies.

'Seth, buddy. I think you're getting your days mixed up.' Thaabit speaks as if it's a simple misunderstanding. 'We will run the morning of the day before the game. You will have a little more than twenty-four hours to recover.'

'We're running 7km the day before a game?' I ask with incredulity.

Yet Thaabit is equally incredulous. There are other players around us. Kalua, Priyan and Banda. I can't undermine the coach in front of them. I give a response to suggest I strongly disagree and remove myself from the situation.

As soon as we're out of earshot Dean bursts into laughter.

'Madness. Absolute madness.'

Despite my protestations, at 7 a.m. the next day I'm running on the beach with my teammates. My legs are already sore from the three-hour training session of the afternoon before. It featured intense possession drills, a bronco test (essentially a fitness test that's a 1.2km sprint) and thirty sets of 10-metre sprints to finish. As I run, I make the calculations in my head. The first game is thirty-three hours away. Over the next twenty-eight days and thirty-three hours we'll play the five other teams in our group both home and away before either progressing to a quarter-final or packing our bags and going home. This is the squad's seventh week of pre-season training.

My hamstring is twinging but I carry on. I'm a vice captain and need to lead by example. I do so by staying at the back and ignoring Priyan and Banda's cries for us to catch up with them.

Thaabit has lowered his demand slightly. We've been tasked with running 4km in twenty minutes, which would be fine on grass. And if we hadn't trained the night before.

I feel for Dean. Having promised to hang at the back with me, he's been set the task of pacing for the rest of the group. Within seconds of starting, the others had steamed ahead of him. He had no option but to keep up.

My teammates don't think. They don't see that we have a game tomorrow, that they need to go slow. They just see pride and a desire to impress the coach. And so I stick to the back with Balaya, Anushaht and Kaps, who has just completed his degree in sports science. At one point Balaya urges us to speed up but we immediately tell him to relax, there's a game tomorrow. He listens. Kaps agrees.

'We have to go slow,' he insists.

We end up running several hundred metres less than the leading pack and taking several hundred seconds more. But that's not important; as long as my legs are fine for tomorrow's game I don't care.

The afternoon session is decent, though still relatively intense. We go over wave after wave of attack-versus-defence scenarios. Thaabit gives the attacking team some good patterns of play but they're complicated by the stones and bobbles and uneven surface of the pitch. They don't succeed in penetrating our goal. In ninety minutes we concede just three times. And two of those were goalkeeping errors. At the end of the session Dinesh's watch tells him he's run 8km, in addition to the morning's 4km.

The boys' legs may be tired but their spirits are so high they're almost delirious. Many agree to meet at 8 a.m. tomorrow to set up the stadium. Everyone has to be there by 1.30 p.m., a full two hours before kick-off. We're told we have to report in long trousers and club t-shirt. Two hours before kick-off, with no air conditioning in the stadium, stuffed into long trousers and with even the shade providing 35 degree heat. But why would I expect ideal preparation?

* * *

Priyan believes we'll win easily. He assures us that Mannar, our opponents, are 'no problem'. He knows their players and knows that we are better. The only team we may have an issue with is Valvai, he tells us, who we play second. They've invested lots of money, have four national-team players and possess a powerful influence over officials. But that's fine. We can still beat them and win the whole tournament. I appreciate his optimism, but still want to wait and see the standard before deciding whether to believe him or not.

We eat Rimzy's specially prepared food at midday and arrive bang on time. The nerves are clear. Thaabit refuses food, too nauseous to get anything down. The players who meet us at the ground are like nervous balls of energy, bouncing all over the place. They've done a good job, though. The lines have all been painted, the nets and corner flags are up, and giant posters of me and Dean have been hung from the stands.

The changing room has also been decorated. Thaabit allows all players three minutes there to take as many selfies as they want, then insists they put their phones away until the game has finished. Ask a Sri Lankan to take a selfie and they aren't likely to refuse. It feels like a fashion shoot. Each player has their own chair with their kit immaculately laid out and a sticker of their face plastered on the wall above. On one wall is a poster of the league table from last season, which Thaabit has printed to try and motivate the squad.

Mannar, I note, lost just one of their eleven games last season, conceding only eleven goals. Trinco, meanwhile, conceded forty-four and lost seven. And that was despite having two highly paid Nigerian professionals in the team. Already I'm sceptical of Priyan's words.

We're left to get changed. Players strap their knocks, stare at the league table, wait for the toilet to become free, slip in their shinpads, tighten their laces, breath deeply, focus. Then, all of a sudden, Thaabit rushes in: 'Go! Go! Go! All or nothing for Trinco!' It's like an army drill and he's the sargeant: excited, nervous, impatient.

'These boys need to calm down,' Dean notes. He's not wrong.

On the other side of the pitch Mannar are also going about their work. I note their soft touches of the ball, their confident control, and know we're going to be in for a tough match. They're tall, too. Not like the Sri Lankans I've met before.

In the tunnel I get a closer look. When they finally arrive, that is, because Thaabit sends us out at 3.20 p.m. We stand around and wait, bored, though it helps any teammates' excessive levels of adrenalin to settle. Our opponents provide a bit of interest. Many of them stare at me and point in my direction. I don't know what they're saying. At least three are taller than me and also more built. It looks like there's going to be a serious imbalance at set-pieces.

The two teams remain in the tunnel. We wait but I don't know what for. The scheduled kick-off time of 3.30 p.m. comes and goes. So does 3.45 p.m.

We chat among ourselves. Sakhti goes one further. Nobody in Sri Lanka, it seems, is aware of the age-old trick where you tap someone on the chest, then move your hand up to slap their face when they look down. I've done it repeatedly to all my teammates and now Sakhti has picked on the tallest, biggest opponent and told him there's something on his chest. He looks down and Sakhti slaps him. We go wild: 1-0 to Trinco.

Almost half an hour late, the game starts. And then it really is 1-0. Within three minutes Sakhti robs the ball from an opponent and squares it to Dean, who plays in Aflal for a one-on-one. He makes no mistake.

My whole body tingles. It's strange. Usually when my team scores I stay calm, fully aware of the vulnerability of a lead. Yet now I'm charging towards Aflal with my arms open wide and screaming. Football, eh?

The crowd shrieks and whistles. About two hundred people are in the stands and on the touchline with several armed policemen watching over them. Chinna is one of those on the touchline. He's come with a group of former players, many of whom are hoping to see us lose today.

'Good luck,' one had told coach Rimzy before the game. 'With players like Banda you have no chance of winning.'

Mannar don't panic. They stick to their game plan of passing it out from the back and through midfield, which is commendable given that the terrible pitch has been swept and watered to limit the dust kicked up from players' boots but appears to have acquired more stones and less padding from sand as a result.

We do the opposite. I try and kick long but can't get my foot under the ball on the hard, uneven surface. It plays with my mind. Meanwhile, Ranoos in goal launches his drop-kicks as high as possible, fully aware that it isn't only hard to deal with but is also the best chance of creating a funny bounce that could lead to a goal.

We kick high, Mannar pass short. We play ugly, Mannar play beautifully. They're a good team, that much is clear. The equaliser is inevitable if not questionable. A little dink aimed between Jai and Vithu on the right side of defence sets their striker free. He lobs the ball over Ranoos but it hits the bar. I'm waiting for the rebound when the other striker careers into me, sending me flying. A sharp twinge spreads through my knee with pain running all the way down to my ankle. I hit the ground and am vaguely aware of my surroundings: shouts of offside, footsteps, more kicks then, eventually, the ball in the back of the net. Then the referee is next to me. I hear the calls of 'offside, offside'. He sends for our physio, Mathu, who hits me with some magic spray. I limp to the side as the game restarts, unsure what's just happened. It isn't until half-time I find out the goal was allowed.

And still there's time for one more before half-time. Mannar dominate the play with wave after wave of attack. I give away a silly free-kick, trying to reach my right leg around the striker to clear the ball he's shielding. From the resulting free-kick another ball is clipped between Jai and Vithu, who play for offside. I desperately chase after the striker. I'm gaining on him. He's slowing, taking a touch, then another, then another. On this surface, nothing but full certainty will do. I'm within a metre of him. I could slide but don't think it's safe enough. Too late. He's let fire. The striker is no more than twelve yards out. For some reason, Ranoos is planted to his line, giving the striker plenty of the goal to aim at. Instead, the ball arcs through the air and straight into Ranoos's gloves. But then it's straight out of his gloves and into the path of the other striker, who taps it in. He's at least five yards offside but no amount of protest will change the linesman's decision. The goal stands.

Thaabit remains calm at half-time. He must have used up all his nerves in the first half. He tells the boys they're playing well and to keep going.

Keep going they do. We control the second half. Our opponents continue to try and play out from the back but rarely breach our re-energised defence.

By now the crowd has swelled to at least five hundred. News has spread. They're standing in the shade behind the goal, hugging the touchline and cheering in the stand. When we get the ball in an advanced position they go wild. I even get delirious cheers when I kick the ball out of play to concede a throw-in from a dangerous attack.

I've never played in front of such an excitable crowd. So when Banda taps home to make it 2-2 it's no surprise that they go crazy. And when Banda lashes home an unstoppable thirty-yarder to put us into the lead, everyone loses it. The ball hits the net and he's running and running and the fans are on the pitch and chasing him and he jumps into Thaabit's arms. The squad catches him and we're all together, laughing and smiling and high-fiving.

We don't deserve the win. But none of that matters when the final whistle blows. Priyan collapses to the floor in joy. Just twenty-four hours earlier he'd told me it was 'impossible' that

Banda would score. The linesmen sprint to join the referee in the middle. And the crowd sprints to us. I'm being hugged from all angles, grown men are kissing my forehead and my hands. It's pure madness. Someone lifts me up.

'The best player,' they say. 'Amazing.'

'Very good header,' say others.

They really are getting carried away. I spot my oldest friend, a former postman in his late seventies who supports us at our every training session at the stadium, running laps around the perimeter while we work and then joining in with the kids' game in the corner. Every time we see each other we hug, but this time he runs up to me and I lift him up and spin him round and round. It seems everyone cheers that special moment. I've never known such a buzz.

It takes several minutes to break through the crowd and get to the dressing room, but almost immediately we're shepherded back out for the presentation. A novelty-sized cheque for 25,000 LKR greets us, along with a 5,000 LKR one for the Man of the Match. Who else? It's Banda.

	Team Name	P	W	D	L	GF	GA	GD	Points
1	Valvai FC	1	1	0	0	3	1	2	3
2	Trinco Titans	1	1	0	0	3	2	1	3
3	Mullai Phoenix	1	1	0	0	1	0	1	3
4	Mannar FC	1	0	0	1	2	3	-1	0
5	Tamil United	1	0	0	1	0	1	-1	0
6	Kiliyoor Kings	1	0	0	1	1	3	-2	0

The next day, Dean and I are walking down the road to the shop when a teenage boy cycles past. He slows and shouts: 'Hey!' He motions kicking with his foot and says 'very good' before speeding off. He's not the only person to recognise us after yesterday. I receive more than two hundred friend requests on Facebook, all from Sri Lankans.

The community has been galvanised. The Trinco Titans are putting Trincomalee back on the map. We're representing the town, the region, proving its superiority to Jaffna. Trincomalee always used to be the best region at football, we're told. It was always a great source of pride. With north-east politics forever confused by the north and east factions of the Tamil Tigers splitting in 2005, the formation of the Karuna party from eastern Tigers that then joined forces with the government and attacked the remaining Tamil Tigers, the subsequent acts of violence, and the inability to display true political leaning, sport has become a post-war vehicle for identity. A proof of superiority in a region plagued by inferiority to the Sinhalese, yet also to Jaffna.

Despite all of the positivity around us, in our house a sense of reality has struck. Mannar, it emerges, lost their four best players to Valvai. In addition to that, the referee from the game has a complicated history with Trincomalee. The last time he refereed at the ground he was physically assaulted by members of the crowd. It must have been on his mind when he denied our opponents two stonewall penalties, much to the delight of those in attendance.

There's no doubt, it seems, that success in the tournament will rely on our vociferous and intimidating home support.

JAFFNA

When Thaabit told me and Dean that we'd be sharing a five-bedroom house with twenty-three teammates ahead of our next match we laughed. What a funny joke. But he was being deadly serious. Straight away we took ourselves off to the shop, our stock response when we want to complain to each other. Dean can't believe it. He can't be doing with twenty-three teammates yapping at him and neither can I. We both like our downtime, our isolation from the world and its madness. Disobeying Thaabit's dietary orders – which Dean does spectacularly every day – we buy a 1.5 litre bottle of Coke and sit swigging it in the empty bus shelter like a pair of drunks.

'And here's another thing wrong with this country...' The list goes on. By the time we've finished we're both happier. After all, part of the fun of being abroad is complaining.

By the time we board the bus to Jaffna we've had enough time to come to terms with our situation. It's a seven-hour journey north on a slow single carriageway behind crawling lorries. We're due to stay in Jaffna for just two nights – a reduction on the original five. Costs need to be cut and so we'll return to Trincomalee after playing Valvai in Jaffna, then hit the road north again the next day for the away match against Mullai Phoenix in Mullaittivu.

Valvai, we've been warned by everyone, are the best team in the league. Four Sri Lankan national-team players, four excellent Nigerian professionals and the best of the talent from last season's opponents, not to mention a huge budget. And, of course, Mindron.

It isn't long before the Tamil films start playing. We're lucky – this bus has both a television and air conditioning, so there's no need for the door to be kept open. Since being in Sri Lanka I've seen a few Tamil films and they all seem to have the same plot line. There's a hero who creates some arbitrary rule around love, family or morals. A rival does his (it is always a he, as women are limited to roles as family members and love interests) best to either break that rule or disrespect the hero. The themes are always violence, honour, identity and religion. Invariably the hero and the villain fight several times, with the hero eventually coming out on top and winning the girl. It's predictable, but it is at least preferable to Pitbull.

My teammates are captivated. They whoop and holler when the hero comes on screen, shriek at any key moments and jokes, and when the whole cast break out into song – which is often – they join in, dancing down the aisles. Sakhti has jumped on two chairs and is shaking his bum in the air and biting his lip. Kalua has taken his shirt off and is waving it around above his head. Vithu is doing the Sri Lankan 'snake' dance up and down the aisle.

'I hope these boys have this much energy tomorrow,' Dean notes.

It isn't long before we're up and dancing with them.

* * *

If you look at a map of Sri Lanka it seems to be one connected island, but Jaffna district – as far north as you can go in the island – is a peninsula separated from the mainland by a lagoon. Just two bridges connect the district to the rest of Sri Lanka. And so, before entering Jaffna, we stop at the 300-metre Sangupiddy Bridge. Built immediately after the war, it's full of significance, an olive branch, a joining together of two warring factions. In theory, anyway.

Jaffna has always been a city of conflict. In the last few hundred years it's been occupied by the Portuguese, the Dutch, the British, the Tamil Tigers, Indian Peace Keeping Force and Sri Lankan army. Before the civil war it was Sri Lanka's second-biggest city. But during those terrible thirty years, the city was ravaged by violence and destruction.

The Liberation Tigers of Tamil Eelam, otherwise known as the Tamil Tigers, started in Jaffna, founded by leader Velupillai Prabhakaran. Given the district's long association with Tamils – with the majority of Sri Lanka's Tamils able to trace their origins to the Jaffna Kingdom – it's no surprise.

When the Tamil Tigers killed thirteen members of the Sri Lankan army while they were patrolling, the sparks ignited that would ultimately end in civil war. As many as 3,000 Tamils were killed in revenge attacks by Sinhalese mobs that rampaged across the country. Some 18,000 Tamil properties were destroyed, and 300,000 people were displaced. These events in 1983 are known as the Black July riots.

Where were the police during all this? Well, they were watching on. Sometimes they were even helping. Routine police stops ended with the cars of Tamils torched to the ground with the victims inside. Businesses were ruined. Houses destroyed. Buses were stopped and set on fire if they were found to contain Tamils. And sometimes it was soldiers doing the destroying.

The Tamil Tigers soon took control of Jaffna, which would continue to be a stronghold until 1995. They collected taxes from the local population to aid their war efforts. The Tamil Tigers ran the police force and courts in Jaffna district, using their power as an effective recruitment tool. And if people wouldn't join their cause freely, there was always the option of using force.

As we leave the mainland behind and progress along the Jaffna peninsula, its difference becomes evident. It's as if the salt lagoon that surrounds the peninsula infuses all life here. There is no jungle. The soil is far from fertile. Instead of agriculture, the locals have historically had to rely on education for their livelihoods.

It's been a long journey and, when we finally arrive at our hotel, it seems there's a war about to spark within our team. Nomi welcomes us. He lives in Jaffna and will be hosting us while we're here. He beckons me and Dean to one side and ushers us into a three-bedded room near the entrance, one of the best in the hotel. Ever since we've been in Sri Lanka, Nomi has always made sure we have received the best treatment possible – as every Sri Lankan we've come across has, every single one keen to give the best representation of their country to the two British players.

I'm first in the room and don't spot the double bed. Dean does and claims it straight away. Jai also joins us, claiming the second single bed. We're all buzzing about the set-up. It's far better than we expected. We were told we'd have a five-bedroom house. In reality we have a hotel.

Then Hizam is in the room. He dumps his bag next to the double bed.

'No, lad,' Dean warns. 'No.'

Hizam ignores him and hangs around. Dean looks at us in amazement. Then Hizam gets out his phone charger, plugs it in and looks like he's setting up for the night. Jai and I are both in tears of laughter. Dean finds it less funny.

'No,' he tells Hizam again, only for Hizam to lie down next to Dean on the double bed. It's as if Dean has had an electric shock. He jumps up, grabs his stuff and swears at me and Jai. 'Nah, that's not on. I'm not having it. No way. I'm gone and I'm taking the wifi.' He grabs the portable wifi transmitter as his last furious act and then he's gone.

Dean's anger does the trick. He ends up in his own double bed, sharing a room just with Banda. And he refuses to let anyone else use his wifi.

Jai and I end up with Hizam and Anushaht, who share the double bed. I'm still laughing at the incident but also worrying that Dean won't calm down. And that he won't share the wifi again.

The worry soon turns to frustration. With Dean gone, Hizam won't shut up. He keeps bursting into song and incessantly sucking his teeth. Every fifteen seconds. Suck. Song. Suck. Song. Suck.

This has worked out terribly.

* * *

The next day Dean buys me a coconut. I guess that means no hard feelings. It's about as exciting as my day gets. We're confined to our rooms in preparation for the big game. I spend time with Sakhti, Vithu and Mathu, our new physio and identical twin of Vithu. I have to look carefully at Vithu and Mathu's tattoos to tell which one is which. The three of them are energetic, encouraging me to laugh and joke with them and teaching me typical Tamil handshakes. We share stories of home while a preview of the new Premier League season plays on the screen behind us. Vithu tells us about his wife who lives in Canada. They met over Instagram and have only met in person once. Vithu hopes to eventually join her in Canada. Sakhti jokes about all of his own girlfriends, then asks me how many I really have. Already, they're becoming some of my closest friends within the team.

At 3.30 p.m. we finally leave for the game. Kick-off is at 6 p.m., which feels a bit like Valvai are showing off for the sake of it. Unlike most other grounds, theirs has floodlights.

But it isn't just about the floodlights. The stadium, situated among the hustle and bustle of Jaffna, is full of significance. It's named after Alfred Duraiappah, the former Tamil politician of the Sri Lanka Freedom Party assassinated in 1975. Prabhakaran and the Tamil Tigers claimed responsibility for the assassination of someone they considered to be a traitor. For Prabhakaran, it seemed, violence was always the answer. Even if it was against other Tamils. And even if it was against other Tamil separatist groups. Leaders of rival separatist groups were murdered and their followers absorbed into the Tigers' support. The message was simple: fight with us or die. There can be no doubt that Prabhakaran would stop at nothing to achieve his end goal. By the end of the war 160 Tamil MPs had been assassinated, 1,700 Tamil militants killed, policemen and civil servants dispatched, deserters punished.

Throughout the war, the Duraiappah stadium gained in significance. At first it was a stronghold of the Tigers, then the Indian Peace Keeping Force, the Tigers once more, and then from 1995 the government. In an attempt to normalise life in

Jaffna, a renovation of the facilities in 1999 led to the discovery of a mass grave from the civil war. Twenty-five civilians were buried beneath the proposed changing rooms. Thousands upon thousands more bodies are still yet to be discovered.

We arrive at the infamous stadium in our new tracksuit – long black Adidas tracksuit trousers with fluorescent green stripes, sky-blue trainers and green Titans t-shirt – at 3.45 p.m. Our squad is depleted. Banda's goals came at a price as he limped off injured and is yet to recover. Balaya, Iham and Naleem remain unavailable. Thaabit has responded by preparing us defensively, putting us into a formation with two holding midfielders and just one striker. He allows us a quick pitch inspection and we are delighted to find grass – actual grass! Sure, it's confined to the wings and the centre is one long runway of baked mud but, still, grass! A stand of hundreds of multi-coloured seats runs along one touchline. Beyond the stand, the walls of the historic Jaffna fort are little more than twenty yards away, and beyond that the ocean. The opposite side of the stadium is far less peaceful. A busy road runs parallel to the far wing, with cars and tuk-tuks and lorries and mopeds all trying to sound their horns the loudest. A series of Tube Tamil media company flags flutter in the strong ocean breeze around the perimeter of the pitch, while a small yet distinct kovil – a Hindu temple – has been built by the halfway line. There's scaffolding around it and a Tube Tamil TV camera already perched atop. Just outside the stadium grounds a tall white structure stands out among the chaos at the bottom of the road, top-heavy and proud. It's complemented by a golden statue of S.J.V. Chelvanayakam, a monument to the founder of the Tamil Federal Party. Further up the road a serene white building, its domed pillars giving it the appearance of a temple, dominates the skyline. It's the Jaffna public library, one of Jaffna's most notable landmarks and a site of historic importance. Formerly home to 97,000 Tamil books, the building was burned to the ground by a Sinahelse mob in 1981. The attack proved inflammatory in more ways than one, with residents of Jaffna believing it to be a Sinhalese assault on their culture, freedom and ambitions. It feels as if the modest stadium is surrounded by history.

We're confined to the changing room for a whole hour. Thaabit gives us thirty minutes to relax, then thirty minutes to get changed – which even for a group of players who carefully manage their appearance seems excessive. The gamesmanship begins before we enter. Our changing room is one big block of concrete. There are no chairs and no benches, so we sprawl across the floor. There's a fan but it's only running at half-speed. It's hot and humid with dark clouds gathering. In this weather, being stuck in the changing room feels like torture.

The minutes drag on. After what seems an eternity, we're fully changed and ready to go. That's when a tournament official enters. He wants to check our IDs. My heart skips a beat. I don't have my passport. It turns out that five of my teammates don't have their ID cards. Thaabit is disbelieving. How can we have forgotten something so important? He yells and glares at the sky. All we can do is rush back to the hotel as quickly as possible.

We make it back in time for the final part of the warm-up. We were already sweating buckets from the fanless changing room, and the runs to and from the bus have only warmed us further. Once again there's plenty of energetic shouting and nervous energy bounding around the team and the coaching staff. There's barely time to pass the ball back and forth to Dean before we return to the changing room for some final words

from Thaabit. He bounces around the room, patting players and motioning his arms upwards in encouragement. The
nervous energy is ready to hit the ceiling. In his final moment,
Thaabit names me as captain and tasks me with leading the
team out. It's great to have the armband, but even better to get
out of that windowless, fanless room. The referees are waiting
outside the changing room door for us and they guide us past
the majestic trophy on its plinth, walking a windy route to the
centre circle. K'naan's 'Waving Flag', the tournament's official
song that plays during every walkout, reverberates over the
stadium speakers. As we enter the pitch, the smell of incense
sweetens our nostrils. The soft smoke comes from a tall golden
statue of a bird, a Hindu tradition.

We line up as usual and face the crowd, then are silent for
the flag-raising ceremony that happens before every tournament game. Up goes the official tournament flag, then the Sri
Lankan flag, then the Jaffna district flag. Once they're fully
raised, we all applaud. The ball boys parade past us, holding
a large FIFA flag and another official tournament flag. We're
then introduced to the Tamil league officials and VIPs. There's
a dozen of them for today's game, all dressed in their smartest
gear, including one in military uniform. They seem fascinated
by my presence. The first one asks where I'm from and when I
reply 'London' it creates a wave of nods and smiles. One even
says 'thank you'. It's then my job as captain to introduce the
officials to my teammates. The whole process truly defeats the
purpose of warming up as it takes so long.

With kick-off getting further and further behind the agreed
time, the stands are filling up. Tube Tamil TV are filming the
game live and have done a great job in promoting it to the
local community. The stands are dotted with fans, though most

prefer to stand on the far touchline. Around twenty have made the long journey from Trinco to support us, and they shriek with joy as the official pre-match ceremonies finally finish and we take our places on the pitch.

From there, it's all downhill. Within minutes Vithu directs a thirty-yard clearance over Fasith, who has replaced Ranoos in goal, and into the back of our net. It'll likely be played on Sri Lankan football blooper reels for years. Straight away, our defensive set-up becomes redundant. We need to attack, to score. Then the rain starts. It's torrential, more so than I ever thought possible. The water lashes down with such force that I can barely see. The multiple cameras that were broadcasting the game have to be relocated to the stands and temporarily turned off, which is just as well because we soon concede our second, third and fourth: a header from a free-kick, a counter-attack and a goalkeeping error from Fasith.

Fasith looks so small. The goal looks so big. I turn around and wonder how anyone can fail to score with such propor-tions. The gloves he wears look twice as big as his actual hands. He's nineteen years old, a few rogue hairs on his upper lip the sole sign of adulthood. Everything about him appears to be quivering. With Ranoos on the bench, this is his chance to make the number-one spot his own, yet every time the ball comes his way he flaps at it. A simple pass back to his feet has the effect of an unpinned grenade chucked into his path.

And yet Fasith is far from the only player at fault. His nerves are symptomatic of the entire team. Plenty of mistakes are being made. The runway of baked mud has turned into an ice rink of soft, moving earth. The ball skids under feet. Every time it happens our players scream in anger. The gaps between defence and midfield and between midfield and strikers are ginormous, yet nothing compared to that of the gaps between our centre-backs and our full-backs. Plenty of fingers are being pointed. The body language is terrible.

We somehow get a goal back from an aimless punt forward that becomes a penalty when Inshaht is fouled. The permanently alert look in Roshan's eyes becomes even more alert as he concentrates with all his might to slot home. The half-time whistle blows and for the twenty minutes afterwards we're absolutely dominant. With the cameras back up and running, we play to feet and break through the lines of our opponents' defence with regularity. Which makes it even more devastating when Valvai get a fifth against the run of play on the counter. Positivity is the new order of the day, though, and we brush it off. Straight away we get our second goal of the game, Aflal playing in Dean, who runs on to the pass with such force I fear he's going to flatten both the defender and goalkeeper.

We remain in the ascendency but as the clock ticks on we tire. We had to do a lot of defending in the first half, which saps the legs and erodes the mental energy. Valvai's Nigerian centre-forward is living up to his billing as the best player in the tournament. His movement is sharp and his finishing clinical. Jai, still playing in his glasses despite the conditions, can only chase after him in vain as he races clear for their sixth. Jai is removed from the game and that's when we really fall apart. Defenders stop chasing after their markers. They give up.

Seven... then eight. Madness! I'm the foreign professional playing at centre-back. A foreign professional should not be part of a backline that concedes eight goals. And yet I feel like I've had a decent game. Much better than I played against Mannar, anyway. I even almost cap it off with a goal. We get a late corner and I notice the referee is standing in front of me and facing away from me. The linesman isn't looking at me. Just as Roshan strikes the ball I give my defender an almighty push and dart into the box. Suddenly I'm free and Dean heads the ball straight into my path. I see a defender on the line and so I loop a header back across the goalkeeper. I don't think I've hit it hard enough. Then it starts to dip. Slowly, so slowly. It's going in, isn't it?

No. It strikes the underside of the bar and is cleared to safety. The crowd love it. The man on the gate – who chatted to me so excitedly and politely when I entered the stadium and even asked for a picture – is now hurling abuse at me. He's part of a group of thirty standing on the touchline near our goal, repeatedly calling me 'London' and laughing. Every time I get the ball they whistle me.

'Hey, captain, they give you the number five. You must be a very bad player.'

'London, bad kick, London! London!'

I love it.

'*Poda poda!*' I yell at them, which Sakhti has told me is Tamil for 'go away'. From their shrieks of approval, I guess the literal translation is something a little more forceful than 'go away'. When the referee takes pity on us and blows the final whistle, they run up to me to shake my hand and take pictures. Then suddenly Mindron is there. He started on the bench and I didn't even notice him come onto the pitch. I give him a hug and can't help but be relieved he still has his shorts on.

Back in the changing room Thaabit gets us all together. Don't worry about it, he tells us, let's not speak about it until tomorrow. Nomi is similarly reassuring, as are the rest of the coaching staff. Mahela Jayawardene calls to say exactly the same thing. After all, we've already got a win under our belts.

To help us forget, Thaabit gives us five minutes to get changed before taking us for ice cream. All phones are banned. Nobody is allowed to even touch their smartphone until we've finished the ice cream. This is a time for togetherness, for conversation. The boys race to get their soaking-wet kit off in our concrete prison. My every step is still squelching, there's that much rainwater in my boots. Suddenly everyone stops and stares. They're looking at Dean. Dean is getting changed, as Thaabit directed. Only he's naked. Ihshan quickly removes himself from the room, mainly because Dean's rear end was about to brush his camera equipment. Even Jai, the most western of all the players, can hardly believe what's happening. They stare, open-mouthed, none of them quite sure what to do.

'In England everyone does this,' I shrug. At that, Dean looks up and sees the entire changing room staring at his naked body.

'I'm getting changed, ya weirdos,' he snarls. 'What's wrong with you?'

I'm pretty sure my teammates are all equally fascinated by and terrified of Dean. As one, their eyes are all averted. Five minutes later we're all on the bus and the defeat has been forgotten.

'The Dean very angry man,' Vithu whispers with a wicked smile, prefixing Dean's name with 'the' as many of my teammates do. He's not the only one whose shock has turned to amusement. All around us there are laughs and smiles and jokes. I smile back at Vithu. Who cares about football when you've got ice cream?

	Team Name	P	W	D	L	GF	GA	GD	Points
1	Valvai FC	2	2	0	0	11	3	9	6
2	Mullai Phoenix	2	2	0	0	2	0	2	6
3	Trinco Titans	2	1	0	1	5	10	-5	3
4	Tamil United	2	0	1	1	2	3	-1	1
5	Kiliyoor Kings	2	0	1	1	3	5	-2	1
6	Mannar FC	2	0	0	2	2	4	-2	0

* * *

While in Jaffna, it's been requested that we visit the Trail cancer hospital. A few years ago Nomi was part of a group that trekked from Galle in the south to Jaffna at the very north to raise money to build a cancer hospital. Now, Nomi manages it. The idea to build a cancer hospital in Jaffna district came from Mahela Jayawardene. At the age of eleven he lost his brother to cancer. Since that day, it was his desire to help future sufferers. But it was more significant than that. Mahela is Buddhist. The hospital was built in 2011, two years after the war ended, and aims to treat patients in the north, eastern and central regions of Sri Lanka. In other words, it doesn't discriminate between Tamil and Sinhalese. It hopes to bring the country together, a little sign that everyone is Sri Lankan.

We're told all of this as we walk around the wards. The patients look distant. Many are undergoing harsh treatments. Only a couple smile at us. The nurses, in contrast, are smiley and welcoming, the hospital clean and modern. We're sent into the gardens to help clean up. In the intense Jaffna heat of the midday sun, we work slowly to fill two bags with leaves and abandoned tissues. Out of respect to our surroundings, we're all wearing long trousers, which only intensifies the sweat.

Satisfied, the coaches call us together for photos with the medical staff. This is an example of two of the owners' social projects coming together to work as one. It's a powerful affirmation of what they believe in. Throughout, Nomi smiles. There's nobody better to manage a hospital of such significance. During the war he worked in humanitarian aid, helping civilians in the hospitals situated in war zones. At first, their numbers were significant, but as the war continued – especially towards its end – the demand became almost overpowering. There were shortages of antibiotics, medicine, food, drink. The Sri Lankan army continued to expand, and as its firepower grew along with that of the Tamil Tigers, civilians felt the brunt.

In 1983, the Sri Lankan army was tiny, made up of just 10,000 troops. There was a reason it was kept small and largely ceremonial: to prevent any coups. But as the war raged, the government had no alternative. Twenty-six years later, at the end of the war, the Sri Lankan armed forces were served by 300,000 troops. With unemployment levels high, the armed forces were never short of recruits.

Inshaht sits next to me for the seven-hour bus journey home to Trinco. Almost every day over the last two weeks he's sent me the same WhatsApp message: 'Hi bro.' I reply with a 'hi'. He then says 'how are you'. I reply and he says 'OK, night bro.' The regularity has brought us closer. Slowly Inshaht has gained confidence to speak English to me not just over WhatsApp but also in person.

He asks me about cricket, tells me about his religion of Islam, shares details of his regular job as a fisherman, working six days a week for meagre pay with Friday off to visit the mosque. And then he tells me about the war. The fighting. There was so much of it. Jaffna, he tells me, is still controlled by the army. As the birthplace of the Tamil Tigers, there are still plenty of concerns about the region. I admit that I spotted plenty of armed soldiers in Jaffna but hadn't thought much of it. I ask whether the Tamil Tigers are finished. Inshaht looks panicked, leaning in towards me.

'No, bro. They still there. They just don't fight right now.'

As a Muslim, Inshaht can never feel comfortable going to Jaffna. Though the Tamil Tigers later admitted their expulsion was a mistake, history never forgets.

Later that evening I receive a message: 'Hi bro.'

TRINCOMALEE

On one hand, losing hasn't been such a bad experience. First we were taken for ice cream, then we had a Pizza Hut. And now we're going for lunch at the elusive Iham's house to celebrate Eid, before an afternoon at the nearby tourist hotspot Marble Beach and then dinner at Jai's. All to 'take our minds off what happened'.

The sums start whirring in my head. Just how many games can we lose and still qualify for the knockouts? Four? Five? All we have to do is reach the top four in a group of six. That shouldn't be too hard. On the other hand, maybe it's best not to lose too many because losing just one has been disastrous. Rifts have appeared. The main one is between Priyan and Anushaht. Against Valvai, Anushaht beat two players and then struck a shot that was well saved by the keeper. Priyan shouted at him that he should have scored. It wasn't the first time during the game that Priyan had indicated Anushaht could have done better. Anushaht responded and Priyan unleashed a torrent of verbal abuse at him. Now Priyan wants to give up his vice captaincy because Anushaht 'doesn't respect him'. Anushaht isn't happy with Priyan and had a long discussion with Thaabit about what could be done.

Meanwhile, Kalua is upset with Thaabit. During the hospital visit Kalua made a joke and Thaabit scolded him for being disrespectful. For the rest of the day Kalua refused to get off the bus, staying in his seat while the rest of the team visited Iham's friend and also during lunch. He was scared of another confrontation.

Even Thaabit has been prone to snap. It's obvious for all to see that he's feeling the pressure.

'Soft lads,' Dean says of the situation. 'Just get on with it.'

I can't think of a better way to put it. All the niggles and arguments are only going to intensify with another negative result. And tomorrow's opponents, Mullai Phoenix, have won both their games so far. Last season they finished second.

It's a cliché that in football there are no easy games. But because of the way the leagues have been drawn, we really don't have any easy games. All the teams in our group are ranked above us, yet the other group contains the three teams who finished at the bottom last season.

Maybe it's a win–win situation. If we do win then it's great: we get our win bonus and team spirit soars once more. And if we lose we get to 'take our minds off it'.

In the owners' minds, we've already won. Following our visit to the cancer hospital, an article appeared on Score-Heros.com, titled 'Trinco Titans Lose the Match but Win the Hearts of the People'. It's shared widely, including by the league itself. That ticks off both elements of the owners' social projects. Perhaps other sports clubs will now work harder to benefit their community. Perhaps they too will seek to bring together different demographics. Or perhaps they'll just give everything to beat the club with the media attention and owned by some of the most famous men in the country. I fear it's the latter.

MULLAITIVU

Mullaitivu: the Tamil Tigers' last-ever stronghold. An area of mixed terrain, its ample jungle within the Vanni providing plenty of hiding places for those at war. The place where they inflicted the government's biggest defeat of the entire civil war, killing more than 1,000 Sri Lankan army troops as they took the army base in the 1996 Battle of Mullaitivu. The small strip of land that they held to the very end. The tiny town of no more than 40,000. The base for the Sea Tigers, the naval arm of the LTTE. The area filled with refugees and no-fire zones at the bitter end.

It's no wonder the football team refers to themselves as Mullai Phoenix. In few places in Sri Lanka have there been more ashes from which to rise.

After talking Thaabit out of holding a morning training session, we leave at 9.30 a.m. The journey is due to take three hours. Kick-off is at 4 p.m.

We hug the east coast as we head northwards, travelling past bays and beaches, army camps and naval bases. As we get to Mullaitivu, signs of the war are everywhere. Inshaht points out a gigantic statue of a golden soldier, arms in the air in

celebration, machine gun held aloft, standing tall in the field of
one of the final battles between the state and the Tamil Tigers.
He's adorned with the Sri Lankan flag and surrounded by lions.
Every couple of minutes I'm tapped on the shoulder to be told
another story, to be shown another landmark.

At 1.30 p.m. we pull into a school, where we're invited to
relax in the rudimentary classrooms for forty-five minutes.
That's when the heavens open. Within minutes the ground is
waterlogged. There's nowhere for the water to go and so it sits
on top of the surface, growing in volume with every minute.
There's no way we can play the game if the pitch is like that
too. But as we lie on the handful of floor mats and sprawl across
chairs, no news comes through so Thaabit decides he may as
well do the team talk. We're marched into a classroom with
enough chairs for everyone to sit, where Thaabit announces that
Priyan and Anushaht are both dropped. There's little reaction
from either, suggesting they've been forewarned. Kalua is on
the bench. Banda remains injured. We're going with a defensive formation again, Sakhti the sole striker. Ranoos returns in
goal. As a team, we need a reaction, Thaabit announces. We're
coming off the back of a heavy defeat and we need to show
what we're made of. The mistakes can't happen in the defence
again. Seth and Jai need to be solid. The whole team turns to
stare at us, as if we're the sole reason we lost 8-2. And then we're
off, back into the bus for the final few kilometres to the ground.
Despite Thaabit's motivational words, few of us believe a game
is about to take place.

Yet when we arrive at the ground there's no standing water.
Yes, it's still raining, but the sheer quantity of sand on the pitch
has absorbed most of the water. It's a confined space with no
stands and just metres between the chain fence and the touch-

line. The pitch's lines are marked by the blackest of greases, its interior littered with cow pats and goat droppings. The club's safety officer must be on holiday.

We're in Iranaippalai, a small settlement 17km north of Mullaitivu. After the final battle, many Tigers hid in the thick bushes around us. Just a few kilometres to our east lies Putumattalan, where the infamous no-fire zone began. It seems incredible that such a brutal war ended in such nondescript surroundings. Iranaippalai is characterised by nothingness. Not much is going on. The streets are open, the landscape green. People are few and far between. And yet the land surrounding us holds such significance, the subject of ongoing UN investigations into human rights abuses.

We spot our opponents' foreign professionals first. It's never a hard job as their body type is always so different: much taller, more powerful and self-assured than the Sri Lankans. Mullai have three Nigerians in their ranks, all of them dwarfing every player on the pitch with the exception of me and Dean.

The game starts and almost the only people in attendance are the league officials. There can't be more than thirty others. I lose myself in the action, making sure our defence holds its line and anticipating danger. Dinesh, the latest vice captain to be given the armband, goes down injured within the opening ten minutes and I'm handed the captain's armband once more. Suddenly I realise several hundred people have materialised from thin air. They hug the touchline, standing not more than a metre from the pitch down both sides and immediately behind the goal.

Despite the twenty supporters who have once again travelled from Trinco, the crowd is providing an overwhelming home advantage. With their immense powers of intimidation, they're proving to be the decisive twelfth man. Menacingly flanking the linesmen and taunting the referee, the crowd succeed in making every fifty–fifty go our opponents' way. I remain calm; this is just how it is in Sri Lanka. Not more than a week ago we benefited from such officiating in our first home game.

The backline is forced to drop deeper. We can't play an offside trap when met with a linesman who either refuses or is too scared to signal offside. That creates gaps in the midfield, and Mullai open the scoring when their central midfielder drives with the ball and plays a lovely pass between Jai and Inshaht at right-back.

We're dominating possession but struggling to break our opponents down. They're playing on the counter-attack, over-loading the wings and playing plenty of diagonal passes to catch us off guard. Which is exactly what they do just before half-time. They break from our corner, and just Vithu and Inshaht are left in defence. I race back but I can't run faster than the ball. A pass is played forward to a striker who's at least ten yards offside. Sri Lanka has taught me to always play to the whistle, so I carry on running while raising my hand to the linesman. Nothing. I almost get there. I'm within metres when the attacker pulls back his leg and strikes into the corner. The crowd goes wild. I turn once again to the linesman – surely he was waiting until the striker touched the ball to raise his flag? But no. The linesman would much rather anger the eleven players in blue and white than the hundreds standing within a breath of him. His flag remains unraised; the goal stands. I go to remonstrate but am pulled away. My teammates know that to argue the decision is pointless.

As always seems to happen, we come out fighting after half-time. It's one-way traffic, save for another counter-attack from our corner. Ranoos gives away a penalty then saves it. I remain paranoid about playing offsides and camp our backline almost on the edge of the area. Our frontline, fortunately, is spending more time in the final third. Naleem, the 'master' who has shaken off his injury, is subbed on for the first time in the tournament and his physicality proves a nuisance. He distracts several defenders when I go up for a corner and the ball makes its way through the bodies. As it bounces I step forward as if to hit it first time, then open my body. The move fools the defender. The ball runs free and I slide in and connect with all of my might. I'm not sure what happens next. It may take a deflection or it may stay straight and true. All I know is that the ball nestles in the net and there's utter silence until my scream – 'YES!' – breaks the air. We've got a goal back. Before the game I'd promised Sakhti and Vithu we'd do the Sri Lankan snake dance if we scored but it seems wrong while we're losing. Instead I sprint back to my position and urge my teammates to follow. We've got a game to win.

We push and push for the equaliser that we hope will lead to the winner. I have a volley that whistles past the post. Naleem heads against a defender on the line. A defender then makes a clearance that hits Naleem and forces the keeper to make a fingertip save. We have several penalty shouts.

It isn't enough. The whistle blows and we're condemned to another defeat.

Dean leaves the pitch with a swollen ankle and a bag of ice. Dinesh is already in the treatment room. I've got half a bottle of cold spray and a fair amount of Kinesiology tape around my sore thigh. Thaabit is fuming about our rough treatment. He feels that me and Dean were singled out by our opponents because of our foreignness. The two of us are more fuming about the result.

We were so close. 2-1. Beaten by an outrageously offside goal. There's no anger from my Sri Lankan teammates at such injustice, just a shrug of the shoulders. This is just the way it is in Sri Lanka.

'We didn't lose,' Thaabit sums up, giving us his very best Sir Alex Ferguson impression. 'We just ran out of time.'

Led by Sakhti, Kalua and Vithu – all three of them so full of life – my teammates sing for the entire three-hour journey home.

	Team Name	P	W	D	L	GF	GA	GD	Points
1	Valvai FC	3	3	0	0	16	3	13	9
2	Mullai Phoenix	3	3	0	0	4	1	3	9
3	Trinco Titans	3	1	0	2	6	12	-6	3
4	Mannar FC	3	1	0	2	8	6	2	3
5	Kiliyoor Kings	3	0	1	2	5	11	-6	1
6	Tamil United	3	0	1	2	2	8	-6	1

TRINCOMALEE

Today's the day Dean and I were supposed to be flying home. Instead we still have at least seven games remaining, no idea of when the tournament will end, and we don't even have possession of our passports. Ihshan has taken them to Colombo to be stamped with a new business visa. Our current visa expires in the next few days.

Because of the original plan, Dean's girlfriend lands tomorrow evening for a holiday in Sri Lanka. Dean still hasn't told the coaches that he's not only going to pick her up from the airport – missing a game in the process – but is then going to stay with her in Galle for two days. So in some ways, he couldn't have timed his ankle injury any better.

Meanwhile we're plotting how to win the next match, against the Kiliyoor Kings, who are yet to win a match of their own. Our number-one supporter and local barber, lovingly referred to as Power Anna (Tamil for 'big brother'), who travelled on the team bus to Mullai Phoenix, is concocting a plan as to how the crowd can suitably intimidate the linesmen and referee. Thaabit is deciding on whether to revert to 4-4-2 or go with a 3-4-3, which is still an important factor but far less so than Power's plans.

All of Thaabit's formations include Dean, who spends the entire morning stressing about how he's going to break the news.

'How's your ankle?' Thaabit asks him. This is Dean's moment, his chance to tie everything together and come out smelling of roses.

'Grand,' he replies.

That's his first mistake.

We head to the shop to talk tactics. Dean agrees to speak to Thaabit after lunch. I go for a swim with Kaps and stretch my sore thigh. It's getting worse and worse. I know I can play on it but I also know that playing on it will only do more damage. Kaps offers to massage it. He's trained and does a good job.

I return to the house to find Dean with his head in his hands. Thaabit says he has to play. The owners – including Mahela – are all coming to watch the match and will be disappointed if Dean isn't there. Dean maintains that he can't play and Thaabit is surprised. Sri Lankans never talk back. He isn't used to this.

'The boys will be let down,' Thaabit continues. 'Call me the bad guy if you want but you have to play.'

Dean does call him the bad guy. He calls him far worse, too. We sit in the bus shelter where we always do our complaining as Dean reveals all. Thaabit has offered to get Dean's girlfriend a taxi or a hotel and has allowed Dean to go and meet her after the match. That isn't an option as far as Dean is concerned. She's his priority and he can't let her arrive in a foreign country without a friendly face. His words come fast. We've been so lenient since arriving, he points out. Things have constantly changed and we've just smiled and got on with it. We could have both left when we were supposed to and screwed over the team but we didn't. It should count for something.

He feels like a body in a relentless meat market. Welcome to the football industry, I tell him, which I don't think helps. He ignores my statement and says how I was told the tournament would finish on the 10th yet he was told it'd finish on the 13th. They obviously never had a clue, he reckons. They just wanted us out there as soon as we could come.

I establish that it is possible for him to pick up his girlfriend, who lands at 4 a.m., and make the match. He'll just have to miss their planned trip to Galle. Maybe he can miss a different match and do Galle then? Perhaps he could go over Thaabit's head and speak to Nomi?

Together we draft a message to Dean's girlfriend, saying there's been a change of plan and Dean has to play in the match. A minute later her name flashes up on Dean's screen and he's visibly panicked, like a rabbit in headlights. He has to answer. Nervously he places the phone to his ear. Immediately I can tell something is wrong. She doesn't sound happy. She points out that everything has worked against her holiday since she booked it, which is entirely fair. It's a terrible situation for her to be in and she even suggests not coming.

All Dean can do after that is speak to Thaabit. A deal is struck: Dean will play the next two home games and then miss the Mannar away match, giving him and his girlfriend a five-day break. As he touches his girlfriend's name into his phone, I cross my fingers and wish him luck. He's going to need it.

* * *

'Hello, my friend… hi!'
    'Hi!' I shout back to the men.
    'How are you?'
    'Good. How are you?'

'My friend, come and sit.'

There are four of them sitting under a tree, drinking in the shade. Three of them are older, approaching their sixties, while one looks about my age. Their smiles draw me in as they motion for me to sit on one of the bricks surrounding their makeshift table.

'My friend, where are you from?' they ask.

'London.'

'Wow!' The response is always the same. 'That is very good, my friend.'

'I am here to play for the Trinco Titans,' I say to speed the conversation on. This sets them off.

'Mahela Jayawardene, Mahela Jayawardene!' they chorus. 'Your sponsor.'

'Yes, very good cricketer,' I reply, which sets them off again.

'Cricket. You like cricket? England World Cup final very good.'

'Drink, drink,' they urge, shoving bottles of Coke and spirits in my face. Chicken is produced from a plastic bag and offered: 'You want rice?'

'You very good defender,' the oldest one adds. 'I watch the match. 3-2.'

I smile and nod and interact. My new friends are fishermen relaxing after the morning catch. I ask if they're coming to the game tomorrow.

'Yes, yes,' they all agree. 'What can we bring you? What do you want?'

These are men who earn peanuts for back-breaking work, men who can barely rub two rupees together, going out of their way for a white kid from a developed nation on the other side of the world. I tell them that I have everything I want in

Sri Lanka, that everyone takes very good care of me. But it isn't enough.

'Tomorrow we will bring you chicken, we will bring rice.' They're so insistent I just nod and agree.

Time is wearing on and I'm conscious that training is soon starting. I've come to the beach to stretch my troublesome thigh and relax it in the sea water. I'm sitting out of training but need to be at the session.

'My friends,' I say. 'I must leave to swim. I have training soon.'

There's uproar but they understand. After all, they're Titans fans.

'First, picture,' they insist. One of them puts his arm around me. 'You are the best footballer from Australia,' he says.

His friend clips him round the back of the head. 'Australia?! He is from England.'

'Australia. England. Sri Lanka. We are all the same,' the man muses. 'We all have red blood. We are all human.'

Two minutes later I'm swimming in the ocean when I hear a new voice: 'My friend, hello! Where are you from?'

* * *

Dean leaves for Colombo in a van that Thaabit is funding. A round trip is costing 19,000 LKR, or half of our wages. With that covered, a big weight is off Dean's shoulders. Everyone is happy. The van will make sure he's well rested and will get him back in time for the game. As for his girlfriend, well, he's sure he can make her happy.

While he sets off, the rest of us visit Dinesh in his family home. He sustained an injury against Mullai and had to be carried off the pitch after just ten minutes. With no stretchers available, four players had to pick him up and jog him over to the sideline. The referee wouldn't allow them to walk.

He doesn't look in a good way. There's a bandage wrapped around his knee and he winces as he goes to get up. The coaches immediately tell him to stay rested. Chairs are plonked around him by various family members and we sit. They talk in Tamil so I smile and take in the surroundings.

The room is five metres square and appears to be a shed. Bits and bobs are everywhere. A bicycle here and there, a box of tools, food. The walls are exposed stone and the roof is corrugated iron. This is Dinesh's bedroom. There is no TV, no laptop, nothing really beyond a bed and a light and all the random pieces of stuff. Dinesh is one of the most respected players in the team, highly respected in the town itself, always laughing, joking and smiling. And yet this is his reality. These four exposed walls are what he comes home to every day.

When he's not playing football, Dinesh works as a painter. For six days a week he slogs from 7 a.m. to 5 p.m. For his ten-hour days he's paid 1,500 LKR – less than £1 per hour. In the winter he often can't work due to the rain. The evenings are spent looking after his ill mother. There's no girlfriend. No wife. Hardly any of my teammates are in relationships. But at thirty years of age, Dinesh is running out of time. How can anyone in Trinco ever meet a girlfriend? The schools are separated by gender, and women don't venture outside. The only future Dinesh can envision is the life he's living now. There can't be much joy in that for somebody who's always so happy. That's why football means so much to him. It's a chance to escape, to succeed.

I leave Dinesh's house even more determined to win our next matches.

* * *

Thirty minutes until kick-off. There are twelve players in the dressing room and no goalkeepers. Nor are any of the owners in attendance. Thaabit is pacing around frantically, rapidly losing patience: where is everyone? Hizam has boycotted the match because Thaabit didn't play him in the last match. In response Thaabit will boycott Hizam's Trinco Titans career. Banda is back, his knee heavily strapped but apparently recovered. It's our one source of positivity. We make our final preparations under a cloud of uncertainty. The team sheet needs to be submitted but we don't know who is playing because we don't know who is going to turn up. It's Rimzy's job to keep the league officials away while we wait, holding the changing room door firmly shut. Ihshan is desperately tapping away at his phone, chasing the players who are yet to appear. Thaabit's backwards baseball cap and sunglasses are doing nothing to disguise his emotions. He's so angry that he refuses to even come out and lead the warm-up. Instead, Kaps and Rimzy are given the task. Back in the changing rooms, Thaabit calms himself enough so that he can attempt to motivate us, but he can't give any tactical guidance without his players. Inshaht arrives and is met with an icy glare. Sensibly, he rushes to his usual spot in the dressing room and hauls on his kit. By the time we get round to lining up in the tunnel Inshaht has been joined by four others and we have seventeen – including a goalkeeper.

All or nothing for Trinco.

The timing is spot on as usual. As we line up in the tunnel the court next door to the stadium starts its legal hearings, meaning we need to wait fifteen minutes for them to finish so we can then play the official tournament anthem from our speakers. That then means that that kick-off will be delayed, as usual. It's a long time to wait in a tunnel and so our opponents, Kiliyoor Kings from Kilinochchi, start speaking to me.

'My friend, where are you from?'

Within minutes we have our arms around each other. Two are from Jaffna while the other, standing at around six foot six, is from Ghana. We laugh and joke and they ask me about the Middlesex Tamil Club, which I admit I've never heard of. One is coming to visit next year and somehow we agree to meet up in London.

Eventually we're allowed out. The temperature is at 35 degrees and the sun's heat hangs as heavy as the expectation from the watching crowd. They've come to see their team triumph. There's no other option.

The usual line-ups and introductions to Tamil officials play out before the captain's toss. Their captain carries more than just scars from the war. There are two big ones running up his face and into his shaved head. But it's his torso that brings most attention. He has just one arm, his left arm cut off at the shoulder. He looks terrifying. He turns out to be anything but.

'A true gent,' Dean repeats over and over.

Their captain, it turns out, was a former sports instructor for the LTTE. He operated from the Tamil Tigers' official training base in their proposed Tamil Eelam, located in Kilinochchi. Here they educated new recruits in the art of killing, training them for a couple of months before sending them out to fight for Tamil Eelam. Here they taught recruits to fire guns, pioneered the use of suicide bombing and made all swear allegiance to the supreme leader. Recruits cut all ties to their family, abstained from cigarettes and alcohol, and agreed to carry a cyanide capsule at all times. It was better to die than to be interrogated, they all agreed. At first the recruits came voluntarily. Soon, though, the Tigers insisted that each family in the north-east send at least one family member. Failure to cooperate was a death wish.

The LTTE weren't fussy. They accepted anyone who wished to fight for the cause. A substantial number of female fighters joined up and there were also many child soldiers, who they found to be highly valuable due to their element of surprise in attack. But there were never enough recruits. As the government pushed the Tigers back further, they went back to the same households to take a second member of the family, sometimes a third or even a fourth. Vans waited outside schools and snatched children as they left, relocating them instantly to Kilinochchi. Parents begged them to have mercy. They rarely did.

Yet life at the training centre wasn't all killing. There were activities and sports, for which the Tigers employed a number of instructors. There was also the official Tamil Tigers football team, which the Kiliyoor Kings captain also captained. I can't imagine they lost many matches.

It doesn't look like he's going to lose this one either. We concede within minutes, which is what tends to happen when your teammates turn up late. There's no time for preparation and it shows. A poor clearance by Inshaht leads to a poor clearance by me. The ball falls straight to their winger and as it's bouncing Anushaht charges in. The ball cannons off his head and moves directly into the path of their striker, who would have been several yards offside. A catalogue of errors.

Minutes later I almost give Kiliyoor another goal. I pass square to Roshan at left-back. I strike it true but it holds up in the troublesome sand. Roshan waits and waits for it to arrive. I scream at him to come to the ball. He doesn't. The winger intercepts but fortunately he can't capitalise.

'Get rid of the white girl!' a lone cry comes from the crowd.

Thaabit is tearing his hair out and is getting his own fair share of abuse. This is far from the twelfth man that Mullai

Phoenix benefited from. The match officials get a rare respite as the crowd's ire turns on their Titans. The expectation that hung so heavy is now a toxic mixture of frustration and aggression. When things are going well the crowd is great, but when they're not…

'Get rid of the coach! What does he know about Trinco? He's putting on a bad show! He's bringing shame to Trincomalee.'

That's something. At least they don't think I'm bringing shame to the town. They only want to get rid of me.

If they actually did get rid of me, I'm sure the score would be far worse. Balaya, playing his first match after injury and our new captain, is like a toy with broken batteries. He's all over the pitch, impossible to control. He charges forward at every opportunity, which would be great if he wasn't playing at centre-back. I urge him to stay disciplined but the armband has given him a level of authority I can't compete with. I mop up as best I can but fear he's going to give me a heart attack. To counter his waywardness, I sit deep and end up feeling comfortable. Kiliyoor aren't a great team and even their foreign professional up front doesn't offer much threat. I don't even need to jump to win my headers. I'm rarely challenged.

Every time Priyan gets the ball the crowd lights up, though not necessarily in the way we'd all hope. There are fewer people in the crowd today, perhaps around two hundred, and it's noticeable. They aren't driving us on as they did in the first game. They aren't intimidating the match officials as we so need them to. Priyan runs the ball out of play on two occasions and almost everyone inside Ehamparam lets loose, calling him all kind of names and expressing their anger. Locals are always quick to point the finger, and the most vociferous fingers are those wearing the white and blue of the Titans. Why take responsibility when you can blame someone else? As a centre-half – a position that can feasibly be linked to every goal conceded – I've often found that, to my detriment.

'Roshan! Move forward. Leave the defence. You are too good to play there!' I look over to the bench, trying to work out the owner of the strange voice as it's joined by more strange voices who agree. It definitely came from the bench, but it's a voice I've never heard before. That's when I see the commotion, or rather the scuffle. Rimzy has his arms around a member of the crowd who has managed to make his way into the technical area. The member of the crowd continues to shout as if he alone can fix the Titans' woes. Thaabit refuses to look at him, his eyes resolutely following the ball like a hawk. He knows that Roshan is one of the best local attacking players. He knows that the crowd wants him to play Roshan further forward. But that's not what the team needs.

Thaabit receives the rare approval of the crowd when Iham is substituted on for the first time in the tournament, which also immediately energises us as a team. Thaabit wanted to build the team around him and it's obvious to see why. With his first action he dribbles past two players and plays a through ball for Priyan, who receives blame once more when he can't quite get on the end of it. Minutes later Iham has scored. A long punt upfield is never a bad idea on the terrible surface of our home pitch. Inshaht does just that and the defence panics. Iham steals in to head the bouncing ball past the onrushing goalkeeper: 1-1.

We control the game. It's just a matter of time until we score again. That is, until our substitute Sahkti gets sent off. He's not been on the pitch for more than a minute when he chases after a through ball. The keeper comes out and slides to smother it in his arms. Sahkti carries on running, connecting straight with the keeper's face. There can be no argument; it's a straight red. A wild man leaps from the crowd, runs to the pitch in his sarong and flip-flops and squares up to one of our opponents who applauds the decision. He's ready to fight for the honour of Trinco. Rimzy, once again the saviour, rushes after him, pulls him back and pushes him off the pitch. He's the only one with any fight in him. Power's plans of intimidation haven't materialised. The rest of the crowd has faded and is now far too lethargic, not angry or passionate enough. Even Power himself looks more exasperated than aggressive.

A chance to even out the dismissals is presented immediately. Our opponent's left-back commits his third bookable offence. This is where we need the crowd to apply pressure. They don't. Even the wild man remains defeated, now disinterested. It's just our luck to get the only referee who doesn't give home advantage. Instead he's calm, collected and fair. Yes, he should have sent the left-back off at some point, but mistakes are going to be made.

Kiliyoor race up the other end and force Ranoos into a wonder save. The resulting corner is only half-cleared and the following shot deflects cruelly off Naleem and straight into the goal: 2-1.

There's nothing we can do. Three consecutive defeats and the crowd is limp. Many disappear, and no one high-fives us as we leave the field. They even avoid eye contact. Balaya is in tears. The team strengths that once seemed so robust have disappeared. Every game seems to bring with it a new weakness, an area in which we're lacking. The problems are mounting up. We're getting worse.

In the changing room Thaabit gives his frank opinion. He doesn't raise his voice but speaks calmly, which has the effect of making his words seem even more cutting.

'The attitude stinks,' he says. 'What right do we have to turn up late, to moan at Priyan, to tell him he's terrible? It's unacceptable. This is not a school game. This is supposed to be an elite competition. Professional. You're getting paid. Paid! I don't understand why you can't take yourselves seriously and show up on time for a fixture. Preparation is key. I have to ask myself, the fact that you haven't turned up when asked: how well prepared are you mentally? You cannot be. I knew straight away we had lost that match before we had started.

'So we have to move on. The shouting at Priyan has to stop. I am sick of it. For me, Priyan is one of the most hard-working players in the squad. He's fit, determined and ambitious and best of all he loves the team. He puts in a lot of effort. Never misses training. Comes to the coaches' house every night and wants to talk football and ask for advice. The entire team is screwing up but nobody is saying anything to the other ten players. You pick on him because he's always been picked on. Well, from this point onwards, the bullying of Priyan has to stop. If you don't have anything nice to say then you shut your mouth. If someone makes a mistake you have to encourage them, support them. If you're being yelled at for ninety minutes by teammates and your own fans, do you think you can play a good game?'

The silence speaks loudest. Thaabit speaks for six minutes without stopping and I don't blame him. Players aren't taking this seriously enough. They're professionals. They need to start acting like it.

	Team Name	P	W	D	L	GF	GA	GD	Points
1	Valvai FC	4	4	0	0	18	3	15	12
2	Mullai Phoenix	4	3	0	1	4	3	1	9
3	Tamil United	4	1	1	2	7	8	-1	4
4	Kiliyoor Kings	4	1	1	2	7	12	-5	4
5	Trinco Titans	4	1	0	3	7	14	-7	3
6	Mannar FC	4	1	0	3	8	11	-3	3

The discussion continues back at the house. It's hard to emphasise just how let down Thaabit feels. None of the local players dares to join us in the house this evening. Even Priyan mumbles something about dinner with his family. Dean goes off to a restaurant with his girlfriend. Banda heads straight upstairs and refuses to come down. Kaps relaxes. And so I sit around the table with Thaabit and Ihshan as Thaabit continues to vent.

'Perhaps I cannot blame them,' he says. 'This is their culture in Trincomalee, their way of life, their style. It's so deeply ingrained. I don't think they've ever been told it's wrong when they're late. They don't respect authority. In the past they've had bad authority figures over here. Those in authority misused their power with favouritism, corruption and personal agendas. So when someone like that gives out a command they don't respect that person and don't follow that instruction. Mistakes aren't corrected. This is the way things happen here. It's normal. That, for me, is hard to accept.

'I'm not from this culture. I'm from the same country but it's not the same culture. I have my own culture, along with my own practices and standards. I don't think my standards are exceptionally high. They're normal. Turning up on time isn't a good quality. It's just what you have to do. It's nothing special.' He sways back and forth as he talks, his words enhanced by gestures. I nod along with Ihshan, struggling to disagree. 'Once the stuff outside the pitch is fixed I'll guarantee you results on the pitch. On the pitch we're fine. Not much needs to be improved. Off the pitch so much needs to change. The culture of Trinco football has to change. I hope this is the season that we can spark that change. I don't know if I can fix things in two months. You can't change things overnight. But I hope they will learn something.'

The only sound is the slowly rotating fan above us. It's hot in here, too hot. Me and Ihshan look at each other, unsure of what to do next.

'Anyway,' Thaabit saves us, looking up and pulling an expression between a genuine smile and a grimace, 'let's take our minds off it.'

Ihshan takes us for ice cream. Dean returns but decides to stay in the house with Meghan. He seems happier than I've ever seen him. Smitten even. I don't blame him. Meghan is bubbly, a joy to be around and thankfully very understanding. This feels a million miles from her life in Ireland. They plan to make the most of every second together.

With the pair happily reunited, we decide to leave them to it for the rest of the weekend. The next morning, our minds having moved on from the terrible defeat, we finally go to visit the elephants.

After a 65km drive to Kaudulla National Park that takes two hours, I'm charged 3,000 rupees at the entrance to the national park. The others in the car – Thaabit, Kaps and Ihshan – are all residents of Sri Lanka and are charged accordingly: 100 rupees. Still, Thaabit insists that we all share the costs. No amount of protest can convince him otherwise.

We're part of a 200-jeep convoy that winds through turbulent dirt tracks for forty-five minutes before finally emerging onto an open plain. An elephant walks out from the nearby woodland but we carry on. It's just as well – round the corner there's a gathering of eighty-nine elephants. Two are fighting, two are procreating and the rest are slowly moving towards the water to feed and bathe. I'm told it's the largest natural gathering of Asian elephants in the wild. It's absolutely incredible. Truly majestic.

The next day I'm awoken early and invited to Banda's niece's 'welcome' presentation. Throughout the day 150 guests arrive to stand next to his niece, who's presented in an illuminated cradle. They pick her up and have a picture with her before eating chicken and rice. There's no shortage of talk about the Titans.

By mid-afternoon I'm in the sea, where I remain until the sun goes down. My mind is well and truly off football. Losing isn't so bad. The only problem is that we're running out of games we can afford to lose.

* * *

Rimzy receives a phone call on the eve of our match against Tamil United: can he go and open the ground so our opponents, arriving at midnight after a seven-hour journey from Jaffna, can sleep in the stadium? The whole twenty-five-man squad plus five backroom staff have brought mats that they plan to lay down on the stadium steps.

Rimzy is shocked. So are all the other coaches. How can a team's owners treat their staff so badly? But Rimzy is a man with a good heart. He doesn't just open the stadium. He also opens the changing rooms so Tamil United can benefit from the slowly rotating fans.

In the morning, on our way to the game, Banda seems to know everyone. Now that Meghan is here, Dean travels by car and I go everywhere with Banda. It's slow progress because every few hundred metres we stop to chat to someone, slow down to wave or even ride side by side with another moped so Banda can hold a conversation on the move.

We arrive two hours before the game and get changed straight away so Thaabit can work on a new tactic without being seen by Tamil United, who are away eating lunch. Thaabit had wanted to cover the new tactic in a morning session, but mercifully Tamil United's arrival put paid to that plan.

I stand in defence so Thaabit can work with his forwards on crossing and getting bodies into the box. The standard is high and the crosses are consistently put into good areas. Then the game starts and everything changes.

We barely get the ball into the box. Passes are wayward. And worst of all, Tamil United are probably the best team we've played so far, with the exception of Valvai. It turns out they didn't sleep overnight in the stadium. That was the original plan, but they ended up staying in a house. The good news has obviously put a spring in their step. Their defence is solid, the midfield covers serious ground and their strikers are sharp – their foreign striker especially, who I rank as the best player we've played against so far.

Fortunately our defence is holding firm. We repel attack after attack and eventually start to get more of the ball. We're working well together and praising each other, just as the rest of the team is doing. Finally we're sounding like a team, even if we're not necessarily playing like one. Certainly not a professional one. Jai is replaced by Inshaht after twenty minutes. He's not playing badly but Inshaht is first choice. He would have started if he wasn't late again, along with Fasith, our reserve goalkeeper. At least Fasith has an excuse: after the Colombo bombings, a nationwide search that disproportionately affected Muslims took place, and a knife was found in Fasith's possession. Under the emergency laws made after the bombings, he is now required to attend a court hearing. Understandably, football isn't necessarily the first thing on his mind. Yet still Fasith, along with the other substitutes, roars us on from the bench. They have to, because there's not much of a crowd to cheer for us – and even what few supporters there are find themselves confined behind a new line of rope held by hurdles, ensuring they're several paces away from the technical areas and even further from the linesman.

The positivity works. We score on the hour, and when we do it's a goal symbolic of my teammates' newfound kindness. Substitute Inshaht hits a remarkable strike from thirty yards that the keeper does well to save. From the resulting corner, Priyan, who without the burden of his teammates' criticism has played with a smile on his face for the whole game, heads in a rocket from the edge of the area. As the ball hits the back of the net, all of Priyan's inhibitions disappear and the weight visibly lifts from his shoulders. Flanked by all of us, he sprints to the bench, thumping the logo on his chest and screaming with all of his joy to the heavens until he's in Thaabit's arms and the two are twirling round and round.

We're in the ascendancy. The chances continue to come. Dean misses two good ones, the second from a matter of yards. Naleem should do better with a shot. I cross for Iham, who manages to connect with his heel, sending the ball back in my direction when it was easier to score.

A rare attack sees Tamil United break behind our defence. I'm there to cover but, as I slide to stop the cross, I land on one of the millions of stones on our pitch and sustain a deep cut that won't stop bleeding. After defending the corner, I go down for treatment. A plaster doesn't work. Instead Mathu wraps a bandage around my leg. Iham screams at me to hurry up. Dean screams at me to hurry up. Mathu ties a knot and we scream for the referee. But the referee is following the play.

Tamil United have the ball on the edge of the box and our defence is disorganised. A shot trickles in and Ranoos has his body safely behind it. Then, just before reaching him, it takes the cruellest of bounces – an off-spinner that Muttiah Muralitharan would be proud of – and changes direction, fooling Ranoos in the process. The ball nestles directly next to where I've just finished my treatment. 1-1.

I feel sick. That wouldn't have happened if I'd been on the pitch.

Winning is a habit. Losing is a curse. Tamil United are playing fresh off the back of a 5-0 victory over Mannar. Their tails are up while our heads go down. The game evens out. There are just a few minutes remaining when I close down a shot and the ball deflects for a corner. Tamil United throw bodies forward. The cross comes at the six-yard area. It should be the keeper's ball. It should be our defenders' ball. But it isn't. Tamil score once again. 2-1.

Five group-stage games done. Three points. Four points behind the qualifying places.

Losing in such a manner is terrible. I walk off the pitch, feeling totally dejected. I avoid eye contact with the fans. There's only one exception – the old postman who comes to watch every training session and every game.

'Burkett!' he cries and gives me the biggest, most gentle hug.

He asks for a quick photo and I oblige. But then it's back to

the reality of the defeat. I can feel the fans walking behind me.
They aren't calling out to me. They're walking with purpose.
Suddenly I realise I'm the only Trinco Titan remaining in the
open. The others feared what was to come. And as I see the
crowd gathering, it suddenly dawns on me. I break into a jog
and fight my way through the crowd that is no longer a crowd.
It's a mob. Tension fills the air. People – our own fans – hold
rods and sticks and whatever weapons they can lay their hands
on as they shout in anger. I know they won't do anything to
me, but my teammates might not be so lucky.

Nomi ushers me into the changing room. The door opens
a crack and then slams shut, the lock immediately fastened.
Inside it's deafeningly silent. Everyone is staring at the floor.
Nobody laughs. Nobody smiles. Balaya is in tears. So are
Priyan and Vithu and Iham. We all know it was a game we had
to win. That we should have won.

'Come on, come on. Let's go!'

Cries reach us through the window. A bang suggests the
mob has thrown something at us. Another bang, followed by
a jeer. They've jumped onto the ledge and are rattling the bars,
trying to find an opening. Nomi shouts from outside the door
that we have to stay put. They're aggressive, booing and calling
out individual players.

'Team of girls,' comes the chant. Then again, louder: 'Team
of girls. Team of girls.'

These are supposed to be our supporters, our twelfth
man. We are Trinco; they are Trinco. And yet we've done the
inexcusable: we've lost again. Even worse, we've lost against
a team from Jaffna. And we didn't even let them stand in
their usual positions, making them huddle behind a rope like
animals! How can they be proud in their community? How

can they feel superior to Jaffna? They can't, and for that they want trouble.

It isn't safe, and so we remain locked inside the changing room. Not that anyone wants to move anyway. The floor is still universally being stared at. Bangs continue to puncture our silence, though the window and door hold firm. Still the yells come: 'Come on, come on. Let's go.'

'Coach, why don't you shout at us?' Balaya asks through the tears. 'We have lost four games in a row.'

Thaabit looks at him in a way he hasn't looked at a player before. He already suspects that his players have never heard kind words before, that their default setting is the finger-pointing and aggression that Priyan has suffered so much from.

'You are too used to yelling,' he responds, every word measured to the millimetre. 'What good would yelling do? Don't listen to them outside. They shout and abuse but they do not know anything. Today we saw what can happen when you change your attitude. You supported Priyan rather than yell at him. Priyan played happy and scored. When a player changes his attitude, I can get so much more out of him. There is still time in the tournament. There are still matches to play. If we keep on changing the attitude, we will see improvements. We are a team. Now we will suffer as a team. We are locked in our own dressing room in our own stadium with our own fans outside, waiting to hurt us. But things will change. We will wait until it is safe. And then we will start again.'

It's almost an hour before we leave the changing room together. There is only a handful of disgruntled fans remaining, yet at their centre is Chinna. He isn't joining in with them. Instead he's attempting to calm them, making sure we're protected. In that moment my respect for him goes even higher. Nobody is happy, but at least we're all safe.

	Team Name	P	W	D	L	GF	GA	GD	Points
1	Valvai FC	5	5	0	0	20	4	16	15
2	Mullai Phoenix	5	3	0	2	4	7	-3	9
3	Tamil United	5	2	1	2	9	9	0	7
4	Kiliyoor Kings	5	2	1	2	11	12	-1	7
5	Trinco Titans	5	1	0	4	8	16	-8	3
6	Mannar FC	5	1	0	4	9	13	-4	3

That evening, Balaya arrives at our house. He's come to resign as the team's permanent captain. Thaabit guides him up to the balcony where we have all our deep chats. Balaya sits down on one of the plastic chairs and gazes out at the coconut trees. He looks like he hasn't stopped crying. Gently, Thaabit prods him and words soon spill out.

'I was born in this city and grew up in this city,' he begins, speaking in Tamil. 'For the last fifteen years of my life I've been playing football seriously for this city, and also for the district. Being captain of the Titans is a great honour for me. To be given the responsibility was a very happy moment.

'However, being captain of the Titans is not something I like. I prefer to play as an ordinary member of the team. Losing today, it has put me under pressure and that is pressure I cannot handle. Trinco fans are crazy football supporters. In the past, football was at its best in Trinco. Trinco had the best players and there was a lot of football being played. But in more recent times a lot of conflict has been caused by spectators. Due to their violence, the competitions stopped. Football was killed in Trincomalee until the North Eastern Premier League started last season.

'Part of the crowd are already angry that their friends were not selected for our Titans squad. That is why they refuse to turn up, and if they do turn up they hope to see us lose so that they can laugh at us and boo us. I can feel it from the pitch when I'm playing. They are happy that one of their own has become captain, but I feel that only adds further to the burden on my shoulders. I know my teammates want me to be captain and are supportive of me wearing the armband, and I don't want to let them or the coaching staff down. However, I have to be honest that this is now becoming more of a burden than a matter of happiness.

'That is why I want to return the armband. I want to return the armband and I want you to remove us from Ehamparam stadium. Let us play in private, away from fans. It is for the good of everyone. I hope you will accept my requests.'

Thaabit doesn't. He tries to calm him, putting a soft arm around his shoulder and reminding Balaya that he's the manager and it'll be his decision. Balaya's mind already appears made up. For what seems like hours we all sit together. Priyan and Kalua and Ihshan and Banda all join us and we talk and talk. Balaya tells personal stories about the death of his father in the war, of his work as a painter but his sole focus as a footballer. The others discuss the tendency in the north for the local community to come together and donate money to pay the salaries of promising athletes. The players we play against from Jaffna, they claim, are all essentially professional all year round as part of a 'village tax'.

Inevitably, talk moves on to the war. Balaya was born in 1992, just after the navy base had been won back from the Tamil Tigers by the army. He tells us how he was scared when he first saw rockets being launched from the base but soon got used to it. How he was sad, knowing that people on the receiving end were going to get hurt but that there was nothing he could do about it. There are still tears in his eyes. There may be for some time.

We sit and discuss Balaya's words long after he's gone. The overwhelming mood is one of sadness. We all strongly agree with Thaabit that the decision regarding the captaincy should be the manager's and not Balaya's, but we have to make sure he's proud to wear the armband.

Thaabit calls it a night and I'm left with Ihshan, who I'm quickly becoming close to. He tells me that Sri Lanka suffers from something called Kuveni's curse. Sinhalese legend has it that Kuveni was the Yakkini queen of Sri Lanka who seduced Prince Vijaya, himself banished from India and arriving in Sri Lanka on the day of the Buddha's death. Yakkhas, along with the Nagas, were the first inhabitants of Sri Lanka according to the *Mahavamsa* – an epic poem chronicling the legendary beginnings of the country – and were considered to be nature spirits, while Prince Vijaya was a direct descendant of a lion. 'Sinhalese' translates as 'of lion'. Having seduced Vijaya, Kuveni decided to drive the Yakkhas from her land and make Vijaya the first Sinhalese king of Sri Lanka. Together they had two children, but Vijaya went on to betray Kuveni's oath by deciding to marry a princess from Madhura, thereby bestowing on her the honour of being his new queen. In her rage, Kuveni laid a curse on the land that prevented any of Vijaya's descendants from sitting on the throne. As she did so, a tiger cub jumped into her lap.

The curse is widely associated with all the political instability, violence and death that has followed. It has gone beyond the royal line, beyond politics, seeping into every corner of Sri Lanka resulting in colonialism, war and division. The only solution, it is agreed, is an exorcism. But until that comes, the island will continue to be cursed. And, from Balaya's words, it seems that the curse goes far beyond the Sinhalese people of Sri Lanka.

*   *   *

I go to bed looking forward to a day of snorkelling at Pigeon Island followed by an evening of takeaway pizza at Jai's with the whole team. By the time I wake up it's been decided that we'll have a 'heavy' training session instead. It's not the end of the world – my legs are holding up surprisingly well and the need to train seems obvious. After all, we're running out of strengths, picking up new weaknesses and we keep losing.

The session is scheduled for 3 p.m. – earlier than usual so that we avoid our fans who will expect us at the usual time. But by 3.45 p.m. only seven players have turned up. Ranoos comes at 4 p.m. Balaya shows up but he's not training. He says that he's got a groin injury. Thaabit loses it.

'This is why Trincomalee football will never improve,' he rants. 'The attitude is terrible. What can I do? Where are my players?'

We spend half an hour doing various shooting and crossing exercises but that doesn't help. The skills that we practised so freely before the tournament no longer come naturally.

'Go home, Jai! Go home!' Thaabit screams after Jai's third consecutive cross spoons out for a goal-kick. Wisely, Jai doesn't go home. We finish with a penalty shoot-out.

I'm part of a team that's too scared to turn up to a training session in case they encounter angry fans. A team whose captain is too scared to wear the armband. A team cowering in fear. What can any of us do in such circumstances?

*   *   *

I'm snorkelling with sharks. This isn't some kind of metaphor for the angry home fans that surround us. I'm actually snorkelling with sharks. The locals tell me they 'only bite occasionally'. I'm pretty sure that's a joke but I don't want to get close enough to find out. A vast coral reef stretches below me, home to fish of all colours of the rainbow. Kaps is behind me; Ihshan and Thaabit are in front.

'Turtle!' Thaabit yells and we all head towards him.

A call from Mahela Jayawardene has changed everything. This morning he told Thaabit that he's very happy with the work being done and that it doesn't matter if we keep losing. For the owners, it matters most about what's happening off the pitch, about building bridges, planning for the future.

'But if you win once, you'll win again,' Mahela reassures Thaabit. 'This is a young team and they'll be in an even stronger position at next year's tournament.'

With that in mind, Mahela wants us to carry on playing at Ehamparam. So what if the pitch is terrible? So what if the fans aren't supportive? This is professional football. We need to be embedded in the community.

A weight has been lifted from Thaabit's shoulders. He no longer needs to worry about being sacked mid-tournament. Instead he needs to start planning for next year's edition of the North Eastern Premier League. Longevity and stability: two factors that haven't often been seen in Trincomalee.

And so to celebrate we head to Pigeon Island, a nature reserve just 2km off the coast of Nilaveli. Thaabit and co. are charged local rates of 50 LKR for entry. I'm charged 3,850 LKR. I'm starting to see why Sri Lankans like white people so much.

The coral around Pigeon Island is shallow, making it ideal for snorkelling. It goes on for 200 metres and is made up of more than a hundred species of eye-catching coral. There are two tiny islands, handily called Large and Small, that are a nesting area for rock pigeons – hence the name – while rock pools and powdery sand provide entertainment for the other tourists.

Visiting hours are tightly controlled to prevent extensive damage from tourists, so after our allotted time with the sharks and turtles we return to our house. Straight away, Kaps comes into my room, brandishing two green 1,000 rupee notes.

'From Pigeon Island,' he explains.

'But my ticket cost 3,850 rupees and then I owed you for the boat and snorkel hire too. If anything I owe you more money,' I tell him.

'Seth, this is my country. You shouldn't have to burden the costs. Instead, me, Thaabit and Ihshan will share your costs. We must always make you feel welcome.'

That evening the house fills with footballers, as it always does. The usual culprits arrive: Priyan, Balaya and Kalua. We're also joined by Aflal and Ranoos, both of whom are staying overnight to make sure they arrive on time for tomorrow's away match. Their homes are an hour away yet they have been ever-presents at training. This despite Ranoos sitting his A-level exams. This despite Ranoos living in poverty, his house walls made of just iron sheets. It's no coincidence they're two of our best players.

Spirits are once again high. Ihshan has adopted two squirrels that were found in the kitchen and the players pass them round, kissing and stroking them.

'Breakfast?' Banda suggests. 'Shall we boil the squirrels or fry them?'

Mahela is right: this whole project is far bigger than football.

VAVUNIYA

'Suicide,' Balaya says. 'Today's match: do or die.'

I don't point out that such sentiment suggests die. Still, there's plenty of good news ahead of the game. With the first round of group games done, we're into the second and final round, meaning that we're playing against Mannar, the only team we've beaten thus far.

An island off the north-west coast that sticks out towards India, Mannar is the place where many Muslims believe Adam and Eve are buried. Adam's Bridge, a series of sandbanks that stretches for 30km, used to link Mannar to India, allowing people to walk between the two countries. Though the natural bridge was destroyed in the sixteenth century by a cyclone, the sea level remains low. The climate is dry, the land arid. Locals have to rely heavily on fishing for their livelihood, even more so after the LTTE destruction during the civil war.

But we won't get to see Mannar. We're playing away from home, far from the pressure and expectation of our fans. We're also playing far from the pressure of their home fans. There's a reason for that: Mannar's fans are infamous for their violence. They have to be kept away. When people have grown up with murder and war being normalised all around, violence at sporting events must seem trivial. And so the game is taking place instead in Vavuniya, a traditional Tamil town that pretty much falls halfway between Trincomalee and Mannar.

Those are the positives, but there's also one big negative: we have a hugely depleted squad. Dean has been allowed to miss the game so he can travel with Meghan – 'honeymoon', Vithu suggests with his usual wicked smile; Jai is ill; Sakhti suspended; Iham, Balaya and Priyan only half-fit; Dinesh injured; Hizam erased from Trinco Titans history after not only boycotting our last game but actually turning up and supporting the other team. All his photos have already been removed from social media, his dispute referred to the owners' lawyer.

Our house is filled with players by 9 a.m. when I emerge bleary-eyed to make myself a breakfast of Samaposha, the Sri Lankan version of porridge. Despite my drowsiness, I can feel the eyes on me. I notice Aflal filming me eating, and several others are watching me. This is my new norm. Everywhere I go, people covertly take photos of me. And when we stop off at a cafe on the way to Vavuniya, a group of children react like they've never seen someone with white skin before. They nudge each other and point. I smile and wave and eventually they even wave back to me.

It's a two-hour bus journey north and throughout I sit with Sakhti and Inshaht. Much of the time is filled with Sakhti telling me to say rude words and Inshaht imploring me not to.

I can barely hear either above Banda's singing. Since his return from injury, he hasn't stopped singing and dancing. He only stops briefly when I call Sakhti a 'bad man'.

'Bad man? Bad man? I am Batman!' Banda yells, thrusting his fist into the air with a wide smile.

As we approach Vavuniya the frequency of Buddhist shrines grows. In post-war Sri Lanka, such shrines are increasingly common in the traditionally Hindu heartland of the Tamils. They're a sign of the Sinhalese victory, as is the commemorative bronze statue of a soldier immortalised in celebration.

The town wasn't always full of Sinhalese victories. The Tamil Tigers have a long history with Vavuniya. In Poonthoddam, a northern area of the town, Prabhakaran established his first training centre on a 40-acre farm. As the Tigers militarised further and sent trainees north to Kilinochchi instead, Vavuniya acted as a border town, complete with entry and exit permits. To the south lay government-controlled areas. To the north lay the Tiger strongholds and the bulk of the A9 road stretching all the way to Jaffna, which for a long time held the status of the bloodiest road in the world, frequently used by the Tamil Tigers for booby traps, ambushes and landmines. By the end of the war, Vavuniya had become more than just a border town. The largest refugee camp, Menik Farm, covered 700 hectares of Vavuniya and housed 200,000 displaced people. Further military-guarded government welfare centres around the town held almost 100,000 more. Determined to find Tiger combatants, these centres were relentlessly searched by government forces. If they were lucky, such combatants would end up at one of the rehabilitation centres set up in Vavuniya at the end of the war. But only if they were really lucky. Most were never seen again.

The stadium we're due to play at isn't far from the town centre, and from the road the pitch looks good. Most importantly there's grass, but it also appears flat. We pull to a stop and I excitedly hop off the bus to inspect the pitch. Which is when I realise I've just been seduced by the greatest act of deception.

This is up there with the worst pitches I've ever seen, which in Sri Lanka is quite an accolade. Running straight through the middle is a raised surface, like a speed bump, 25 metres long and 10 metres wide. It's about 30cm high, its epicentre on the centre spot. The whole area is dusted with a thin layer of gravel, the only protection from the rock-hard surface beneath. In moulded studs it's like running on ice. To the left of the centre circle lie three large dumps of larger gravel, sharp edges sticking out at all angles to protect players from the holes below. But one area has been missed. There are ten shallow holes in close formation, each of which is a potential ankle-breaker. Forget the three points; I'd rather just get out of this place without injury. Happy and healthy: it's my mantra in Sri Lanka. As long as I come back happy and healthy, that's all that matters.

With such a depleted squad, Kaps makes his debut as sweeper. I'm moved to the left of a defensive three. In Sri Lanka, however, that means I essentially play as a normal centre-half with Kaps five yards behind me. Thaabit gives me instructions to man-mark, following my attacker wherever he goes, but I ignore them. The tactics are so different from what I've been taught and I'm sceptical they'll work. Instead I hold my position and attempt to maintain defensive strength. That doesn't work either.

Mannar have made two new signings since our first match: a Nigerian striker and a Cameroonian striker. They're fast, skilful and intelligent, curving their runs and timing them well. They don't even need to time them to perfection. After all, they're the 'home' team and have to be at least three yards off to be flagged. And on such a surface it isn't easy for a defender to turn and chase them. Most problematic, though, is the seem-

ing telepathy between the two strikers. Their link-up play is
phenomenal. Within minutes they're running us ragged.

We can't keep possession. Iham and Naleem don't look
at all fit. At central midfield and striker they're the spine of
our team and so our play is confined to the wings. Banda and
Priyan are working their socks off to make something happen. I
intercept a pass and drive forward, releasing Banda and making
my way into the box. Nobody covers me in our defence and
Mannar almost score on the counter-attack.

I return to my position but am temporarily blinded by a
huge gust of dust blown up from the pitch. When I regain my
vision the ball is coming towards me. Fast. I chase after the
Nigerian forward and stand him up in the corner. *Don't let
him beat you, don't let him beat you*, I tell myself over and over.
So when he crosses backwards I'm satisfied; it isn't a dangerous ball. There's a midfielder approaching but he's outside the
area. The midfielder connects with his head. Still no danger;
he won't score from there. But hold on. Ranoos has slipped on
the thin gravel as his body weight has shifted. He's lying helpless on the floor. The ball is trickling towards him… slowly, so
slowly. Ranoos makes a desperate leap and – just as it appears
he might stop the ball with his skinny outstretched arm – it
takes a funny bounce and cannons off the surface, soaring over
him and into the empty net.

Our heads go down. And when a losing team's heads go
down it always signals danger.

The second comes quickly after. The Nigerian striker I'm
supposed to be man-marking pulls on to Priyan, who is covering for Roshan at left-back. I hold my position in the centre.
The Nigerian rolls Priyan and I make my way over to stop the
cross. He shoots and I'm satisfied. No danger; he won't score

from there. I don't take into account that Sri Lankan goalkeepers aren't great at dealing with powerful shots. The ball flies directly through Ranoos's body at the near post. 2-0.

Our heads go down further and the third goal comes even quicker. It's a regulation hoof over the top. It's easy to defend. I see it coming but, as I turn to start running back, my feet go from under me. Realising his man-marker is face down in the gravel, the Nigerian saunters up to Ranoos and lobs him majestically.

There are still seventy minutes left of the match.

Thaabit reacts by withdrawing a heavily breathing Kaps. He hasn't played poorly but is carrying a knock and doesn't possess the pace to deal with such a tricky pairing up front. From being at sixes and sevens, the introduction of Vithu steadies our defence.

Half-time comes and everyone is blaming everyone. The defenders blame the attackers, the attackers blame the defenders, and the midfielders blame all of us. In these situations the keeper also usually blames everyone, but Ranoos barely says a word. Even now he's smiling. He's one of the few who does take responsibility, and it's no surprise he's come on in leaps and bounds as a result. Already he's transformed from a shy keeper who never kicks the ball to screaming at me in the first half for clearing the ball out of play rather than passing back to him.

I try and rally the troops, using all my powers of persuasion to tell them that we've all made mistakes and we have the next half to put them right. There's a brief silence as they take in what I've said. 'But the attackers...' Balaya starts and once again all hell breaks loose. Nobody but Ranoos is willing to take responsibility for what has just happened. It's the same trait that sees them all race to stand on the post instead

of mark at corners, the same trait that means players arrive
late, the same trait that's holding the whole of Trincomalee
football back.

But somehow the arguments and shirks of responsibilities
work, and we're like a team transformed in the second half. Aflal
replaces Naleem and straight away he misses a golden chance.
And another one. And another one. From cautious optimism
comes frustration. Things get more and more heated. Players
are openly shouting at each other and refusing to track back.
Banda is fouled and the suspended Sakhti leaps from his seat
on the bench to push the perpetrator. There's a wild look in his
eyes and several people have to hold him back as he attempts to
lay hands on the perpetrator once more.

After the game Thaabit laments the chances we missed.
Eight clear-cut goalscoring opportunities, he claims. Still, 3-0
is the right result. We don't deserve anything from the game.
Ranoos saved us on multiple occasions, with the two forwards
continuing to run us ragged. Even when I tried to kick the
Cameroonian forward out of sheer frustration, I couldn't catch
him. The hoots from the crowd plague me for hours.

Rimzy starts shouting. It's the first time I've heard him raise
his voice. He accuses us of lacking pride in our city, of lacking
fight. Then, on the bus, Nomi makes a speech. He speaks in
Tamil but it's clear he isn't happy. Bits get relayed to me. Fellow
owners are saying we're the worst team in the tournament. It's
reflecting badly on Mahela. He doesn't like this. It's the first
time I've seen Nomi unhappy. As punishment Nomi refuses to
let us eat at our post-match restaurant.

Banda is in tears the whole way home. Balaya wasn't quite
right – there was nothing self-inflicted about today. It wasn't
suicide. It was murder.

	Team Name	P	W	D	L	GF	GA	GD	Points
1	Valvai FC	6	6	0	0	22	5	17	18
2	Tamil United	6	3	1	2	11	10	1	10
3	Mullai Phoenix	6	3	0	3	5	9	-4	9
4	Kiliyoor Kings	6	2	1	3	12	14	-2	7
5	Mannar FC	6	2	0	4	12	13	-1	6
6	Trinco Titans	6	1	0	4	8	19	-11	3

TRINCOMALEE

What happened bro, the match?
Burkett super defender of trinco.
You are the best defender in trinco titans… good luck frd.
Not your fault bro. The attackers no good.

Facebook provides respite. I have more than five hundred new friends in the two weeks since the first match and many send me messages of positivity. I reply to all of them. I say 'Thanks, bro' but it comes out wrong. This is the problem with Ihshan's phone. Mine has broken and I'm having to use Ihshan's spare, which is still fresh from its factory settings. It hasn't yet learned how I text. 'Thanks, Brian,' I tell multiple Sri Lankans before heading downstairs.

The man who made it all happen has arrived in Trincomalee. Andrew Mollitt comes early the morning after the Mannar game, following an overnight flight from Singapore. He's here for less than thirty-six hours before flying back, due to return to Singapore at 7.20 a.m. and start teaching his first lesson at 8.20 a.m.

With him comes Giles Jacobson, a fellow maths teacher at their international school and another link in this whole process. Giles coached Thaabit at under-15 level. Andrew then coached Thaabit at under-19 level. Andrew also taught Owen Amos when he was an eleven-year-old student in Richmond, Yorkshire. Andrew was the one to convince Thaabit to go into coaching. Since that day, he's acted as his mentor. They chat for hours. I find them all, along with their portly driver, at 11 a.m. when I come down for breakfast. Andrew gets up immediately to greet me with a firm handshake as if we've known each other our whole lives. He's shorter than me with a shaved head, dark stubble and gruff voice. Giles, in contrast, is tall with the build of a long-distance runner. Both seem full of life. They've been there since 6 a.m. and haven't moved from the kitchen table, reminiscing and discussing the whole Trincomalee experience.

I wash up the blue bucket that is used as a bowl, fill it with porridge oats, make a Ceylon tea and then pull up a chair.

Both Andrew and Giles are great talkers. As international school teachers they're men of the world with experiences to match. Andrew talks with pride of his time playing football in Sri Lanka. He stayed in the country for four years, captaining Sri Lanka's most successful team: Saunders Sports Club. That gave him a unique insight into the country. Saunders played and trained in Pettah, one of Colombo's roughest districts. He tells us how his colleagues would warn him that he'd be killed, advising him not to go into Pettah. He didn't listen to them. After school he'd hop onto his pushbike and cycle past kids swinging rats around by their tails. At the training pitch there were open sewers behind either goal. A missed shot often landed into the sewer. The keeper would then retrieve the ball and kick it as far as they could to restart the game. As a centre-back, that meant the kick landed directly on Andrew's forehead. He'd return home with faeces on his head, having narrowly avoided the flying rats. An hour later he could be at a dignitary's house enjoying a dinner party. And all because he was a suda – a white man. In Sri Lanka, white skin allows you to be accepted by both the lowest and highest rungs of society. And to make the most of Sri Lanka, you have to make the most of such acceptance, Andrew insists.

He listens with interest as I share my stories. There are so many similarities. Giles chips in and before I know it it's lunchtime and we're off to Jai's.

We drive in a convoy of two cars. The roads are busy, as always, the drivers cavalier and the horns constantly sounding. A bull is walking down the road and suddenly charges at a young girl in red riding her bike. It headbutts the frame but not with enough power to knock her off. She finds it hilarious. We drive past an entire family on a struggling moped. There are five of them, the mother at the back, two small children between her and the father, and another sitting at the front. It's a new record.

At the beach we get straight into a game of beach football: players against non-players. Depressingly, the non-players race into a two-goal lead. They've got the portly driver in goal. He can barely kick a ball but in goal he's phenomenal – so good we even have to make the goals wider. Banda is treating this like a cup final. He's playing his heart out and even shouting at Jai and me when we make mistakes. In the end he scores a hat-trick, celebrating each with pure unadulterated joy, so we avoid embarrassment.

Andrew and Giles are having the time of their lives. They wonder why they ever left Sri Lanka. Singapore just doesn't compare. This country is beautiful, they say over and over. This beach is their favourite in the whole world. I don't disagree.

As we jump back into the sea under the perfect circle of the sun, everything seems right with the world. Then, with the flash of a phone, the serenity of that world is flipped on its head.

Mathu sends a photo on our Trinco Titans WhatsApp group of his twin brother, Vithu. He's lying unconscious in hospital with a tube in his nose. A flurry of voicenotes follow, all in Tamil. We're desperate to find out what's happening. Love-heart emojis are sent. Ihshan is asking around. Thaabit is making urgent phone calls.

Vithu has tried to kill himself. Vithu: our life-loving, funny, kind defender. One of my best friends in the team. My centre-back partner on the pitch. The short Sri Lankan who always greets me with either a cheery 'Hi friend!' or a wicked smile. And he's tried to give up all that he has.

Information trickles through. He had an argument with his mother. She claimed he had brought shame upon her. Distraught, Vithu reacted in the only way his jumbled mind could see fit: he went to the cupboards and took out a box of his mother's diabetes pills. He swallowed the whole box. It wasn't enough to kill him, but the whole team is alarmed. His psychological state worries us all. Vithu needs counselling. We need our happy, healthy defender back. Football isn't important. Life is.

He hasn't been discharged from hospital, which isn't surprising. They want to keep him in for monitoring. But Vithu doesn't want to be monitored. He wants to play for the Trinco Titans. So the very next day he does.

Not even twenty-four hours after the incident, he's sitting next to me in the changing room. He's frail, devoid of energy. A plaster covers his hand where the canula was inserted. He's pouring a concoction into his water bottle. There's a distant look in his eyes. I fist-bump him and there's not much of a reaction. I ask how he is and he wobbles his head in the classic Tamil manner.

'Mmm,' he replies, then bursts into laughter.

'After death,' Priyan laughs and puts his arm round Vithu. He keeps it there for a long time.

'My friend. Last night I try suicide,' Vithu tells me, his eyes down. 'Fight with my mother. This morning my sugar very low. Seventy-eight.' He downs his second consecutive energy pack and smiles, as if the whole thing was little more than a routine argument.

The chair on my other side is empty. It's Balaya's, who called this morning to rule himself out with a groin injury. It's an exaggeration at best, an outright lie at worst. He can't face the crowd. He won't even come to the ground because he claims the fans will shout at Thaabit. Thaabit doesn't care but Balaya is adamant. He won't come. He'll be fit for the next away game, where he'll also be able to captain the side. Thaabit tells him that if he doesn't come today he won't play for the Titans again. He comes just after the meet time.

All or nothing for Trinco. Balaya and Vithu are the embodiment of that statement: two starkly different actions but both the result of one vulnerable mindset.

The importance of the match underlines this. It's a mustwin but we're playing against Valvai, the team that beat us 8-2 and contains a smirking Mindron. They've won every game so far. We need our full squad to put in a shift. We get a collection of individuals so fearful of failure that they'd rather not try in the first place. Before the game Thaabit was pulling his hair out. Nomi, who travels five hours by bus from Jaffna for every home game was feeling badly let down by players such as Balaya. What point is all this effort if it isn't reciprocated?

And yet the spirit in the dressing room is high. Vithu's presence has lifted everyone, as has Andrew's, who Thaabit has named on the bench. My teammates aren't the most sensitive to Vithu – 'counselling' is said throughout – but Vithu smiles more and more as he becomes increasingly comfortable in their company. He even manages to ask Dean how his honeymoon was. When we're told to change, Balaya looks coy. He offers to massage my legs and then strokes Vithu's hair affectionately. It's obvious he's feeling a sense of guilt.

The warm-up is delayed while Banda shovels cow poo from the playing surface and the rest of us do our best to remove the sharpest stones. Before we know it, we're in the tunnel side by side with Valvai. We thought they'd be resting players, taking the bottom team lightly as they look towards the knockout stage. They aren't. Their full squad is playing, including their right-back who added me on Facebook after our last match.

'Tomorrow you'll let us win,' I had typed to him on Facebook Messenger last night.

'Yes of course my friend,' he replied.

As we walk out I notice their badge on a board that includes all the teams in the North Eastern Premier League. The names all scream of war. There's the Titans (obviously), the Warriors, the Avengers, the Kings, the Conquerors. Valvai's badge, though, is the only one to feature two roaring tigers.

They certainly don't start like tigers. We control the game against our unbeaten opponents and grow in confidence. Priyan is released by Iham and is through on goal, only to be tripped on the edge of the area. It could be a red but the referee produces a yellow. We push and push. Dean and Iham control the midfield, Dean huffing and puffing while Iham takes on the role of creator. We need to score the goal we deserve.

Instead it's Valvai. Roshan and Priyan are defending against one player but he still manages to get the cross in. It loops towards me on the edge of the six-yard box. I know their Nigerian striker is lurking. Just as I'm about to head the ball, someone jumps into me. My header goes somewhere. I don't know what's just happened. In my confusion I can hear Dean scream 'Seth! Seth!'

It turns out my header went straight up in the air. The person who jumped into me was Ranoos. He said 'keeper's ball,' but he didn't shout it. His child's frame bounced straight off me and was catapulted to the floor. And while the two of us attempt to make sense of what's just happened, a Valvai attacker sneaks in and heads home from a tight angle.

Still, we're playing well and continue to control the game until half-time. We just need to stay in the game until the final ten minutes, that's what Thaabit emphasises.

My thigh is giving me problems. It's the same issue I had at Mullai Phoenix. At half-time I get it sprayed and massaged. Vithu, who's had a great first half, is brought off for Kalua. There's no chance he can risk playing a full game in his condition. Everyone goes over to congratulate him. Once again Balaya affectionately strokes his hair.

I stretch and stretch but it's doing nothing. Every step since half-time is making my thigh worse. Kalua is struggling to keep track of his Nigerian opponent and it's making my job harder. The opponent spins and plays a wicked through ball before I can shut him down. Ranoos spots it but doesn't call loudly enough, crashing into Roshan who's attempting to clear. There's a tangle of bodies and out from it emerges the loose ball. Straight to a Valvai player. 2-0.

I last another five minutes. I'd been desperate to play every minute of every match but the twinge I feel when I sprint is too much. I just about manage to kick the ball out of play and then hit the deck. On the bench, Thaabit turns to Andrew and nods. Andrew starts to remove his tracksuit bottoms. The crowd give me a warm clap as I limp off the pitch. It's the largest crowd since the opening match, though at least half is made up of Valvai supporters. I clap them back, but when Andrew takes the field there's a real roar. One white man replaced by another white man – this is too much for them.

We concede immediately. I feel helpless from the sidelines as our defence parts willingly. 3-0 and Mindron is the scorer. He wheels away to the corner flag, a mark of respect to the ground that played such a role in his formative years. Minutes later it's 4-0.

The bench is a lonely place. Nobody talks to each other. The game happens in front of us but it feels so distant. The taunts are so clear. There's a lone voice carrying from within the stand. It's in Tamil but I can tell it isn't complimentary. Later I find out the majority of the calls were from players who were cut at the early trials. They're the same ones who watched all our training sessions, who've been to all our games and are always the first to criticise. They tell us we're terrible, accuse Rimzy of stealing player wages, and tell us to leave their city. They've found out that we wanted to play behind closed doors and have allowed it to fuel them. They don't want us anyway. They wish we didn't represent Trinco. They threaten to burn the banners Ihshan has stuck all around the ground. I don't know how Thaabit can shut them out.

Another goal: 5-0. From dominating the first half, we've ended up humiliated. It's a cruel sport.

Yet the fans don't go crazy. At the full-time whistle I get up to shake hands and am hugged by every Valvai player, including my new Facebook friend. I apologise to him. After my Facebook friend pretended that Dean had stood on his toes to try and get him carded, I told Dean to actually stand on his toes at the next set-piece. He didn't need asking twice and my Facebook friend went down screaming in pain. The referee merely waved him back to his feet.

Even if the referee did see Dean step on the player's toes, it's doubtful anything would have happened. In our seven games so far, not one foreign player has been shown a card by the referee. Not me when my handball prevented the Mullai forward from entering the penalty area for a one-on-one. Not on any of the multiple occasions Dean has gone in with too much force. Not Valvai's Nigerian centre-forward when he shouted insults at the linesman for giving him offside and continued to shout after the referee warned him to stop. Not Mullai's Ghanaian centre-back when he kicked Sakhti in the head. And yet Sri Lankans are carded for the slightest of incidents: an arm on an opponent to keep them away, a coming-to-gether, a fifty–fifty. I'm not complaining.

Thaabit, meanwhile, is publicly congratulated by Valvai's captain. He tells him that we're the most organised, disciplined side they've played to date and says 'good job, coach'. Then Mindron arrives at Thaabit's side and bows in front of all in attendance to kiss his feet. It's the ultimate sign of respect – a sign that he's sorry for the way things ended with the Trinco Titans and a slap in the face to all those who have booed us. Thaabit can only hug him in response. He's too shocked to do anything else.

Back in the changing rooms Thaabit gets us all together and claps us. He's proud. We did ourselves proud. Every player gave it their all and for forty-five minutes we were brilliant.

'Today we don't lock ourselves in the changing room,' he announces. 'We go onto the pitch and stretch with our heads held high.'

It's easier said than done. I try to get back out but fans are coming from all angles. They swarm me, asking me for selfies, high-fiving me and saying how happy they are I'm their Facebook friend. I don't get these people. We lose 2-1 to a last-minute goal and they threaten us and attempt to attack us. We get popped 5-0 and they are all happy. It doesn't make sense. But not much makes sense on a day like today. Today isn't about the football. It never was.

	Team Name	P	W	D	L	GF	GA	GD	Points
1	Valvai FC	7	7	0	0	27	5	22	21
2	Tamil United	7	4	1	2	12	10	2	13
3	Mullai Phoenix	7	3	1	3	6	10	-4	10
4	Kiliyoor Kings	7	2	1	4	12	15	-3	7
5	Mannar FC	7	2	1	4	13	14	-1	7
6	Trinco Titans	7	1	0	6	8	24	-16	3

* * *

Later I get a WhatsApp message from Vithu: *Hi my friend, how is your leg is it ok?* This is a guy who tried to end his own life twenty-four hours ago, now asking me if I'm the one who's OK. I send him a love-heart emoji. He tells me he's speaking with his mum, that everything is OK. They're going to rebuild the relationship. I invite him for dinner but he isn't allowed to eat for three days. All he can ingest is fruit juice.

'Very sad,' he concludes. 'The match today, again we lose.'

I tell him it's the least of our worries.

Banda is another. He's becoming increasingly withdrawn.

He goes to bed at 8 p.m. and doesn't rise until midday. When he is around he doesn't sing. He often disappears for large chunks of the day.

'The other players are treating this like a regional tournament,' he laments. 'They come and get their free kit, their free food, their money and they laugh and joke. They don't understand this is much bigger. This is our greatest opportunity.'

That afternoon the team arrive at our house to collect the next 20 per cent of their wages. It comes to 8,000 rupees, though many have been fined 2,500 rupees for punctuality issues.

'It is the fault of us, not the coaches,' Ranoos shrugs. 'They're learning.

Banda doesn't surface. While he shuts the world away, Thaabit has come to terms with the reality of our situation. Together with Ihshan, we go for a drive once the team has left our house, stopping off at the Cinnamon hotel bar, where we watch the Premier League, drink mocktails and play pool. Recently it's become a ritual. Dean spends time with Meghan. Kaps gets an early night so he can rise at the crack of dawn to meditate. We finish our pool games then return to the house, where we brainstorm ideas for the documentary and discuss team tactics late into the night. A 3-4-3 is at the top of Thaabit's mind, an attacking move that may help us score but comes with the worries of whether we have the personnel to play such a system along with the knowledge. Most importantly, it's questioned whether such a formation will do enough to hide our ever-growing number of weaknesses. There's no such question about making the most of our rapidly diminishing strengths.

Qualification still isn't impossible. If we win our final three games we should make the quarter-finals. We've improved as the tournament has gone on, but we've now played seven games and no player has scored more than once. Two of our final three games are away from home. The odds are stacked against us.

We all agree we're ready to go home. It's been an incredible experience. It's just a shame it couldn't have worked out better.

With home in mind, I take one of the biggest risks of my life: I tell my football-hating girlfriend to book her flight to Sri Lanka for a week on Saturday. If we qualify she'll have to twiddle her thumbs in Jaffna until we're eliminated. I'll never hear the end of it. But surely we can't qualify. We're four points behind the two teams in front, we need to win all our remaining three games and that means we need to actually score some goals. At eight goals in seven games – and from eight different goalscorers – we're far behind the other teams. We could do with a clean sheet, too. There's no point in scoring goals if you keep conceding them.

I'm sure the gamble will pay off. And if it does, there's an even bigger gamble that I'm planning.

* * *

We've barely paused for breath by the time the next game comes around. Support around the city has dropped to an all-time low. It's clear that we've become the city's burden. The secret that everyone knows but nobody wants to talk about. As far as Trincomalee is concerned, it has no Titans.

We drive to the ground past the green domed mosque where Inshaht's six-foot banner was once proudly displayed. Now it's gone, ripped down in a rage. None of the posters around the city still stands; only the ones in the stadium remain untouched. If we lose against Mullai Phoenix today, it's almost certain the banners that adorn the ground will be set on fire by the fans.

We arrive after the meet time and find an almost full squad awaiting us. 'Hi friends!' they shout when they see me and Dean. A round of fist-bumps follows, the sun glinting off Vithu's wedding ring as our hands touch.

The squad remains almost full but numbers are low for the game. Ranoos is unavailable, Priyan has had to go to Jaffna to register for his second semester at university, and Vithu is suspended. There are just four players on the bench and one of them, Balaya, claims he isn't fully fit.

My thigh hurts. I'm not fit. Yet I have to be fit. The warm-up proves problematic. My thigh is twinging all the time. I tell the coaching staff and Kaps hands me a pink tablet: 'Painkiller.' I don't want to take it but it's my only option. I wince and swallow it, then ask Mathu to spray the affected area. He massages the spray in and after a minute I can feel something change. There's a numbness, enough for me to at least give the game a good go. I fist-bump Mathu in thanks and slip my shinpads into long socks. Thaabit gives me a thumbs-up as I leave the dressing room. He has already told everyone he can't have any injuries.

Twenty minutes later Naleem is walking off injured. He's replaced by Aflal, who's tasked with continuing to chase Dean and Iham's through balls. Five minutes after that, Jai goes down – his knee hurts. He's told to get on with it, but now we have two centre-halves nursing injuries. Not that it matters too much, as Mullai prove toothless. Their buzzy Sri Lankan strikers have been relegated to the bench in favour of a foreign player up front. He's strong and holds the ball up well but is nothing to worry about. Mullai's goalscoring problem rivals ours and so it's no surprise when the teams go in 0-0 at the break.

Thaabit tells us to keep going and to stay in the game. Mathu works overtime on his makeshift physio table, attending to me, Jai, Naleem, Sakhti and Banda. Balaya makes himself useful by providing massages and avoiding Thaabit's gaze.

After half-time we return to a cheer from the crowd. There are only a couple of hundred in attendance and many of those are balaclava-clad Mullai fans, but Chinna is attempting to galvanise his former troops from behind the goal. He continues to do so throughout the half and eventually it works: a long-range free-kick from Roshan takes a wicked deflection and soars into the net. Most of the team go wild, as if they've long forgotten what scoring a goal feels like. As much as I'd like to join them, I return to my position. My leg is in no shape to run to the other end of the pitch.

I play deep to minimise my running and try to avoid kicking the ball at all costs. Kicking with my left is painful; kicking with my right is agony.

The second goal is welcome. A poor corner from Roshan bounces around the box before Aflal's miscue falls to Iham, who converts from close range. This time I forget my thigh. I let out a roar and join the celebrations. Sakhti turns to me and indicates it's time to do our dance. Before I know what's happening I'm mimicking a cobra, my left arm holding up my right elbow and my right hand jabbing back and forth in time with my head. Sakhti does the same and we move towards each other before acknowledging the laughs from the crowd.

Mullai look like a beaten team. Their body language is terrible. A substitution that saw their foreign forward removed in place of a foreign midfielder had given them something of a spark, but all that has been lost. Now they are rattled. Banda outmuscles their right-back and when the referee blows for a foul the right-back throws a pile of sand from the pitch into Banda's face. It deserves a red card. It gets a yellow card. Mullai have been let off and they know it.

The clock ticks on. We constantly ask the referee for the time. Cries of 'sir!' ring around the ground. Twenty minutes. Fifteen minutes. Mullai's striker is taken off and their centre-half moved up front. I smile to myself. They're desperate. The clean sheet is getting closer.

And then the most surprising thing happens: the centre-half scores. It's all down to the foreign midfielder, the number eight. He runs on to a wicked through ball. I spot the run and go to cover Jai and Inshaht, both of whom have switched off. Fasith, replacing Ranoos in goal, also runs out. But first he hesitates.

The hesitation is all Mullai need. Fasith is a fraction of a second late to the ball. I was never going to get there. The number eight squares for his centre-half and all of a sudden Mullai are back in the game. Surely we can't let it slip.

Dean drops deeper to help out. Our defence drops deeper. We've stopped playing, instead preferring to hoof.

Once again the number eight breaks free. He moves to the left wing and beats Inshaht and Jai. Dean closes him down and forces him into a mishit cross. We watch as it loops over Fasith. There's nobody attacking it and it's heading out of play. Until Roshan panics. For some reason he attempts to clear the ball. It slams into his shin and spirals off in completely the wrong direction: into the empty net. 2-2. I have to turn Roshan and forcibly push him out of the goal, he's in such shock. If it wasn't for such an intervention he'd stand there all day.

Now our heads have gone. Roshan's especially. He's one of our best players, our goalscorer, but all he can think about is that fatal mistake.

When the referee blows the full-time whistle an eerie silence descends over the ground. A draw is no good for either team; we both needed to win.

Nobody from the crowd shakes my hand. The old postman gives me a hug but it's out of routine rather than any passion.

'Why?' he asks with arms outstretched, as if his whole world has come crashing down. 'Why?'

Other fans are taking more direct routes.

'Apologise!' an elderly man in a Chelsea shirt, all gums and no teeth, demands of Roshan. Roshan can barely even look at him and so the man turns his attention to me. 'How defence?' he asks. I tell him I don't know.

Suddenly we're being crowded. We try to stretch away from the action but the fans are edging closer. They're staring and it's hostile. Words are being said. The old man in the Chelsea shirt continues his rant. Players who were cut at trials stand there, smirking. One of the fans says something that proves the final straw. Kaps cuts through the crowd and drags us all back into the changing room.

This is our safe haven. Or it should be. Inside we find an irate Anushaht. He's squaring up to Sakhti and drawing his arm back as if to throw a punch. Sakhti is standing up to him, willing Anushaht to try it. Tears are rolling down Anushaht's cheeks. He was an unused sub and it hurts. He wanted to contribute to the team. Worse, after the game the fans descended on him too. They laughed at how he isn't even good enough to play for such a terrible team. They pushed him. They humiliated him. Sakhti, who's good friends with many of those laughing, seems the obvious target. It takes a long time to calm Anushaht down. We drag him away from Sakhti without much resistance and instead he throws his moped helmet on the floor and curses his people. He lets out more tears. Then it's over, and he accepts his fate.

Fearful of another attack from our own fans, we wait a long time and then leave the changing room as a group. Strength in numbers. Dinesh bundles Thaabit out, protecting him from the lingering crowd by throwing an arm around him. Those in the crowd who want to be hostile hang around at the exit but don't approach us. The threat of violence feels very real but never quite manifests. We keep our heads down and jump in the car while Kaps locks all the doors from the inside. They eyeball us as we slowly make our way forward. There's a tuk-tuk blocking the exit. This time they don't throw anything at the changing room or tell us to leave our city. They talk and stare and scheme and hate, but it doesn't translate into action. We're uncomfortable but unharmed.

They turn their attention to Rimzy, who's taken it upon himself to shepherd us all to safety by attempting to move the tuk-tuk. As Rimzy moves among the madness, the threats begin. Rimzy – well-respected, well-meaning Rimzy Nana – becomes the centre of their anger. There's nothing he can do. They want to beat him up, tell him they want to give Thaabit a good kicking. Dinesh returns to the throng with Banda and Naleem to guide a shaken Rimzy to safety.

They carry on staring. It feels as if we're in a standoff. I sit in the back of the car and stare at the seat in front. I don't want to make eye contact. None of us speaks a word. Kaps remains motionless at the wheel. Eventually the crowd backs off. Eventually the tuk-tuk is moved. We're safe. We drive out of the home ground for the last time with a huge sigh of relief. The banners still flutter from the gates as yet unburned. Ihshan will return to get them in the morning once the crowd has long gone and their anger has subsided.

As we drive back along the road, I take one last look at the pitch that offered so much hope and potential, that grazed my knees and condemned us to defeats. The old postman has returned to his laps. Slowly, so slowly, he walks around the pitch. He'll continue to do so every day until the next time the Titans start up, until he has new idols to support and new hope that Trincomalee football will put itself back on the map. I smile as I watch him. He's what I'll miss most about this beautiful, terrible stadium.

	Team Name	P	W	D	L	GF	GA	GD	Points
1	Valvai FC	8	8	0	0	30	6	24	24
2	Tamil United	8	4	1	3	13	13	0	13
3	Mullai Phoenix	8	3	2	3	8	12	-4	11
4	Kiliyoor Kings	8	3	1	4	14	15	-1	10
5	Mannar FC	8	2	1	5	13	16	-3	7
6	Trinco Titans	8	1	1	6	10	26	-16	4

* * *

Other results go our way, meaning that – remarkably – we can still qualify with two games to go. That evening the house is inundated with players. Iham and his brother are the first to show up. Then Dinesh and Kalua come for dinner. Then Inshaht and Aflal. Then Sakhti and Anushaht, who's come to apologise to Thaabit, having already made up with Sakhti.

We sit up on the balcony and look into the coconut trees. Everyone is laughing. Jokes are made about the game. Football comes and goes but Trinco always moves on.

The next morning Ihshan returns to the stadium to find the banners have all been torn down. Any trace of the Trinco Titans has disappeared from the city. Banda has a more successful trip. He returns to the house carrying a huge box on the handlebars of his moped and an even bigger grin. Gleefully he shouts that it's a package from France – from his girlfriend. All this time Banda has been telling us he has a girlfriend in France. He's also told us he had another girlfriend in Germany and so none of us believed him. Yet here's the proof.

He opens the parcel and it's a Pandora's box of product. There are two pairs of Nike football boots, neither of them the fake version. There's a pair of running shoes. A box of Celebrations. So many packets of crisps. Moisturisers, shower gels and creams. Clothes.

He wears his fresh new football boots down to the dining table for lunch. Everyone congratulates him and asks if they can touch the boots. His misery is eased. Happiness spreads across his face.

'You have to marry her!' we declare.

* * *

The never-ending tournament now has an official end date: 5 October. Two months after the original date. The quarter-finals won't start until ten days after the end of the group-stage games. When I tell Dean his mouth hangs open. Any disappointment at conceding those late goals against Mullai is gone.

'Imagine,' he repeats over and over.

It's impossible to step onto a football pitch with the intention of losing a game. The ebb and flow and desire to excel prove overwhelming. But it's certainly possible to want to go home. Right now we all want to go home – me, Dean, the coaches, Ihshan. It's time to resume our lives that have been put on hold for too long.

Dean retires to his room in shock. It's the hottest day yet and everyone else is resting from the sun, so it's down to me and Banda to do the familiar drive into town to get lunch from Rimzy's house. The horn beeps every few minutes as Banda waves to friends and acquaintances.

Within ten minutes we're at Rimzy's, where his wife welcomes us into the home. We're invited to sit, and Rimzy's mother comes to ask me questions in her broken English, with Banda doing the translation where necessary. She asks me all about Sri Lanka and throws her arms in the air when she says 'no points!'

Little Razan returns from the mosque in his skull cap. It's Friday and the streets are filled with Muslims pouring out from the mosque. Razan jumps straight up to the TV to turn on his beloved cartoons, then begs me to play slaps with him. Dean first introduced him to the game and he's taken to it well, flinching only on occasions and hitting with force. It helps that Dean never goes easy on him. Not wanting to be embarrassed by an eight-year-old, I give as good as I get, and after a time Razan wants to play rock, paper, scissors instead. We have a few rounds and then Rimzy's wife returns with the food. It's time to leave.

As we ride off on the moped, the whole family stands in the door to wave at us. We wave back with our thumbs up, warmed by the goodness of those we're fortunate to associate with in this city.

Later that afternoon the results come in from Group A, which always plays the day before us. Tilko Conquerors beat Mattunagar Super Kings 12-0. Maathodam, with a goal difference of -27, win their first game of the tournament, beating Vavuniya Warriors 2-1. Vavuniya are still in second place. Mattunagar are still in fourth place, their qualification almost confirmed.

Neither Mattunagar or Maathodam are paying players. Nor Ampare Avengers, also in Group A. All their owners are giving them is win bonuses. All teams in Group B are professional. The luck of the draw. If we'd been placed in Group A we would certainly have qualified. But it doesn't matter. Tilko and Valvai are so far ahead of everyone else that it seems we're all bystanders in their inevitable marches to the final.

The Trinco Titans are delighted, our WhatsApp group abuzz with jokes. One of the players cut from the Titans squad at trials, also a long-time tormentor at our games, played his first game in the North Eastern Premier League today as a second-half substitute for Mattunagar. He came on in defence with the score at 4-0. He left the field forty-five minutes later having conceded eight goals.

'The best defender of Trincomalee,' reads a photo sent by Naleem of the player in football kit with thumbs up. Voicenotes spring from everywhere. No matter how bad we are, we'll never be as bad as our tormentor. What goes around comes around.

I go to Dinesh's house for dinner with Meghan and Dean. We arrive to find an absolute feast. Newspaper is covering bowl after bowl. There are three different types of bread, noodles, sweet-and-sour chicken, eggs, daal, coconut sambal. Plates are piled high but Dinesh is never satisfied. 'Eat! Eat! Eat!' he insists, shoving bowls in our direction at the slightest sign our plates aren't full.

Sussy and Manisha, Dinesh's sister and niece, rush around. They give us everything we didn't even know we needed and are on hand to constantly fill up our glasses with water. 'You're beautiful,' they tell Meghan over and over.

When dinner is over it's insisted that we sing. I say the one line I know of a Tamil song and then Dean does his party trick of singing the whole chorus of a Tamil hip-hop number: 'Enna Nadanthalum' by HipHop Tamizha and Kaushik Krish. All three of us then do Shaggy's 'It Wasn't Me'. The cameras come out. Video calls are made and selfies are taken. The family is so proud to host us. We're so proud to be hosted.

Dinesh takes me on the tour. The kitchen we're eating in is basic but comfortable. There's a shrine to Jesus and an old

TV with a large screen. The walls are light blue and peeling. Beyond the kitchen there are several buildings in various states of disrepair. A large family lives here – cousins, grandparents, children – and all are supported by Dinesh's 1,500 rupees a day as a painter and one of his uncles' takings as a tuk-tuk driver. It's not extreme poverty but money is hard to come by. All ceilings are corrugated iron sheets. There's just one toilet and it's outside – a hole in the floor with a shower fitted above, both covered by more corrugated iron sheets. People of all ages smile at us, intrigued by the foreigners they've welcomed.

We return to the kitchen and the photo albums come out. We see Dinesh growing up from a child, through the 2000s and up to the thirty-year-old man he has become. A running commentary indicates what could have been: 'This my friend move to Canada. This my friend move to Australia. To Switzerland. To France.' In an area plagued by war, the safest option was to run. Heartbreakingly, Dinesh shows us his former girlfriend, who was forced to flee to Canada.

'She looks like a model,' Meghan notes. Dinesh smiles distantly.

'Now married a Canadian,' he laments. 'Me, never again.'

The next page shows a young Dinesh parading a trophy around Ehamparam and the awkward silence is broken.

When it's time to leave, an uncle is dragged from a room to drive us home in his tuk-tuk, Dinesh's Trinco Titans sticker still proudly glued to the rear. He drops us home and refuses to take any money for doing so.

People who have so little yet give so much.

KILINOCHCHI

'What do you think the score is going to be?'

'Well, we always concede two goals and we struggle to score, so I'm going with 2-0.'

'I think it'll be six,' Dean replies.

There's a method behind Dean's thinking. Although we can still qualify, the players are waving the white flag. Priyan is unavailable through injury – 'acting', it's widely agreed. Iham has to go to university for registration. Hizam is long gone. Dinesh is actually injured. Nobody knows where Jai is. And of the fifteen players who have actually turned up, four – me, Dean, Naleem and Balaya – are carrying injuries.

We head north on the well-trodden path of the A9, making our way through Vavuniya before arriving at Kilinochchi, 65km south of Jaffna. The city is flat, brown and dry with no distinguishing features. Its buildings aren't in a state of disrepair but nor does there appear to be any recent sign of repair. It's quiet on the wide streets. Few people are out, and the tuk-tuks – painted red, I note, rather than the green of Trinco – are in short supply. Even the most vivid of imaginations would struggle to see this place as a major settlement, let alone the capital of a separatist state.

We stop to eat lunch at the Friends Inn, a hotel near Kilin-ochchi's centre. Large helmets decorate the grounds, all of them covered in flowers. The message of peace and unity is every-where. Kaps hands out the unclaimed wages, including my own, and then we sit for lunch and watch as two boys splash about in the hotel pool, indifferent to what's going on around them. Sakhti finds a mango tree and soon enough everyone is throwing stones to try and knock down the best pieces of fruit. As we share around our catch, everything seems right with the world.

We head to the ground and pass a newly erected Buddhist shrine – as always, a mark of Sinhalese success in the Tigers' heartland. Two policemen stand by to create a checkpoint. Even ten years after the war, the military presence in the north-east remains high. There are army camps everywhere, all ready to stop any signs of a breakout of Tamil Eelam separatism. We pass another landmark: a large concrete block with a bullet hole in it. A Sri Lankan flag flies proudly atop. Suddenly we're out of the city and what's brown becomes green, the vegetation thick-ening. It's as if Kilinochchi is the city forgotten by nature.

We carry on past farm fields set on fire by their owners, thick white plumes blinding the bus as it drives forward. Peacocks line the side of the road. I try to picture the battles that must have raged right here not long ago. I can't. Even though the history is right in front of me, the thought of war is so far removed from anything I've ever seen that it proves impossible.

Yet war was synonymous with Kilinochchi from 1990, when the Tamil Tigers first captured the town, until almost the very end, in 2009. As the Tigers' administrative capital, LTTE flags were previously everywhere, police and civilian cars carried the green stripes of the Tigers, all of them obeying the 40km/h speed limit of Tamil Eelam as they made their way to their appointments that ran to LTTE time, half an hour ahead of the main Sri Lanka time. Locals paid their taxes directly to the Tigers. There were Tamil Tigers-owned restaurants, businesses and even an LTTE TV channel, all operating from Kilinochchi – at least, in the 'good days' because, by the time 2008 came around, the Tigers were on the back foot. When the United Nations and all other foreign aid workers were ordered to leave Kilinochchi because the government could no longer guarantee their safety, the writing was on the wall. It wasn't the beginning of the end, it was almost the end of the end.

Once foreign eyes were gone, the government stepped up their offensive. Three attempts were made to take Kilinochchi, with the third, in January 2009, proving successful. With Kilinochchi under control, the Sri Lankan army managed to win the rest of the A9 back from the Tigers, as well as the strategically important Elephant Pass that joins the north to the rest of Sri Lanka. The Tigers, in contrast, retreated further into the Vanni, eventually ending up in their tiny spit of land at Mullaitivu with as many as 200,000 civilians surrounding them. Some of those civilians were there voluntarily; many had no other option. The last few months of war proved truly shocking. To this date, the United Nations are still investigating war crimes alleged to have been carried out by both the Sri Lankan state and the Tamil Tigers. The Tigers, it is claimed, used civilians as human shields and shot dead any who attempted to desert them; the Sri Lankan state, meanwhile, is accused of targeting civilians, as well as blocking food and medicine from entering the war zone. Whatever the tactics, the Sri Lankan army got their wish on 19 May 2009 when Prabhakaran, the supreme leader of the Tamil Tigers, was found floating face down in the mangroves. The war was over.

Eventually we reach the stadium and it's worth the drive. The pitch is by no means Wembley but it is at least largely flat, and the best we've played on so far. The rock-hard surface barely protected by a thin layer of sand gives the ball a wicked, unpredictable bounce but it also means the ball runs fairly true when passed along the surface. As I walk across the pitch, I'm very aware of a recent statement I read that it will take the Sri Lankan government until 2020 to clear all of the estimated three million landmines scattered in the civil war. I'm even more aware that the year is 2019. A rural area just outside the Tamil Tigers training base? It surely must have been a prime location.

I hear a call from the stands. I look up to see several of our opponents waving at me. Instantly I remember what a friendly team they were at our previous encounter. Three of them run down to meet me on the pitch. They're enthusiastic, their questions coming rapidly. I answer as best I can and ask some of my own questions, then it's time to pose for multiple selfies and share my Facebook name with them.

This is supposed to be a bitter rivalry. This is a six-pointer if ever there was one. If we win today and then win our final match – and Kiliyoor lose both – we will qualify ahead of them. But it hasn't even crossed my new friends' mind. I continue talking to them until forty-five minutes before kick-off, and then when we're in the tunnel we resume our conversation.

'Kilinochchi is a very poor place,' they tell me. They're all from Jaffna, with just four of their team hailing from the Kilinochchi area – the captain being one.

The first half maintains its friendly nature. Rather than a battle for the honour of qualification, we find ourselves taking part in a leisurely stroll back and forth. Neither team, it appears, has been told that the aim of the sport is to shoot the ball into the opponent's net. Kiliyoor have plenty of possession, treating it as a chance for everyone to have a touch without ever trying to break past our defensive line. We appear happy simply to be there, our experimental front line of Kalua and Anushaht just two of the players jogging around a lot but not actually doing anything. On the rare occasions that we get control of the ball, we do so apologetically, quickly kicking it aimlessly forward so that Kiliyoor can have possession once more.

Kiliyoor bring on their star striker for the second half, replacing one foreign pro with another. I exchange knowing glances with my other defenders. It's been well documented that this is the top scorer in our group. But the vertically challenged Vithu, playing alongside me at centre-half, isn't fazed.

'I will break him,' he says in full seriousness.

He doesn't quite break him, but he does keep him quiet. The clock keeps ticking and our elusive clean sheet becomes more of a possibility. The game is evening out. Roshan releases substitute Aflal with a deft flick and he's one on one with the goalkeeper. Aflal strikes the ball true and it soars past the keeper. Then cannons off the bar. When you're bottom of the table you have to take your chances. But when you're bottom of the table you have a habit of missing your chances.

My thigh is still sore. I still avoid kicking long and am several paces slower than normal. Under such pressure, though, I can cope. As long as the game doesn't go on for much longer.

'Sir,' I ask the referee in the same style as the Sri Lankans, 'how long?'

'Ten.'

Fate considerably tempted, we concede a corner. Kiliyoor's six-foot-six Ghanaian centre-half trots up. He's a head taller than Dean, who's marking him. The ball floats in and both rise. Dean does well to block the centre-half's header but the ball bounces up invitingly. None of our players is willing to stick their head where it hurts. Instead Kiliyoor's right-winger bicycle-kicks the ball tantalisingly over all five foot four of Vithu, helpless on the line. 1-0.

And then it's 2-0. Substitute Balaya, playing without the armband, wins a free-kick by our own touchline. He attempts to take it quickly, passing down the line along the ground. It goes straight to an opponent, who for some reason floats it straight back to the isolated Balaya, who has nobody around him. For some even stranger reason, Balaya opts to head the ball rather than let it float harmlessly out of play. The last ten minutes has a habit of making our players act a bit strange. Balaya's header doesn't go forward, instead it goes backwards for a corner. The routine is repeated. Kiliyoor's defenders trot up. Dean and I mark while our teammates rush to stand on the posts. This time the ball doesn't come in our direction. The Kiliyoor corner-taker kicks it straight out of play from the corner.

'That has to be the worst thirty seconds of football I've ever seen,' I say to Dean.

Now fate has really been tempted.

The ball has landed in the side netting and Ranoos, desperate to get an equaliser, attempts to take a quick goal-kick. In his haste he mishits the ball straight to an opponent on the edge of the area, who takes a touch and mishits his own effort. It floats towards Ranoos, who goes to catch the ball. He doesn't judge it right. The ball brushes against his fingertips and then bounces behind him. Ranoos still has enough time to redeem himself, but he's so shocked that he hesitates. The linesman flags that the ball crosses the line.

If matches finished at eighty minutes we'd be a decent team.

I turn to Dean once more: 'Make that the worst forty-five seconds.'

Kiliyoor's supporters are dancing on the sidelines, their hands clasped together and hips shaking. They're ecstatic, and continue to be so long after the referee blows his whistle for the final time.

It's official: we've been eliminated.

It takes me a long time to get off the pitch. Everyone wants a hug and a chat. Fans come up to me. Ball boys ask for a fist-bump and when I give it they react as if they've seen a ghost. I can only imagine what the reaction would have been if I'd actually played well.

I'm almost at the changing room when my friends from the other team catch up with me once again. They want more selfies. I pose and smile and feel bad for my teammates on the other side of the door. If I was in their shoes I wouldn't be happy about someone smiling with the opponents after a defeat. But what can I do? It's the constant conundrum in Sri Lankan football.

'Seth!' Thaabit calls me as I finally make it into the changing room and begin to remove my socks. 'Come quick.'

We spoke about this before the game. Both of us said how much we'd like to interview Kiliyoor's captain for the book, and now Thaabit has only gone and secured an interview. The captain smiles when I emerge with my dictaphone. As Dean always says, he's a gent. Up close I see his dark goatee and brown-stained teeth, I feel his presence and see his scars more clearly. A part of me is scared. He looks like a Disney baddy, but he has a good heart.

'What do you want to ask?' Thaabit says.

I say it's obvious what I want to ask, but Thaabit suggests he doesn't want to talk about it. Instead I hint. I ask him how long he's played football for and he tells me seven years as a professional thanks to the tax paid by the locals. He's had no other job. What did he do before? He doesn't say. Did he always want to be a footballer? Yes. What was it like growing up in Kilinochchi? Yes. I start to wonder if he has a clue what either of us is saying.

He has a history, but he doesn't want to talk about it and I can't blame him. He's been rehabilitated. In this post-war Sri Lanka, it was his only option. I can't be sure of his real feelings and nor can I ask. So instead Thaabit finishes with one question: 'Who is your favourite footballer?'

His face lights up and he flashes his stained teeth: 'Cristiano Ronaldo!' We fist-bump and call it a day.

There's still time for tens of selfies with my opponents. It's no surprise when I'm the last one to board our bus home.

	Team Name	P	W	D	L	GF	GA	GD	Points
1	Valvai FC	9	8	0	1	30	8	22	24
2	Tamil United	9	5	1	3	16	14	2	16
3	Mullai Phoenix	9	4	2	3	10	12	-2	14
4	Kiliyoor Kings	9	4	1	4	16	15	1	13
5	Mannar FC	9	2	1	6	14	19	-5	7
6	Trinco Titans	9	1	1	7	10	28	-18	4

JAFFNA

We don't go straight to Jaffna. First we return to Trincomalee. It's not ideal but neither is having to stretch a two-month budget over three months.

Meghan has left. She went to the airport straight from the game, leaving Dean to navigate his final few days in Sri Lanka alone. Now that there's an end date in sight, Dean doesn't mind so much.

'Some experience this, eh?' he repeats over and over.

We both feel the same, knowing we've been lucky to have encountered such a wonderful place.

The next morning I make the short walk to the beach alone. The sun is already hot yet the beach is empty. Fishing boats line the shore while palm trees sway back and forth in the mild breeze. Nobody is in the sea. This is perfect solitude. It isn't long until I have to return to the pollution of London, its tall buildings and perpetual busyness, the mad rush of people always in a hurry. And so I stay on the beach, breathing in its peacefulness and enjoying the time alone.

When it's time to leave I politely turn down the offer of beer and chicken from the fishermen under the tree. Instead I accompany Thaabit and Ihshan as they drive the short distance to Roshan's former football club, where hordes of people are awaiting us. They're in football shirts and cricket whites, some in Islamic skull caps, and as we park they run up to the car. We get out and open the boot, where bags upon bags of donated kit lie. The club's senior leaders usher us onto a stage where we hand out the kit and pose for photographs. Children are running around wildly, grown men are shaking their heads in disbelief. This is the difference that our owners intended to make to the local community.

And as far as Thaabit is concerned, it's only the start. A donation is to be made to Ranoos's school. Mahela's cancer hospital will also get something. Money will be set aside to reward the players who have shown the most commitment over the weeks.

But all that is to come. First, there's a tournament to finish.

We leave late so that Naleem can leave with us. It's his first day teaching back at school and he arrives a little before 4 p.m. Our trip has been made compulsory for the whole squad. The threat of reduced salary results in a good turnout. Dinesh doesn't show up and neither does Priyan; other than that we have a full complement. Which is a shame because our bus is tiny. We're wedged in, a mass of limbs, each trying to reach for space.

The bus heads out of Trincomalee and snakes up the Vavuniya road. It's a new route, more rural than our usual one. Thick jungle greets us on the roadside, dots of houses marking breaks in the trees. Many are long abandoned, either totally empty or boarded up, left in a hurry many years ago and never returned to. Buddhist flags – rectangular blocks of colour flowing both horizontally and vertically – hang from buildings that surely used to be Tamil strongholds. Blue, yellow, orange, red and white. Sri Lankan flags, in comparison, are in short supply.

At Vavuniya we meet the A9, our familiar path north-bound. Not that my teammates notice. They're all distracted by the Tamil films Ihshan plays on the screen at the front of the bus. As usual, they whoop and shriek at the smallest of plot developments. Sakhti is the loudest, his shrieks only eclipsed by Vithu's manic laughter. Together with Kalua, they dance and dance the whole way to Jaffna, stopping briefly at Elephant Pass for a toilet break. As we let loose into the firm ground, we take in the last outpost before the Jaffna peninsula. Little more than a decade ago this was the most violent stretch of land in the country, witnessing the heaviest fighting of the entire war. Now a calmness grips the landscape. We embrace it, and then it's back onto the bus for more Tamil film madness.

When we arrive in Jaffna we find our most cramped hotel yet. Dean, Jai and I are guided into the largest of the player rooms but it's soon worked out that the arithmetic done for room allocations isn't correct. Having bagged myself the best bed, I now find Banda pitching up next to me. Things only get worse when I go to the cupboard to get a bedsheet: the first one has bloodstains on it and the second has large brown marks. It's just one night. It's just one night.

Boys flood into our room. Universally topless and many solely in sarongs, they play music and dance. When they bring word of women out on the streets charging just 1,000 rupees, Banda is straight out of the room. He comes back ten minutes later carrying Anushaht's shorts. I don't ask.

Back in the room, Banda doesn't stop moving. First he starts banging the bed in frustration while playing a shooting game on his iPad – a fake. Every few minutes it comes: bang... bang... bang. And then, when he finally puts the fake iPad down, he starts squirming. I tell him the corridor is comfy. He squirms some more.

It's just one night.

Dean starts talking in his sleep. But at least Banda's finally asleep. Then he also starts talking in his sleep.

Jai and I are still awake, our faces illuminated by the glow of our phones. It's well past midnight.

It's just one night.

I barely feel as though I've drifted off to sleep when a noise awakes us with a start: '*Yeeeuuuuuurrrgh!*' The sound comes again, more urgently: '*Yeeeuuuuuurrrgh!*' It's from Dean, sitting bolt upright in bed. 'What is that?' he screams, pointing at the curtain. 'Rat!'

We're all wide awake now. Banda is sent to the curtain because Banda is always the person to tackle this type of situation. Carefully he lifts it up, the rest of us fearful in expectation. He finds nothing but a cotton thread. Dean, a vivid dreamer, imagined the whole thing.

There's no chance we're getting back to sleep now. Vithu comes in to offer us all tea. Then Kalua barges in and heads straight for our bathroom in the hope of finding toilet paper. Music is blaring from next door. It's not even 8 a.m., still several hours before I usually rise.

Still, it's just one night.

I admit defeat and get dressed. The hotel doesn't have breakfast facilities so we eat out. As is common, the restaurant we eat at has no soap, which isn't ideal for tackling our greasy deep-fried breakfast. Those in Jaffna, though, must be used to not using soap. Throughout the war, the government made soap a banned item in the north-east because of the Tamil Tigers' tendency to use it to make their landmines watertight. When you've washed your hands with only water for twenty-six years, I suppose it becomes habit. 'Hey, Machan,' Vithu yells to a waiter. 'More for my friend here,' he puts his arm around me and beams. I protest that I'm not hungry but he won't take no for an answer. Neither will Sakhti who is sitting opposite. He either forces me to eat or teaches me new swear words to say to the waiter.

When we return to the hotel a friend is waiting for me: Gershon, the Kiliyoor Kings centre-back. He lives in Jaffna and has time before needing to leave for his match in Mullaitivu. We hug like old friends and he calls me his best friend, which seems a bit extreme. A red baseball cap sits back to front on his head. His hair is swept across his head in fashionable style, accompanied by a perfectly manicured beard and soft facial features. Tattoos run down his right arm. Self-confidence oozes from him.

Dean excuses himself, rushing to our bathroom in the hope that toilet paper has appeared. It hasn't. The hotel has none. I've barely said hello to Gershon by the time Fasith races out of the hotel entrance on a pushbike.

'Toilet roll for the Dean!' he hurriedly explains. Dean, it turns out, is hammering down Sakhti's door. Sakhti's room is the only one with toilet paper, albeit wet and stained, and Sakhti has wisely locked the door. Dean howls with impatient rage.

Gershon laughs and shakes his head. We're sitting under the trees in the garden with Balaya. Occasionally the two of them slip into Tamil, but mainly Gershon asks about my life and we discuss the other teams in the tournament. He tells me that he's been a professional footballer for the last few years and is being paid 150,000 LKR for the group stage. Kiliyoor Kings' Nigerian striker, meanwhile, is earning 100,000 LKR. Either way, the salaries dwarf ours. It's no wonder we're below them in the table.

'Your team defend well, dribble well, pass well,' he analyses. 'But shooting…' he bursts into laughter.

I change the subject and ask him about growing up in Jaffna during the war. I'm greeted with much the same response as that of his captain: 'Yes... Yes.' It seems those most involved want to talk about the past as little as possible, and for that I can't blame them. Instead we go back to talking about the North Eastern Premier League and the future.

The Kiliyoor Kings team bus comes an hour into our conversation. We hug once more and Gershon excuses himself. He has a match to win. We wish each other the best of luck.

As Gershon leaves, Priyan turns up on the back of a moped. We fist-bump and then he hurries to speak to the coaching staff. Our next salary payment is 16,000 LKR, but Priyan's next fine is 16,000 LKR. He had told the coaching staff that he was still injured, but photos have appeared of him playing football for his university team. It's one thing to lie about injury and play for a different team; it's another to then put the photos on Facebook and tag yourself. He comes to an agreement with the coaches: his fine will now only be 15,000 LKR.

* * *

There's a party mood in the camp, a sense of finality. Ninety minutes against Tamil United, sitting second in our group, and then it's all over. Ihshan takes official team photographs and then the players all get their phones out for their own selfies. Eventually we warm up but nobody is taking it too seriously.

Inshaht is given the captain's armband for his impressive work rate throughout the tournament. Along with Roshan, he's been our best player. Inshaht's reaction is amazing. His mouth breaks into an expression of sheer ecstasy and he's instantly mobbed by his teammates.

There are no masts so no flags can be raised, and just one dignitary is in attendance, so for once we start on time. Thaabit starts with his strongest team:

Ranoos

Inshaht   Jai   Seth   Sakhti

Banda   Roshan   Dean   Priyan

Iham   Aflal

Yet soon he has to make changes. The pitch looks great from the sidelines: full of grass and flat. Up close, though, the lumps of sand and divots are obvious. Within fifteen minutes Jai goes to turn and breaks down. He's twisted his ankle and needs to come off. Vithu is his replacement.

'Now you see the old Vithu,' he promises.

We do. I note that he's decided not to wear shinpads. It doesn't matter. The defence holds firm. My thigh has started to throb but it's controllable. The attack, however, is non-existent. We fail to register a single shot despite often getting into decent positions. Then Inshaht switches off for a long ball and suddenly the left-winger is hitting the ball past Ranoos to make it 1-0, which may as well be 10-0 given our toothlessness going forward. Whatever we try, it seems the scoreboard will forever read 'Titans 0'.

'Have some pride,' Thaabit urges us at half-time. 'At least make an effort to win the ball back. At least run.'

Dean and I frantically nod our heads in agreement at this most basic of instructions. But Thaabit's words fall on deaf ears. As the game goes on, I get angrier and angrier. Iham, shifted into midfield, refuses to chase back. Aflal watches as opponents stand next to him with the ball. I scream and scream. I begin to lose it. For the first time I truly feel a sense of hopelessness. What can I do? What can Thaabit do? What can any of us do if players aren't even going to try? It's the minimum requirement of any footballer – let alone a professional.

The second goal comes and it's a catalogue of errors. Aflal gives the ball away cheaply and stands still. Priyan doesn't press. Iham stays in his position. The ball is switched to Tamil United's left wing and they put a poor cross in. I call my name to show I'll clear it. Vithu goes for the header and misses it. His movement puts me off my clearance and I miss it. Fortunately the ball bounces safely to Sakhti, who has an easy clearance to make. He stands and waits for the ball to come. He stands and watches an opponent steal in to claim the ball. We all watch as the ball goes past Ranoos.

Energy levels go down further. My anger rises. Their winger shows me the ball and I slide in, not caring if I get man or ball. Fortunately I get ball. My head isn't right.

The final whistle brings closure. Yet I'm the angriest I've been in Sri Lanka. We're lucky to score 0, yet my teammates join together and laugh and applaud the effort for the whole tournament. I feel dislocated from the process, distant. I'm asked to sing with Dean in the changing rooms for Ihshan's documentary. I can't bring myself to.

'Seth very angry!' Vithu observes, throwing his arms up in the air to mimic my actions on the pitch. Sakhti copies Vithu, standing next to me and grabbing hold of my manhood. People start to look concerned when I don't react.

'It's OK,' I attempt to half-smile, 'but now I don't sing.' I pick up my stuff and leave them to celebrate. They shrug their shoulders and do just that.

'My friend!' the Tamil United manager calls. I meet him halfway as he walks over and shake his hand. 'You are from the UK?'

'Yes, London.'

'Me too.'

He goes on to tell me how he coaches in the Tamil Football League played on Wimbledon Common. That's how he got to know the Jaffna owner, who then asked him to help the team. Before coming to Sri Lanka, he flew to his native Uganda to recruit three players. That was back in May. Now it's late August and his flights, along with the three professionals he selected, are booked for 17 September. Thanks to the constant delays and questionable organisation, their quarter-final will take place on 18 September. There's nothing they can do; flights are expensive to change and all of them have jobs and seasons they need to return to. Not that it matters much. He tells us of the corruption he's seen, the questionable decisions made by officials in favour of Valvai. It becomes even more obvious that this whole tournament is a charade for an inevitable final between Tilko and Valvai.

The bus toots its horn and we agree to meet in London.

The final thing I see in my career as a professional footballer in Sri Lanka is three of my opponents driving away from the ground on the same motorbike.

	Team Name	P	W	D	L	GF	GA	GD	Points
1	Valvai FC	10	9	0	1	35	9	26	27
2	Tamil United	10	6	1	3	18	14	4	19
3	Mullai Phoenix	10	5	2	3	12	12	0	17
4	Kiliyoor Kings	10	4	1	5	16	17	-1	13
5	Mannar FC	10	2	1	7	15	24	-9	7
6	Trinco Titans	10	1	1	8	10	30	-20	4

TRINCOMALEE

We go home straight after the game.

'Aflal play very good,' Naleem laughs sarcastically, patting him on the shoulder. My teammates are often brutally honest in their assessments.

My anger subsides as we go further into the night. Naleem feeds me biscuits. Iham strokes my hair. Sakhti asks me to swear in Tamil. Vithu prods my shoulder with his snake dance. When Thaabit produces several bottles of fizzy drink, they go wild then insist that Dean and I are the first to drink. I can't stay mad at my teammates; without them, this whole experience would have been nothing.

My phone buzzes whenever Ihshan lets me use his portable hotspot for wifi. Messages are flooding in.

> *Bro I'm so proud of you. Trinco Titans player.*
> *Super player.*
> *The best!*

Even after eight defeats in ten matches, messages on Facebook from supporters of Trinco are still great for the ego. Vithu

WhatsApps me from the back of the bus. His new WhatsApp name is THE KING. The photo he's chosen for his profile? A selfie of the two of us, both smiling. Long live the King.

Just before midnight we arrive back at the coaches' house for one final night. Iham, Aflal and Ranoos are staying overnight too. They'll return home in the morning. I stay up late with Ihshan, Thaabit and Iham, talking about how it all went wrong. We come up with many answers but they only lead to more questions.

We rise the next morning to find disappointing weather. Great blocks of cloud obscure the sun, giving a muggy full stop to our final day in Trinco.

Over breakfast I read an article in the *Guardian* that details the disastrous impact the Colombo bombings have had on Sri Lanka's tourist industry. Around 80 per cent of hotel bookings have been cancelled, tourist numbers are down by 71 per cent, and people's livelihoods have been taken away. In response, there's growing clamour for Sri Lanka to elect its own Trump or Modi. Such a move would be disastrous for the Tamils and Muslims of Sri Lanka, comprising 11 per cent and 7 per cent of the population. A lurch further towards Sinhalese nationalism, the article makes clear, is likely to increase ethnic tensions. The war may be over but the conflict isn't. There are growing suspicions of Muslims. There have always been suspicions of Tamils. Gotabaya Rajapaksa is the front-runner for any such election. A Sinhala nationalist, he acted as defence minister for the final part of the civil war. As a consequence, he faces two lawsuits in the US for human rights abuses. Investigations into the 'disappearance' of Tamils, attacks on civilians and torture are ongoing.

I think of the friends I've made here, the welcomes I've received. I think of the Trinco Titans, a sign of unity: a squad filled with Christians and Muslims and Tamils and Europeans, led by Muslims and Sinhalese, owned by Tamils and Sinhalese, playing against Hindus and Christians and Buddhists and Muslims, all in harmony, and I think how this is the real Sri Lanka. The Sri Lanka of the future.

I know that newspapers prey on fear to sell copies, but it doesn't make the report any less scary. Sri Lankans don't deserve this. So much has been done over the past few years by the government to promote unity. Homes have been rebuilt, land returned to its rightful owners, a ban on Tamil organisations lifted, suspected Tamil Tigers released, and families with missing members able to claim compensation. All the good work doesn't deserve to be undone in favour of aligning with Trump or Modi. Sri Lankans don't deserve further conflict. The teardrop island has done enough crying.

I head to the beach alone with my thoughts to swim and stretch my injured thigh, which feels like it's hanging on by a thread. There's just one couple frolicking in the water. A group of fishermen are heaving a boat into the water, their cries of when to push and hold punctuating the silence. A man stops by me, bearing necklaces. He's tried to sell me one at least three times a week since I've been here. He goes over his story, telling me how he dives many metres to the bottom of the ocean at Pigeon Island to collect these rare stones. I nod my approval and decline. Eventually he lets me get on.

Waves attack the shoreline, making entry to the water hard. Once I'm in, stray dogs follow my progress, mimicking my movements on the beach. Shoals of fish fly out of the ocean and into the air right before my face. I have the same target as always: the brightly coloured Hindu kovil a few hundred metres down the beach. After a while the dogs give up, preferring to play among themselves. Thick plumes of smoke start to enter my nostrils. They're from the mounds of rubbish being burned at the side of various hotels. Still, I plough on. And then I'm past the temple, instead aiming for the plain white church that stands just 20 metres further on.

After my swim, we have one final lunch of Rimzy's, this time eating at his house. His wife spoils us with her selection of chicken, daals and rice. Not a speck is left.

When we return to the beach in the afternoon, we are greeted by a commotion. Hundreds of fishermen are in the water. There are people snorkelling, a dozen boats surrounding the nets, and the usual complement of fishermen manually dragging the catch in by hand, mechanically stepping and pulling in rhythm, just as they have been doing all their lives. This is their biggest catch in months – the kind of day they pray will come, and now it's finally arrived. The owner sits regally on a plastic chair and watches the madness unfold around him. Pressure is high. Some fishermen are pushing each other. Those hovering in boats pull up nets and cut fish free into their soon-filled baskets.

Reinforcements arrive. The catch is so big that fish are jumping from the main net. The reinforcements then cast their own nets to catch the escaping fish. More boats arrive. The air is filled with yells of excitement from the fishermen. There's rumoured to be 4,000kg of fish in the net. If those rumours are correct, the profit will be more than a million rupees.

The main net is pulled ashore. Fish writhe around frantically on the sand, searching desperately for the ocean water they've just been snatched from. Spectators get splattered by the sand that the fish spray about. Fishermen start to place the catch into baskets, throwing rogue puffer fish back into the ocean. Hundreds of crows and stray dogs wait patiently around the catch, knowing from experience that any other castaways will be thrown in their direction.

The action goes on and on. When it finally ends, just before sunset, there's an immense air of satisfaction. A vast crowd has assembled – not of the usual tourists, but this time of locals. Old women hold cloth they have made to sell to tourists, boat owners stand by, friends and even family look on with pride. It's the biggest catch of the year.

*   *   *

The boys turn up for our farewell party in an assortment of Thaabit's clothes. Eventually, that is. Even with the promise of their final salary, the majority are late.

They congregate on the balcony. Vithu and Mathu, our identical twins, come wearing identical outfits. Even now I can only tell which one's which by looking at their tattoos. 'Music is life,' their shirts read and they go about proving that theory by instantly choreographing all of us in their Tik-Tok videos. The whole squad mimes and dances, then performs the snake dance on camera in honour of the celebration Sakhti and I had planned from game three but only got to use once.

The phone goes on charge and the impersonations begin. My teammates laugh about my anger at Aflal and throw their arms in the air. They turn their attention to Dean, who they feared was going to murder Anushaht in the Tamil United warm-up after he blasted a ball at Dean's head. Vithu pretends to be an irate Dean while Sakhti assumes the role of Anushaht. 'Sorry, sorry, sorry,' he whimpers, cowering in mock fear. More impersonations are done and stories are told. We laugh and reminisce about recent events that feel like they happened a long time ago.

We settle into smaller groups. Dean is with Banda and Dinesh, who hates the fact that Dean calls him 'uncle'.

'I just boy,' Dinesh insists, 'no uncle.'

Vithu tells me all about his wife. They married two years ago on his twenty-first birthday – four days after they met for the first time. Theirs is a love made over Instagram. After eighteen months of typing back and forth, the wedding was conducted in Sri Lanka. His wife then returned to Canada, where she lives. Their plan is for her to sponsor Vithu's plane ticket to Canada, but the loss of her job as manager of a local KFC branch has complicated affairs. In the two years they've been married, they've only spent one stretch of time together: a sole month in Trincomalee.

Our conversations are interrupted by the call for dinner. The coaching staff have returned from Pizza Hut with gifts of thin crust and Pepsi. While we tuck in, the evening is outlined. First we are to collect our salaries. We are also invited to vote for our players' player of the tournament. At the collection, players then have the option of donating to the prize fund for the play-ers' player. They're also asked if they wish to donate their match winnings – 1,400 LKR each – to the Trail cancer hospital. All but one donate. That sole person, who Thaabit refuses to name, says he wants the money instead. Just ten donate to the players' player prize fund. Thaabit adds the 6,000 LKR left over from fines, and the coaches then contribute a further 9,000 LKR to bring the total pot up to 25,000 LKR.

Then the awards are announced. Sakhti, the only player to attend 100 per cent of sessions, is recognised for his commit-ment with 10,000 LKR. Inshaht wins most improved player.

Roshan gets the coaches' award for player of the tournament. Then the big one: 25,000 LKR for the players' player, the award that everyone always wants. It goes to Ranoos: the young kid who's just finished his A-levels and lives in a house without walls. Naturally, he's delighted.

The inevitable speeches follow. Nomi starts but it soon turns into a free-for-all. This is Sri Lanka, where respect must always be given, and so everyone who wants to speak is allowed to. Thaabit has tears in his eyes as Anushaht and Roshan speak, but he looks less thrilled with Balaya and Dinesh. Balaya blames the younger players, saying they let the seniors down. Dinesh blames many people, chiefly Kalua for always trying to be funny instead of serious, then apologises to me and Dean for those who let the team down.

Time goes on and players shift in their seats. It's left to Rimzy to pick up the pieces. He speaks for several minutes, bringing a close to the seventy-five minutes of speeches we've sat through. Afterwards we all hug each other. 'Sorry... sorry,' the players tell me and Dean as we embrace. It turns out that Rimzy used us as examples, saying that – even though we aren't from the city – we fought with all we had, unlike those actually from the city. We shouldn't be setting the benchmark for playing with heart, he said, that should be down to the Trinco players.

We all hug for a long time. There's real friendship in each embrace. The house is a hub of noise. Ihshan hands out extra player stickers and posters and we all sign each other's. Vithu and I swap ours and promise to display them in our houses.

Nobody wants to leave. Eventually, an hour after originally scheduled, Thaabit decides it's time for everyone to go home. The van to take the two of us and Ihshan to Colombo has arrived. We wheel out various suitcases and boxes of equipment. More hugs are given. We leave Dean and Kaps behind. They're going straight to the airport; Dean's flight leaves in twelve hours. It's the first time Dean and I hug. He's some boy, as they say in Derry. We've complained to each other, tried to solve the world and now it's time to part. I know I've made a friend for life. And he still hasn't got typhoid.

Players crowd the van as we leave. The windows are open and they reach inside to fist-bump.

'My best friend!' they cry.

'*Nanbans*,' I reply, Tamil for friends.

And then we're gone, leaving them behind and escaping this beautiful, unforgiving city in the darkness of night. We're no longer Trinco; no longer Titans.

SRI LANKA

Everything moves so slowly in this country. Getting from one point to another is never fast. But now I have to get places fast. There are loose ends to tie up, bookings to be made, a holiday to sort.

I head to Colombo, where Thaabit puts me up for a few days in his Thaabit Ahmed Football Academy office/coaches' house. It's a shrine to football. Pennants and posters cover the walls. The bookshelves are full of autobiographies and football classics. Kits are dumped in the most random of places. I eat western food, relax and plan. There are two days before my girlfriend arrives and I need to make the most of them. On the first day, I tick off none of the tasks on my to-do list. On the second day, I meet Mahela Jayawardene.

Thaabit makes me dress smart for the occasion. I wear my sole polo shirt, and borrow a pair of trousers that are too big and a pair of smart shoes that are too small. In the tuk-tuk to the meeting I'm roasting-hot, desperate to take off my shoes and socks and step into my trusty flip-flops.

The tuk-tuk is one rattling metal box of fumes, Colombo's infamous traffic forcing us to wait and wait. Thaabit keeps on checking his watch. We're going to be late. Ihshan, meeting us there, is going to be even later. This won't look good. Especially when our meeting with Mahela is to discuss the future of the Trinco Titans. In an hour Thaabit may not have a job.

The road is shut and so we hurriedly pay our tuk-tuk driver and then walk the final few hundred metres to the luscious green Royal Colombo Golf Club. We're in luck: Mahela is already in the clubhouse but Nathan – Mahela's fellow co-owner – hasn't yet arrived. Ihshan joins us and suddenly we're all calm. We're ready.

The staff guide us into the dining area, where Mahela is sitting at a table. He gets up and I note his loose-fitting jeans, his flip-flops and his casual t-shirt. When you're Mahela Jayawardene and you're eating at the Royal Colombo Golf Course, you can dress how you want. Looking entirely at ease with himself in the stuffy company of Colombo's rich and elite, he greets us warmly. After handshakes, Thaabit sits opposite Mahela while Ihshan and I sit on the same side of the table as Thaabit. We're unbalanced, three against one. We need Nathan.

He arrives, a big man with a big presence, a blue shirt with the top button undone covering his hulking frame. He chucks the keys to his white Range Rover aside and then introduces himself to me and Ihshan.

'It's Nah-den,' we're told. Not Nathan.

He's straight to the point. A venture capitalist and former director of Sri Lankan textile firm MAS, the manufacturer of Sri Lanka's cricket kit, he's excelled in the cut-throat world of business. He didn't do so by avoiding tough questions. There's barely time for introductions. He was born in London and returns regularly for business.

'Have you been to Hoppers?' he asks.

'No,' I reply. 'Perhaps we can head there together next time you come.'

'No, I won't have time,' he replies, which isn't great for my ego. 'Why did we lose?' he continues now the formalities are over. More questions follow.

'What stopped us from doing well?'

'What did we do wrong?'

'How can we be better?'

Thaabit – dressed for the occasion in far smarter clothes than I am – presses his hands together and explains as best he can. The players weren't committed. There was no ambition. The pitches were terrible. The fans were hostile. The organisation, or lack of it, halted our momentum.

The back-and-forth goes on for an hour. Mahela sits back throughout, remaining positive. 'Nah-den' stays on the front foot, leaning forward in his chair and taking great interest. Good cop, bad cop. It's a powerful combination.

More questions are asked, more explanations are given. My role is introduced, Ihshan's too. I tell them about the book I'm going to write and they nod their heads. Ihshan mentions his masses of video footage. We each answer our own questions, trying to remain as positive as possible. With a small few tweaks, I assure them, Trinco Titans will be in a much better position next season.

They nod but I don't know if 'Nah-den' is satisfied. The last of the ice cream is barely scooped from his bowl before he announces he has to go. It's abrupt, but he follows up by concluding that next year will be better. They will speak to the tournament organisers. They want a full report on the tournament just gone. They will speak to the other co-owners but don't see anyone else for the job. They'd like Thaabit to continue.

A fellow diner, seeing we're standing up to leave, comes to shake Mahela's hand. 'This is a former cricketer,' he explains to his acquaintance. Mahela smiles; in Sri Lanka he rarely needs introducing.

We wait patiently, and with one final request we ask Mahela to signs our shirts and pose for photos. Mahela agrees and then suggests we meet up for a drink later that evening. We can just about say 'yes' before 'Nah-den' has dragged him out of the doorway and into his Range Rover. He's a busy man with places to be.

As soon as they drive past us, Thaabit lets out a huge sigh of relief. He's got another crack at the North Eastern Premier League.

* * *

I tick off half the tasks on my to-do list but it's the most important half. My flights home are booked. Thaabit's mate who owns an island in the Maldives offers a two-night all-inclusive stay in a water cabana for little more than cost price. That should help me to put back on the 15kg I've lost since being on a Sri Lankan diet of rice and no refined sugar. A gem-trading friend of Thaabit's lends me a ring of blue sapphire, white gold and diamond from his personal collection that I can use when my girlfriend arrives. After all, every book needs a happy ending.

JAFFNA

It's no surprise when the final of the North Eastern Premier League 2019 is Tilko against Valvai. Tilko triumph on penalties.

LONDON

'Hi bro, how are you?'

Sri Lanka has moved on. I've moved on. Yet Trinco remains the same. Inshaht's messages arrive almost daily, always the same. *Your match, what happened bro. OK, now I sleep.*

Life hasn't got easier for him. Football provided an outlet, but the storms of the winter hit the fishing industry. He hasn't worked for months. Money must be tight. But he doesn't linger on any of that. All he wants to talk about is football and our families.

Vithu still has our picture together as his WhatsApp profile image but he messages me less regularly. I see from Instagram, however, that he's still living his life to the fullest. If anything, the trauma has brought him even closer to his twin brother. They wear the same clothes, have the same haircut, and make energetic Tik-Tok videos every day.

Balaya, Priyan and Naleem often pop up. It helps when I post something on social media. Inevitably, it'll get hundreds of likes from Sri Lankans who saw me play, heard of me or even just randomly added me on Facebook. I've now received more than 2,000 friend requests on Facebook. Now that

I'm no longer in Trinco, I don't feel I have to accept them all any more.

Time allows me to see Sri Lanka for what it was. It's funny how you forget all the negatives: the stress, the lack of control, the lies, the rumours, the uncertainty, the disorganisation, the unprofessionalism, the white privilege, the unmistakable tension. I don't remember any of it. As I look back at my photos, I smile. What I'd give to have one more night on that balcony with my teammates, having a laugh about some trivial cultural difference after a good day of training.

Some experience, as 'the' Dean would say.

It's still up in the air whether the experience will be repeated. Mahela's group haven't yet committed to investing again for the upcoming tournament. If they do invest, it isn't confirmed whether Thaabit will be coach. Thaabit himself doesn't know if he wants to coach. And if he does, few of the same players will be selected again.

The door remains open for me to return. As time goes by, I feel more like closing it. Unique experiences are best when they remain unique, unrepeated.

And whether things truly will be the same is still to be seen. The tensions that were always bubbling below the surface are rising. In the run-up to the election, reports surfaced in the west of busloads of Muslims being shot at on the way to cast their votes in Mannar. The representative of the Sinhaelse-Buddhist Nationalist Party, Gotabaya Rajapaksa, was later elected as president of Sri Lanka in November 2019. Extremist Sinhalese nationalists, it seems, feel emboldened.

It feels safer back in England. Everything seems less important. I have it easy. All my teammates can do among the chaos is keep on keeping on, remaining hopeful of a brighter tomorrow. I hope they get there. I hope all of my *nanbans*, those Titans of the teardrop isle, do.

ACKNOWLEDGEMENTS

This book would not have been possible without many people. In fact, none of my books would have been possible without Ian Ridley, who first took a chance on me back in 2014 by publishing *The Boy in Brazil*. Since then, his mentorship and continued support of my writing have been a major influence. I'm proud to be Ian's business partner in Floodlit Dreams.

Floodlit Dreams has an excellent team of people behind it that have helped this manuscript grow from a series of notes scrawled on an iPhone to an actual book. Charlotte Atyeo's editorial work was as necessary as it was thorough. Marion Lawson saved a few blushes with her comprehensive proof-reading. Steve Leard did what he does best and produced another great cover. Thanks also go to Nalini Sivathasan for fact-checking the drafts of this book and helping me to get my head around the complexities of the country.

I first met Owen Amos in a grimy pub on Old Street. The hours flew by as we discussed football, travel and books (Owen was the ghostwriter of a great book with Stephen Constantine: *From Delhi to the Den*). Never did I think our meeting would lead to me playing professional football in Sri Lanka. For that

I must thank Owen, who not only pushed for me to take the opportunity but also provided feedback on some early drafts of this book. Andrew Mollitt, too, played an important part – and not just because it was his tweet that alerted Owen. Andrew's early words of encouragement were important in persuading me to take up the opportunity.

From the minute I got to Sri Lanka to the moment I left, Thaabit Ahmed was the perfect host. He couldn't do enough to help me out, always making sure I was looked after. Thaabit, you're a great person and coach – I hope you go on to achieve amazing things. The same goes for Ihshan Iqbal, who has a promising career in film on the horizon (*Funny Boy* is the most recent he has produced on). I wouldn't have had nearly as many laughs without Ihshan. Kapila Priyadarshana proved a calming influence, so much so that he was present for my proposal. Kaps, I hope you live your dream of being truly immersed in nature (so long as you avoid those leeches and poisonous snakes!).

Dean 'The Deano' Curran is 'some boy'. In a culture vastly different from your own, it's comforting to have someone by your side to experience it with. Dean cracked me up and kept me sane in equal measure. I couldn't have had anyone better to join me in Sri Lanka, though I think parts of my shins are still shaking from some of the challenges he put on me in training.

I left London with a girlfriend and returned with a fiancée. Thanks go to Harriette Cassie for not kicking up too much fuss that I was disappearing for the whole summer (I think she probably enjoyed the break). I promise to at least ask you if another opportunity comes up. And, of course, thank you for saying yes in the mountains of Ella.

To my family – Mum, Dad and Kizzie – thank you for not worrying too much. The phone calls helped.

And finally, to all of my Trinco Titans *nanbans*. You made sure I had a smile on my face every day. So in no particular order, the final words in this book are dedicated to you: Priyan, Banda, Vithu, Mathu, Rimzy, Ranoos, Sakhti, Balaya, Hizam, Azil, Inshath, Iham, Jai, Aflal, Naleem, Fasith, Rifkan, Dinesh, Anushath and Kalua. All or nothing for Trinco.

SOURCES

As much as friends and journalists helped me to understand the country and provided me with facts and figures, I'm grateful for the following sources which furthered my understanding:

de Soyza, Niromi, *Tamil Tigress: My Story as a Child Soldier in Sri Lanka's Bloody Civil War*, Allen & Unwin (2011)

Dix, Benjamin and Lindsay Pollock, 'Vanni: A Family's Struggle Through the Sri Lankan Conflict', *New Internationalist* (2019)

Gimlette, John, *Elephant Complex: Travels in Sri Lanka*, riverrun (2015)

Harrison, Frances, *Still Counting the Dead: Survivors of Sri Lanka's Hidden War*, Granta Books (2013)

Malaravan, *War Journey: Diary of a Tamil Tiger*, Penguin (2013)

Shaw, Chris (Executive Producer) & Callum Macrae (Producer & Director), *Sri Lanka's Killing Fields*, ITN Productions, www.channel4.com/programmes/sri-lankas-killing-fields (2011)

Subramanian, Samanth, *This Divided Island: Stories from the Sri Lankan Civil War*, Atlantic Books (2015)

Venugopal, Rajesh, *Nationalism, Development and Ethnic Conflict in Sri Lanka*, Cambridge University Press (2018)

ALSO BY SETH BURKETT

Non-fiction

THE BOY IN BRAZIL
Living, loving and learning in the land of football

FOOTBALL'S COMING OUT
Life as a gay fan and player
With Neil Beasley

DEVELOPING THE MODERN FOOTBALLER
THROUGH FUTSAL
With Michael Skubala

Fiction

NO FINAL WHISTLE

TEKKERS

THE HITLER TROPHY
Golf and the Olympic Games
By Alan Fraser

FOOTBALL'S COMING OUT
Life as a Gay Fan and Player
By Neil Beasley
With Seth Burkett

RAISED A WARRIOR
One Woman's Soccer Odyssey
By Susie Petruccelli

THE BREATH OF SADNESS
On love, grief and cricket
By Ian Ridley